AMERICAN WITHDRAWAL FROM AFGHANISTAN

AMERICAN WITHDRAWAL FROM AFGHANISTAN

P.M. Kamath

VPM's Centre for International Studies (Regd.), Mumbai
In cooperation with

Indian Council of World Affairs, New Delhi

ISBN : 978-81-212-1319-6
Price: ₹ 890/-

First Published 2016

Published by
Gyan Publishing House
Gyan Avenue 12 Pargati Market Ashok Vihar Phase-2 Delhi-110052
Phones : 23282060, 23261060
Fax : (011) 23285914
E-mail: books@gyanbooks.com
website: gyanbooks.com
Printed at: G. Print Process, Delhi

Cataloging in Publication Data--DK
Courtesy: D.K. Agencies (P) Ltd. <docinfo@dkagencies.com>

National Seminar on "American Withdrawal from Afghanistan in December 2014: Post-Withdrawal Puzzle of Policy Options for India, Pakistan and Afghanistan" (2014 : Mumbai, India)
American withdrawal from Afghanistan / [editor], P.M. Kamath
pages cm
Revised and Updated papers presented in a National Seminar on "American Withdrawal from Afghanistan in December 2014: Post-Withdrawal Puzzle of Policy Options for India, Pakistan and Afghanistan" held by the VPM's Centre for International Studies at Mumbai during 29-31 July 2014.
ISBN 9788121213196

1. Afghanistan--Foreign relations--United States--Congresses. 2. United States--Foreign relations--Afghanistan--Congresses. 3. Afghanistan--Foreign relations--South Asia--Congresses. 4. South Asia--Foreign relations--Afghanistan--Congresses. 5. Afghanistan--Foreign relations--2001- --Congresses. 6. Military assistance, American--Afghanistan--Congresses. 7. Disengagement (Military science)--Congresses. 8. Peace--Congress. I. Kamath, P.M., editor. II. Title.

DS357.6.U6A17 2014 DDC 327.581073 23

Contents

Preface 7

List of Contributors 9

1. Introduction 11
P.M. Kamath

2. The Verities of Afghanistan and India's Options 23
Bharat Karnad

3. Global Jihad/Terrorism: New Challenge to World Peace and Stability: A Philosophical Analysis 31
D.B. Shekatkar

4. The American Withdrawal from Afghanistan 2014: Impact on Strategic Mosaic of South Asia 39
Dilip Mohite

5. Afghanistan and Regional Peace Building: Myth and Reality 69
Arpita Basu Roy

6. Russia Returns to Afghanistan-Challenges Persist 85
R.G. Gidadhubli

7. The Afghan Crisis: An Appraisal of UN's Role in Combating Taliban Insurgency 93
B.N. Mehrish

8. 'State of Afghanistan after 2014 and the Policy Options for India and China 111
Subhadeep Bhattacharya

9. NATO Troops Withdrawal from Afghanistan and Its Implications for Regional Peace and Stability 125
Arvind Kumar

10. The Future of Democracy in Afghanistan 135
Mohammad Atta Roshangar

11. Pakistan's Perspective in Afghanistan: Policy Options for India 145
Tej Pratap Singh

12. Pakistan's Search for Strategic Depth in Afghanistan 161
P. M. Kamath

13. US Withdrawal from Afghanistan: Implications for India and the Way Ahead 173
Kavita Sharma

14. Pakistan's Afghan Policy in Post-2014 Scenario: Options for India 187
Sudhir Singh

15. Post-2014: Likely Relapse of Afghanistan to Terrorism? India's Options 203
P.G. Kamath

16. Stability under Threat: Post-US Withdrawal from Afghanistan 219
Navasikha Duara

17. Indian Perception of the American Withdrawal from Afghanistan in December 2014: Developmental Issues and Related Policy Options 233
Amruta Deshmukh

Appendix 243

Seminar Report 249
Anand V and Vineeth Krishnan

Index 253

Preface

Throughout the period since India won national freedom on 15 August 1947, Indian foreign policy has aimed to keep the then Superpowers—the United States (US), and the Soviet Union, away from Indian borders. But the Soviet Union militarily intervened in Afghanistan in December 1979. Indian Prime Minister (PM), Mrs Indira Gandhi, during the heydays of the Cold War, did not in 1980 raise her concerns, directly, on the Russian presence in Afghanistan. In October 2001 when the Americans militarily intervened to dislodge the Taliban government for its refusal to handover 9/11 suspect Osama bin Laden to the US, Indian PM, Atal Behari Vajpayee did not protest. His successor, Manmohan Singh, on the other hand regretted the US decision to withdraw their troops from Afghanistan by the end of December 2014. By then Indian foreign policy towards her neighbourhood had undergone a radical transformation.

Hence, the Vidya Prasarak Mandal's Centre for International Studies (Regd.) held a Three-Day Seminar from 29 to 31 July 2014 on the topic 'American Withdrawal from Afghanistan in December 2014: Post-withdrawal Puzzle of Policy Options for India, Pakistan and Afghanistan'. We were able to bring together a group of eminent scholars numbering around twenty seven from all over the country. In addition to academic specialists on matters concerning US, Pakistan, India and Afghanistan, the group also included diplomats who had practical experience as also military men who had seen service in the region. There were nationals from Afghanistan and Iran. These scholars have aimed at answering some of the concerns of Indian foreign policy in the jigsaw puzzle of Afghanistan played by major powers and Afghan neighbours and have presented a positive picture of emerging political scenario in that country after analysing the roles played by Pakistan, China, US, the Russian Federation and of course India.

We were fortunate that Maulana Abul Kalam Azad Institute of Asian Studies, Kolkata came forward to be the main sponsor of the seminar, with Indian Council of World Affairs, New Delhi and Indian Council of Social Science Research, New Delhi too extending their helping hand.

Of those who attended, we succeeded in motivating in all sixteen contributors to provide us with their updated papers and to bring out edited papers for the final publication in a book. We had asked participants to give their additional comments or suggestions. We have included these in the appendices. In the task of editing we were greatly helped by Professor C Jagannath Paï, Shri Anil Uchil and Ms. Anita Gujran, Academic Research Assistants of the VPM's CIS. These persons have spent several hours and days to see that a flawless manuscript goes to the press.

We are also grateful to Gyan Publishing House, New Delhi for volunteering to undertake the task of publishing the book. While many have extended their cooperation in publishing this volume, if readers still find inaccuracies, editor alone takes the responsibility for them.

P.M. Kamath

List of Contributors

Amruta K. Deshmukh, Associate Professor, Department of Political Science, Chetana College, Mumbai.

Arpita Basu Roy, Fellow, Maulana Abul Kalam Azad Institute of Asian Studies, Kolkata

Arvind Kumar, Professor and Head, Department of Geopolitics and . International Relations, Manipal University, Manipal

B.N. Mehrish, Former Professor of Politics, University of Mumbai and Senior Research Fellow, ICSSR

Bharat Karnad, Senior Fellow in National Security Studies, Centre for Policy Research, New Delhi.

Dilip Mohite, Former Professor and Head, Department of Political Science, Faculty of Arts, M S University of Baroda, Coordinator for Ford- Foundation Programme in International Relations and DSA Programme.

Kavita Sharma, Asst. Prof, Dept of Political Science, VPM's R.Z. Shah College of Arts, Science and Commerce, Mumbai

Lt. Gen. P.G. Kamath, (Retd) PVSM, AVSM, YSM, SM and Adjunct Prof., Dept of Geopolitics & International Relations, Manipal University, Manipal.

Lt. Gen.(Dr) D.B. Shekatkar, PVSM, AVSM, VSM (Retd), President, Forum for India's Integrated National Security (FINS)

M. Atta Roshangar, Research Scholar, Department of South Asian Studies, Pondicherry University.

Navasikha Duara, Asst. Prof, SVKM's Pravin Gandhi College of Law, Mumbai

P.M. Kamath, Former Professor of Politics, University of Mumbai, Hon. Director, VPM's Centre for International Studies and Adjunct Prof, Dept of Geopolitics and IR, Manipal University, Manipal.

R.G. Gidadhubli, Adjunct Prof., Centre for Eurasian Studies, University of Mumbai Former, Director and Prof., Centre for Eurasian Studies, University of Mumbai

Subhadeep Bhattacharya, Fellow, Maulana Abul Kalam Azad Institute of Asian Studies, Kolkata.

Sudhir Singh, Dept of Political Science, Dyal Singh College, University of Delhi

Tej Pratap Singh, Department of Political Science, Faculty of Social Sciences, Banaras Hindu University, Varanasi.

1

Introduction

P.M. Kamath

American overt military intervention happened twice in the case of Afghanistan. First time during the Cold War in 1980, soon after the Soviet military intervention in that country in December 1979; after Gorbachev agreed to withdraw from its own misadventure in 1989, the Americans also withdrew without even batting an eyelid as to the consequences, which could follow. The then American withdrawal was more to force its Cold War rival, the Soviet Union, to withdraw from Afghanistan rather than to make it follow democracy.

The most significant result of abrupt American withdrawal was that Afghanistan was turned into a University to train international Islamic terrorists to conduct acts of international terrorism against various countries, including India. Manpower for that was available in plenty as internationally those who had landed in Afghanistan to fight Islamic Jihad against the non-believers from the Soviet Union were now readily available for a new task. One such influential Saudi billionaire, Osama bin Laden founded Al Qaeda, an international terrorist group, to carry out politico-religious and cultural war against the US, the West and the rest.

Then on September 11, 2001 now popularly called 9/11, attack on the US took place destroying the idea of invulnerability of the American mainland. The US was quick in fixing the blame for organising the 9/11 international terrorist attacks on Al Qaeda led by Osama bin Laden. George W. Bush, the US President was equally quick in asking Bin Laden, who was then in Afghanistan, to be handed over to the US. Taliban, led by Mullah Omar, which was then in power in Afghanistan, refused. The US thus was led to attack Afghanistan for a second time in October 2001, though now directly.

The US has been in Afghanistan since then. While the US as an occupying power was able to introduce a modicum of democratic elections, modernise governance, and subdue regional warlords, it also gave rise to insurgency led by the Taliban and also direct involvement of Afghanistan's eastern neighbour—Pakistan. But when the American dollars and blood did not visibly bring about concrete results, the same public and Congressmen asked the US government to withdraw American soldiers. Then Senator, Barack Obama, as an outsider to the establishment, was extremely critical of the previous US President-George W. Bush. As a candidate, Obama had asked American soldiers to be withdrawn from Afghanistan. He was elected President in November 2008. He had to make good his promise, but such promises by tradition and as a tactic of electoral politics was implemented during his second term in office.

Then in February 2013 in his address to a joint session of the Congress, President Obama laid before them his plan to withdraw the US troops from Afghanistan in a phased manner, by December 2014.

Bharat Karnad in his key note address-"The Verities of Afghanistan and India's options" brings out the facts of the then existing situation that necessitated the US to withdraw its troops. He primarily considers the decision as reflecting a failure on the part of the US to determine as to how to deal with regional developments while refraining from interfering in the larger strategic game of the wider region. Karnad thinks that the new regime of Ghani-Abdullah with a sufficiently weakened Taliban as a military force should help not only to consolidate democratic framework, but also pushing India to become more proactive in its foreign and military policy, it will find itself unable to cope with a hostile reality in the extended region.

D. B. Shekatkar in his paper "Global Jihad/Terrorism: New Challenge to World Peace and Stability a Philosophical Analysis" says that it is a "simple law of nature, and undisputed fact of human existence that if you water and nurture the right roots you will get good fruits. If you water the wrong roots you will get poisonous fruits!" It is true in case of Afghanistan and Pakistan, both nations have not seen any sustained peace for decades. Thousands and thousands of people (especially (women and children) have died every year. There is no sign of any lasting peace in Afghanistan. He goes on to ask a few important and searching questions: Will there eventually be peace in Afghanistan? When will innocent people stop meeting unnatural death due to bomb blasts, assassinations and Taliban atrocities? When will young children, especially girls start going to schools? When will modern education systems replace Madarasa culture and philosophy? When will Afghanistan take its rightful place in the comity of nations? When will the country become normal country again? Why such hopeless and helpless prognosis? Can't the nations of the world find a way ahead towards peace, stability, prosperity and meaningful existence for the young generations of Afghanistan? Pessimists feel that these are unlikely to happen in the near future. Many of them, mostly supported by Pakistan's point of view feel that things are likely to get worse before they start improving!

Dilip Mohite in his "South Asia's Strategic Mosaic after the American Withdrawal from Afghanistan" says that Pakistan considers Afghanistan as a 'life-line-cum obsession'. While Pakistan and India have direct stakes in Afghanistan, US is an extra regional power and China has gained a foothold because of Pakistan factor. As per Mohite, the US has not been able to completely eliminate international terrorism in Afghanistan, at the most it can be credited with partial success.

Arpita Basu in her paper on "Afghanistan and Regional Peace Building: Myth and Reality" explores the possible trajectories of a regional approach to peace-building in Afghanistan, the imperatives necessary to promote greater cooperation amongst traditionally competitive states around Afghanistan, and the scope of multilateral security arrangements given the dynamics of the actors involved and the workable response for India. In her article she mentions, "Although many of Afghanistan's direct and extended neighbours view the existence of Al-Qaeda and the Taliban as critical threats to their national interests they are often locked in various types of security competitions with one another, resulting in their larger rivalries subordinating the common interest of fighting terrorism. She further states, "What is necessary is a synthesis of the multiple interests of the regional states and wider forms of regional cooperation that are in principle desirable to foster stability and development in Afghanistan. They may not be workable and different forms of alliances need to be created".

R. G. Gidadhubli in his contribution on "Russia Returns to Afghanistan-Challenges Persist" brings out how Russia welcomed US decision to withdraw from Afghanistan as that provided it "a golden opportunity to return to Afghanistan and also rebuild on the relics of the Soviet ties and above all to promote Russia's geopolitical and geo-economic interests". At the same time he sees, "there are persisting challenges due to drug trafficking, terrorism... India and Russia have common interests in Afghanistan for promoting socio-political stability and economic development which will facilitate closer South Asia and Central Asia cooperation".

B.N. Mehrish in his paper, "The Afghan Crisis: An Appraisal of UN's Role in Combating Terrorism" raises certain issues on American military interventions that have raised the question of partitioning of Iraq into Shia, Sunni and Kurdish sections. Will American interventions in Afghanistan too lead to a similar fate? The rupturing of Karzai's political alliance with minority leaders has led to ethnic polarisation.

India called upon the international community to fulfil its pledges to rebuild the Afghan National Army and the Afghan National Police. India's concerns are regarding the main threat to Afghanistan's security and its internal stability, terrorism and extremism, said, "US faces same fate as the Soviets", so said Qari Yousef Ahmadi, a spokesman of the Taliban, on the occasion of the 25th anniversary of the Soviet troops' withdrawal from Afghanistan, in line with the so-called Geneva accords.

The Bush administration had deliberately marginalised the United Nations, preparing to operate on its own or with a few allies rather than through the long drawn-out process of building international consensus. This was repeated in Afghanistan. He argues that the US bombing with tons of 'precision' bombs', and

US/NATO forces killed about 10 times more Afghan civilians than they killed Serbs in 1999.

In June 2011, President Obama announced a phased pullout of 100,000 US troops from Afghanistan to end the costly war launched after the 9/11 attacks. But the Taliban dismissed Obama's announcement as symbolic and rejected any talks with the government in Afghanistan.

The bombing of the Indian consulate in Jalalabad and the killing of jawans on the LOC were all part of Pakistan's attempts to exploit the US withdrawal from Afghanistan and undo its strategic reverses of past two decades. The US intelligence had confirmed to India that *Lashkar-e-Toiba* cadres were being moved into the provinces of Kunar and Nuristan in expectation of the US troop withdrawal from Afghanistan in 2014.

Subhadeep Bhattacharya in his paper "State' of Afghanistan after 2014 and the Policy Options for India and China" says that on the one hand, Afghanistan suffered and sustained foreign invasions; on the other it has been ripped with the severe internal ethnic conflicts. The freedom-loving tribes of Afghanistan have clashed with each other time and again to ensure their respective liberty and territorial sovereignty. That helped Afghanistan to remain free from any colonial domination during the era of European colonialism. Afghanistan still holds strategic importance due to its location. It was the 'crossroad of Empires' and the route to both East and West. From Alexander the Great to the American Super Power, the big players who wished to safeguard their regional interests in adjacent Asia, could hardly overlook Afghanistan.

Afghanistan again came under foreign intervention with the Americans hunting the country's length and breadth to smash the Taliban; the way the Soviets did in the concluding phase of the last century. This time, however, the Americans had another job to perform which was to reconstruct this war ravaged and crisis ridden wild territory into a modern state system by rooting the pillars of democracy deep inside its infertile soil and to impress the lessons of Western political thinking in the minds of the 'unruly' populace of Afghanistan.

To ensure that Afghanistan does not become the safe haven of the Taliban or similar fanatic factions who can pose challenge to the global and regional security, is the prime concern of the international community. If Afghanistan is left to itself again with its bloody ethnic strife, there is a full chance of the return of Taliban.

A national army is the prime characteristic of a state, ancient, medieval or modern, which defends the sovereignty and integrity of the state. Creating a working national army was a tough job in a country like Afghanistan, known for its strong ethnic divisions and conflicts.

The future of Afghanistan in the post-2014 period is a matter that concerns both India and China. Ruling the neighbourhood is the prime condition for any rising power. Given the strategic and economic importance of Afghanistan, China wants to play a significant role there and given her rivalry with India, it is obvious that Beijing will disapprove of similar role for India.

India's concern in Afghanistan is Pakistan. In the aftermath of the Afghan War of 1989, Pakistan initiated a proxy war against India in Kashmir and for that, Afghanistan became an important tool. As Zalmay Khalilzad, former US Ambassador in Afghanistan said, "With regard to Afghanistan it (Pakistan) would like to count on the use of Afghan territory and other assets in any confrontation with India. Already Islamabad is using Afghanistan in its confrontation with India in Kashmir. Many Kashmiri militants are being trained in the Taliban regions of Afghanistan and some members of the Taliban have fought in Kashmir".

Arvind Kumar argues in his paper on "NATO Troops Withdrawal from Afghanistan and its Importance for Regional Peace and Stability" that the declaration of drawdown strategy and the time table announced by the US in the year 2013 had raised a fundamental question whether it would be drawing down from a position of strength. The 32,000 American troops in Afghanistan will virtually be reduced to 9,800 troops after 2014. Troops are expected to be stationed at Bagram airfield and in Kabul. US had a desire to move Afghanistan from an economy shaped by war to one that can sustain a lasting peace. But, somehow, such a desire so far has not got culminated into peace and development in the region. The future of Afghanistan depends upon the legitimacy of the Afghan government and its will and capacity to implement the rule of law. Pakistan has a central role to play in the stabilisation of Afghanistan. India too will remain important for the overall reconstruction of Afghanistan. There is certainly a much greater acceptance of India's presence in Afghanistan among influential Pakistani civilians. India remains the most popular foreign country at the local level in Afghanistan. The regional players must desist from the temptation to carve up Afghanistan into local spheres of influence.

Mohammad Atta Roshnagar in his paper "The Future of Democracy in Afghanistan" points out that in the post-9/11 era, Afghanistan has seen the emergence of a middle class youth population, which is considered as a driving force for the success of democracy after the pull back of foreign troops. As a member of this middle class population, he tries to explain how democratic values, free media, higher education, freedom of speech, expression and so on, have influenced the life and world views of younger generation.

The urbanisation and economic development has reshaped Afghanistan, but it does not mean that the country will have a bright political future or that the Taliban won't regain a measure of power after the withdrawal of US troops in 2014. The Afghanistan movie won't just restart where it left off when the Taliban were driven out from power. Afghanistan has seen the most obvious change in urbanisation and its gains. Gross domestic product per capita has increased nearly five-fold since 2002, with an annual growth rate of about nine per cent. Life expectancy has increased from 44 years to 60 in the past decade; the maternal mortality rate has declined by 80 per cent; the under five mortality rate has dropped by 44 per cent. The number of primary health-care facilities has increased nearly four-fold. Afghanistan has rebuilt an educational system that had nearly stopped functioning.

There are many problems as well; high illiteracy, addiction, involvement in drug trafficking, lack of administrative capabilities to fight them, are some. Corruption and poor governance are other challenges in Afghanistan; **Transparency International**, a watchdog group, pointed out that Afghanistan is among the world's most corrupt countries and getting worse.

The group had said that at least $1 billion donated over the past eight years has been siphoned off.

Afghanistan's economy has been almost exclusively dependent on foreign assistance. US and other nations have promised that they will not abandon Afghanistan, which happened in 1989 after the Soviet Union was pushed out. The World Bank has warned that an abrupt aid cut off could provoke a collapse of political authority, give rise to civil war and consequent greater reliance on opium production. The present accomplishments have not been achieved easily; all Afghan citizens have paid a huge price and have been victims to attain them. To forecast Afghanistan's post-withdrawal situation is very difficult, because there are many factors which determine the developments in Afghanistan.

Tej Pratap Singh's paper "Pakistan's Perspective in Afghanistan: Policy Options for India" analyses Indian policy options in the background of the fact that all wars in Afghanistan have historically been unwinnable. During his election campaign, President Barak Obama had criticised Iraq war as a 'war of choice' and so an 'unnecessary war'. But he termed Afghanistan as a 'war of necessity' and so the US has to win the Afghan War at any cost. He reiterated this later also while addressing war veterans on August 16, 2009 and termed Afghanistan War as a war of necessity. "Those who attacked America on 9/11 are plotting to do so again. If left unchecked, the Taliban insurgency will mean even a larger safe haven for Al Qaeda to plot to kill more Americans."

Afghanistan is a landlocked country and has no access to sea either through Pakistan or Iran; hence they have a common destiny. If one nation is destabilised the whole region will be affected. Therefore, India and Pakistan cannot be insulated against turmoil in Afghanistan; like Pakistan, India too has high stake in the peace, security and stability of Afghanistan. However, Pakistan wants to keep India out of Afghanistan and has made it its foremost strategic objective in Afghanistan. Pakistan is conducting its foreign policy in Afghanistan as the zero-sum-game, where any gain for India in Afghanistan is treated as loss for Pakistan.

Pakistan and Afghanistan are divided by the Durand Line. This is a disputed border which was never accepted by Afghanistan and it treats it as an imperial border imposed on it by British India ignoring ethnicity, language and culture. It divides proud Pakhtuns into Pakistanis and Afghanistanis. Pakistan is obsessed with its security, territorial unity and integrity. It feels that east-west depth of Pakistan is very narrow in comparison to north-south and so it wants to compensate this strategic weakness by having a friendly and if possible, pliant government in Afghanistan.

P.M. Kamath in his presentation on "Pakistan's Search for Strategic Depth in Afghanistan," says that Pakistan's search for strategic depth revolves around army's threat perceptions. Pursuit of strategic depth began with great intensity after the loss of East Pakistan as a result of the Bangladesh war of 1971. In the 1980s the Soviet Union was considered as a security threat along with India. But now in Pak's perception, security threat emerges only from India.

Former Army Chief General Kayani argued in favour of western borders being secure; he meant that strategic depth provides Pakistan the ability to concentrate on Indian borders. Former Secretary of State, Hillary Clinton in October 2011 pointed out that the double game played by Pakistan in nurturing terrorists promoted to fight against India and Afghanistan could eventually harm Pakistan as well. The terrorists in Pakistan's background have begun to show their strength by hitting Pakistan as demonstrated by the Peshawar attack on Military High School in December 2014. Treated as strategic asset by the intelligence agency ISI, to be used against India, terrorists are turning their guns against Pakistan itself. Tahrik-e-Taliban Pakistan (TTP) popularly known as Pak Taliban has begun targeting Pak security forces, civilian leaders and military-civil assets. He has also argued that strategic depth might have been relevant in the pre-Nuclear Weapons period but nuclear weapons have reduced the concept of strategic depth to irrelevance.

Kavita Sharma in her paper 'Post-US withdrawal from Afghanistan: Implications for India and Way-ahead" says that the US' flawed stand is actually the main cause of worry in post-US withdrawal period as it would lead to the rise of Taliban. All the stakeholders in the region would have to step up their game plan to counter implications of this folly of US before it becomes too late. India being one of the key partners in reconstruction, development and stability of Afghanistan has lot of stakes and would like to see peaceful establishment of new democratically elected government and swift transition of responsibility of security to Afghanistan National Security Forces.

Afghanistan's internal situation continued to be chaotic. Taliban and insurgent factions had regrouped and posed formidable challenges for the new Afghan government. Prevalent security environment necessitated additional security forces and resulted in the surge of US Forces in Afghanistan. The widely feared scenario of Taliban resurgence post-US withdrawal will once again take Afghanistan to pre-2001 period, which will not be in the interest of world peace.

Sudhir Singh in his paper "Pakistan's Afghan Policy in Post-2014 Scenario: Options for India" points out the obvious: Since the last 13 years despite being a member of the coalition against terror, Pakistan has been supporting terror elements precisely to score points against India. Despite the civilian regime in Islamabad since March 2008 till date, military has been adamant to sustain old Afghan policy which is bound to inflict collateral damage on India if not managed properly. Therefore, we must reformulate our strategy to cope with the impending dangers.

Singh argues that so far Pakistan has used all the negative means to keep Afghanistan turbulent despite international community's consistent request to contribute positively. Today Pakistan is one of the most hated countries in Afghanistan. This hostility is no longer confined to the Northern Alliance or elements in the Afghan government, but now runs so deep that most Afghans have stopped differentiating between Pakistan's military and the general population. Of course, Kashmir is also linked with the project because their dominance over Afghanistan is intended to create anarchy in Kashmir.

P.G. Kamath, in his paper on "Will Afghanistan relapse into Terrorism post-2014? India's Options", says that the Soviet withdrawal from Afghanistan was the handiwork of US, Pakistan and the Mujahedeen. The Americans were known to have given $40 billion in addition to other weapons and equipment and 2000 stinger shoulder fired Surface to Air Missiles to Pakistan. Lt. Gen. Akhtar Abdur Rehman, the then ISI Chief was responsible for directly conceiving and controlling the operations. It was hailed as an Islamic victory–a victory for Jihad, where Islamic freedom fighters defeated a superpower. There is a grave danger of misinterpreting the impending US withdrawal as victory for Jihad, where they would again claim having defeated another superpower to boost their morale.

In case of relapse of terrorism in Afghanistan, he discusses various options available to India. It is in India's interest that Afghanistan has a 'strong and stable' government. Afghanistan needs to see that clergy, warlords and tribal chieftains are brought into the governance system; ANSF is strengthened; efficient police force for internal security is built upon and adequate care is taken of 'pashtun nationalism'.

Dr Navasikha Duara in her contribution: "Stability under Threat: Post-US withdrawal from Afghanistan" focuses on the threat of emergence of Taliban and seeks to reduce and remove Pakistan's patronage to terror group. India-Pakistan need to see success in survival of Afghanistan as in the interest of both and the region rather than treat and see Afghanistan as a zero-sum-game. She foresees the possibilities of ISIS reaching out to Afghan terror groups like Taliban, Haqqani Network etc.

Dr Amruta Deshmukh in her contribution "Indian Perception of the American Withdrawal from Afghanistan in December 2014; Developmental issues and related policy options" focuses on India's democracy and discusses economic development and building democracy as issues taken up by India and the US. The two intend to explore opportunities to work together to promote Afghanistan's development including in areas such as agriculture, mining, energy, capacity building and infrastructure. India needs to promote accelerated completion of long-planned Turkmenistan, Afghanistan, Pakistan and India (TAPI) gas pipeline. The project is a win-win situation to all the nations directly involved.

Without peace, security and stability in Afghanistan, global peace, security and stability cannot be achieved. Afghan peace is linked to global peace. In view of this fact, Pakistan has to rise above its narrow selfish national interests and bring desired change in its perspectives in Afghanistan. This will also be in the larger interests of Pakistan as any instability in Afghanistan will destabilise Pakistan as well. So the need of the hour is that Pakistan must join hands with the US and India and other regional and global stakeholders in stabilising the situation in Afghanistan.

2

The Verities of Afghanistan and India's Options

BHARAT KARNAD

The military fatigue induced by indecisive military operations in Iraq and Afghanistan and in propping up the high-maintenance "democratic" regimes in Baghdad and Kabul has prompted the United States to follow a familiar pattern. It is cutting and running from yet another failed foreign intervention. Two successive failures after the initial highs of taking out the Saddam Hussein government and ending the Taliban rule of the one-eyed Mullah Omar in Kabul, has put the US policy for this region and towards the Islamic world generally at a crossroad. Washington seems unsure about how to deal with developments while retaining a hand in the larger strategic game afoot in this wider region.

The US Secretary of State John Kerry attempted to broker peace and reconciliation between the two presidential aspirants Dr Abdullah Abdullah and Afzal Ghani, the former is Tajik representative and former foreign minister while the latter is the figure head of the majority Pakhtun community and ex-finance minister. Kerry's effort has worked only up to the point that the differences between the political rivals have not ruptured. The scuttlebutt in Kabul has it that Hamid Karzai liked the idea of extending his stay in the President's office so much that he engineered the results of the runoff elections in order to prolong his tenure as President. In the second round of voting a phenomenal increase in voting transpired and two million more votes were cast than the first time around, with most of these votes going to Ghani. Abdullah thinks he was robbed of victory and is adamant that he'll accept no outcome other than his installation as President.

While the impasse is set to continue several compromise solutions are making the rounds. Among these are Abdullah and Ghani taking turns as president. Another solution is for Abdullah being given the defence ministry, intelligence, and police in a Ghani presidency. The reason why eventually this may be acceptable to the Tajik faction is that the coercive power of the state will reside with it besides putting it in-charge of prosecuting the war against the mostly Pakhtun Afghan Taliban headed by the one-eyed Mullah Omar. Things are very much changed on the ground for the Quetta shura. The extent of change may be gauged by Omar's declaration made not too long ago, that should the Taliban return to power programmes for educating the girl-child and employment opportunities for women would not be affected. In any case, the Taliban have been sufficiently weakened as a military force and do not anymore constitute as serious a threat to the Afghan National Forces (ANF) as previously was the case.

The fall-off in the Taliban fighting strength is grudgingly conceded, albeit *sotto voce* by the Taliban leadership. Long years of attritional war against the high-tech resourced US military leading the International Security Assistance Force (ISAF) have taken their toll. The drone war in particular has decimated several levels of leadership down to the grassroots, which the Taliban are finding hard to replace. A good proportion of the Taliban's fighting cadres were seasonally drawn from among the youth in agricultural communities in remote valleys involved in growing heroin poppy, joining in Taliban operations during the non-harvesting season was a paying proposition until the professionalisation of the ANF which heightened the intensity of fighting and increased the risks to them. Tribal youth are now more motivated to protecting their home base and the trade in heroin as cash crop than in restoring a Taliban government in Kabul. Moreover, the generous funding by the Arab Sunni charities for the Afghan Taliban is drying up in the context of the rise of the hideous Islamic State of Syria and Iraq (ISIS) and international pressure on Saudi Arabia and the Gulf states to refrain from financially supporting Islamic extremist groups generally. Thus, constrained financially and manpower-wise, the Taliban are less of a factor in Afghanistan than they were a few years back.

Besides the internal balancing of Pakhtun and non-Pakhtun interests, the future of Afghanistan will be influenced by external players. Among its neighbours, India is well placed to consolidate its presence and role in that country. It enjoys support, trust and goodwill across the board, reflected in the warmth that Karzai, Abdullah, and Ghani feel for New Delhi. Even so India's strong relationship with the Tajik-dominated Northern Alliance is, as always, the fallback option. Kabul seeks continued Indian engagement with more development aid (totalling some $2 billion till date), project assistance from India has seen a brand new Parliament House and a smooth double-lane highway connecting Delaram with Zaranj on the Iran border come up (the latter has even won the friendship of tribesmen growing poppy and using the road to tranship it to heroin processing centres on the border with Iran). Heroin is narcotic substance which has limited positive uses in the field of medicine. The tribal community knows how to grow poppy which has made the agriculture of the region narcotics- based, efforts should be made to train them regarding growing other crops also, under contract farming arrangements or otherwise. Rural marketing networks and support systems should be established and entrepreneurship, business, employment and other wealth creation avenues should be explored and harvested. Poppy should only be grown in limited and controlled amounts after careful consideration and deliberation and only to fulfil its demand by the medical field. More people may want to grow poppy rather than other crops as it fetches them more returns, here the pricing needs to be looked into and redefined. Poppy should be grown only under licensed and well defined contractual agreements and the contracts need to be assigned in such a manner as not to induce a feeling of inequality and favouritism among the folk, due to the high price fetched through poppy farming. Large fields should be avoided for growing poppy, once it was reported that in a land in a village located in Bihar (India), where poppy was being cultivated the parakeets and other creatures who took their food from this plant started showing signs of addiction and after some time perished and this continued season after season. Hence, it may be advisable to grow poppy in pots which will also have the benefit of freeing the land for the cultivation of other crops, or if grown on land, the land crop should be well protected and be made inaccessible to living creatures. Tribal folk should be educated regarding hazards and havoc of addiction, especially opium (morphine) based addiction, on individual lives and the entire humanity (effect on brain, thinking etc.) and should be discouraged from dealing with illegal drug traffickers. Illegal drug trafficking which is also a major source of funds of the terrorist groups should be tackled immediately and with heavy hands. India should align its forces with other international forces who are working in the above mentioned arenas.

India's economic stake in Afghanistan has grown with Karzai's encouragement. Concessions to Indian consortia to mine iron ore in the natural resources rich Hajigak region in the western part of the country are expected to be the vanguard for a still greater Indian presence in Afghanistan's extraction sector. Indeed, Hajigak could become an Indian economic hub connecting India with Russia and Central Asia by means of the north-south rail and road corridors to the port of Chahbahar that India is investing in and developing. In the security field, ANF is provided with the largest number of slots set apart for foreign officers in Indian military training centres. New Delhi is also ensuring that the ANF is not bereft of heavy armaments in their fight with the Taliban. It is not widely known that helicopters, long range artillery and tanks purchased by India in Ukraine and Russia are carted overland using the Northern Distribution Network through Russia and the Caucasus to Afghanistan. More directly India ships small arms and ammunition and other war material as per ANF's requirements.

With its consulates in Jalalabad, Khandahar, and Herat, India is also liaising with various Pakhtun tribes that sustain the Taliban with a view to moderating the Taliban stance against India. The logic being that if Afghanistan's social entities of its ethnic quilt-work of tribes and sub-clans who join Taliban for employment, can be induced to be nice and prefer peace and progress over fighting then India's interests will become safer in that country. Such reaching out has led the former Taliban foreign minister to disavow any interest in fighting India or to join Pakistan in deploying battle-hardened Taliban fighters in

Kashmir. The Pakistan Army's military operations in North Waziristan against the Pakistan Taliban have often spilt over across the Durand Line into Afghanistan, causing bad blood between Pakistan and Afghanistan on the one hand and between Pakistan and elements of the Afghan Taliban on the other hand, the latter sharing tribal loyalties with members of the Haqqani clan and a fragmenting Tehreeq-e-Taliban Pakistan (TTP). In fact, the Punjabi faction of TTP has declared that while it will not engage in armed activities within Pakistan, *jihad* in Afghanistan would be continued. Moreover, Islamabad's inability or unwillingness to fully rein in mobile terrorist gangs for whom international borders mean little has eventuated in Iran warning Pakistan of military hostilities in case the Pakhtun Sunni fighters of various stripes are not stopped from creating sectarian mayhem in Iran's borderlands.

Pakistan finds itself between and betwixt the strategic doctrines of the past that conceived Afghanistan as being able to afford "strategic depth" of the Pakistan military and the imperatives of the future in which it finds itself surrounded by three neighbouring states, which it has alienated – India to the east, Iran to the west and Afghanistan to the northwest. Further, the latest attempt by Islamists to forcibly takeover the Pakistan Navy frigate PNS Zulfikar berthed in Karachi harbour and use it to mount attacks on US carriers in the Arabian Sea adds another dimension to an internal menace transforming into a military threat to others, even the friendly countries. This is the latest in a series of terrorist strikes that earlier targeted the Mehran naval base and the Kamra air force base, and emphasises the world-wide concern of Pakistani nuclear weapons or fissile material (usable in radiation diffusion devices or "dirty bombs") falling into the hands of terrorist organisations. All these developments have created insurmountable difficulties for the Pakistani army which finds its capacity stretched almost to the breaking point.

Such a fraught external situation has combined with the prevailing disorder and political turmoil within the country. The joint campaign conducted by Imran Khan's Tehreeq-e-Insaaf party and the Tahirul Qadri led Minahjul Quran movement has sought to draw the Pakistan army into the ongoing political fight in order to unseat the Nawaz Sharif regime. Till now General

Raheel Sharif has remained resolutely on the sidelines by neither helping the government assert itself nor siding with the opposition, the latter stance would be tantamount to giving marching orders for the dispensation from the Muslim League (N) which is presently in power. With Pakistan so preoccupied, Afghanistan is understandably not as conspicuous on Islamabad's foreign policy radar.

The upside of the situation is that it has convinced the Pakistan army to take a more realistic stance and state that there is no security threat from India, like General Ashfaq Kayani followed by other army chiefs have done. But this tempered view of India has in no way diluted Pakistan's belief that India should not have any significant role in Afghanistan. As it is, Islamabad accuses the Indian consulates in lower Afghanistan of fostering the rebellion in Balochistan and such other anti-Pakistan activities. It is a view that the Pakistan government has been successfully able to sell to Washington. India has thus been kept out of the various forums– Ankara, Chicago, etc—called to discuss the future of Afghanistan post-withdrawal of American military forces. India's being kept away from the negotiating table may have had the deleterious effect of making the Karzai government more adamant. In any case, considering India's time and crisis-tested association with the Northern Alliance, Indian interests will have to be safeguarded in perpetuity. The question is how?

The worst case scenario can be of the US decamping entirely from the country and winding up even the support missions such as drone strikes on Taliban targets, due to which the Kabul government collapses and the Taliban which controls large parts of southern and eastern Afghanistan comes back to power. New Delhi will then be confronted with stark choices. It can continue as before, the bolstering of Tajiks in their northern stronghold where the writ of the Taliban will not run as it did on the previous occasion. Teharan may decide to beef up the Shia fighters around Herat sufficient to ward off Taliban rule.

In all likelihood the successor regime of Abdullah Abdullah or Afzal Ghani will rely more on Indian military assistance and depending on how the fight against the Taliban progresses may ask in essence for Indian military deployment to replace the departed US military forces. Would New Delhi accede to such request, given that it may have a sort of understanding with the Afghan Taliban of Mullah Omar to implicitly protect India's economic investments in the natural resources and other sectors in Afghanistan and even a vague guarantee against interfering in Kashmir affairs? No. Even so, let's suppose the Indian government decides that it is in the long-term interests of the country to place Indian military units in the line of fire in Afghanistan, problems will arise with the Indian military sustaining an active role at a distance. While the Indian Navy regularly traverses the oceanic highways and logs in long sea-time, neither the army nor the air force is experienced in expeditionary missions. Also there is no infrastructure to support a big Indian military presence in Afghanistan.

This leaves whichever regime is in Kabul to try and survive the best it can with material support from India and other countries as the conflict with the Taliban enters the protracted and attrition stage of warfare. Such warfare, if the Afghans are ready to wage it, can be sustained for a long time. After all, the *jezail* (and now the Kalashnikov) wielding Afghan and his love of fighting is a figure of lore who, when he didn't tangle with outsiders, fought his cousins (to wit, a Pakhtun proverb that cousins are the worst enemies!). The fact is that with the north-south rail-road corridors through Chahbahar, India has direct access to Afghanistan and Central Asia and does not anymore need to transit through Pakistan to reach the Central Asia Republics. With Pakistan thus bypassed, its suspicions of India may only grow as Islamabad fears Indian use of Afghanistan to destabilise Pakistan (as many Pakistani hardline charges are being put up with respect to Balochistan). This possibility gives Pakistan all the more reason to keep India out of Afghanistan to the maximum extent possible or to minimise the Indian presence and role in that country if the former endeavour fails.

For the US and the West, Afghanistan is important for two other reasons. One, because with ISIS seemingly taking wing in West Asia, it won't be long before Taliban fighters and professional *jihadis* are drawn to Abu Bakr al Baghdadi and his promise of the caliphate to fight under the ISIS flag and use Afghanistan as the channel. The extremist Islamists will then become an uncontrollable and cascading threat that will spread throughout Eurasia. The other reason is the possibility of a revived

Russia reclaiming Central Asia as its area of influence and staking its interests in Afghanistan as leverage for potential use against NATO in Europe. Extremist Islam is also emerging as a potent danger to China in the Muslim Uyghur majority province of Xinjiang thus tying Chinese security interests into the future of Afghanistan especially because Pakistani Sunni proselytisers have been accused by Beijing as radicalising the Uyghurs and initiating *jihad* against the Chinese regime.

In a sense then southern Asia with India centred in the region and straddling many fault lines may be going back to the past when it was a contested ground between various ideologies and clashing interests. Unless India becomes far more proactive in its foreign and military policy, it will find itself unable to cope with a hostile reality in the extended region.

3

Global Jihad/Terrorism: New Challenge to World Peace and Stability: A Philosophical Analysis

D. B. SHEKATKAR

The Jihadi/Terrorists of today who operate in different parts of the world can be categorised as: Non-state supported, state sponsored and supported and state directed groups. Such groups operate across the world. It is unfortunate that some of the self-projected, self-sponsored and self-supported experts in counter-terrorism and unconventional warfare have not bothered to understand and analyse the philosophy and concepts of *jihad*/ terrorism. In the Indian context and against USA, non-state supported groups, all operate from Pakistan. Pakistan is an exporter and advocate of Jihadi concepts/Terrorism across the world.

The Jihadi Concepts of War which are a product of misinterpreted religious teachings are being redefined and followed by most of the terrorist organisations all over the world. Jihadi concepts are basically based on anger, intolerance, hate, revenge and destruction. I shall deliberately avoid discussing the religious fundamentalism, relation between religion and terror and the difference between *jihad* and terrorism. When it comes to the question of peaceful existence of the human kind, it makes no difference under the influence of which philosophy of *jihad* the innocent human beings (especially women and children) are being killed all over the world every day.

Age-Old Problem

Jihad, terrorism, fundamentalism are not a new problem. This is a challenge that will continue to confront the nations (specially the liberal democracies) of the world till human society survives. The Zealots of Palestine used *jihadi* (terrorist) tactics in their struggle against the Roman occupation during the first century AD. Over the century the term '*jihad*' got associated with the struggle against foreign domination and occupation. It is a phenomenon that evolved into a highly developed strategy allowing nations and in some cases small groups to conduct undeclared covert warfare. It is a strategy that is used against the nations that are otherwise at peace. In the twenty first century in areas experiencing extensive conflict, it has proven to be an effective tactic that is often used by both sides of the conflict. Modern day Jihadi/terrorists have moved beyond simple assassination and bombing, they have capabilities that provide them with the potential of killing thousands of people at a time in targeted nation and as a result threatening the political and economic stability of entire nation. From being people-friendly technology has become an agent of brutality that is being used for slaughtering people at a terrifying scale. The same technology is now being used by terrorists as well! 9/11is a glaring example!

Types of Jihadi/Terrorist

The concept of *jihad* in simple terms evolves from the philosophy of struggle for peaceful and meaningful existence against an evil. However, over the centuries and especially in the twentieth and twenty first century the concept of *jihad* has been totally misinterpreted and misunderstood. It has now become a *loose term* used by ill-informed and mentally sick people. The Jihadi/terrorist of today who operate in different parts of the world can be categorised as: Non-state supported, state supported and state directed groups. Such groups operate across the world. It is unfortunate that some of the self-projected, self-sponsored and supported experts in counter-terrorism and unconventional warfare have not bothered to understand and analyse the philosophy and concepts of *jihad*. In the Indian context against USA and Europe non-state supported groups, state sponsored Jihadi groups and state directed groups operate from Pakistan. In actual fact there are hardly any visible dividing lines. The Inter-Services Intelligence of the Pakistan army controlled, financed and directed by the Pakistan government have perfected and mastered the philosophy and the art of *jihad*. A Jihadi/ Terrorist movement must have effective leadership and an extensive support structure if it is to survive for any length of time. The leadership needs to have dedicated followers within the group and they need people outside the Jihadi/Terrorist groups who will provide over ground support such as intelligence collection and fund raising etc. Since 1980 there has been an increasing involvement and participation of women in *jihadi* movements across the world. Since the beginning of twenty first century most of the *jihadi* groups have been enrolling a large number of women for *jihadi*/terrorist activities for obvious reasons. Women are perceived to be highly suitable for collection of information, intelligence, transmission of small weapons, carriage of money and infiltrating into government mechanism as well as security forces. Though it is a wrong perception, terrorists seem to be convinced.

Conduits and Carriers

While combating terrorism in Punjab in 1990-1992, and in Kashmir during 1994-1996 and later combating insurgency in north-east India, I came across many cases when women and young girls were involved in passing information and small weapons. When I encouraged the concept of surrender by the terrorists we found many women surrendering themselves and their communication equipment and radio sets to the security forces. In Kashmir, the terrorists have a Ladies wing named as "Dukhtatan-e-Millat" which has been the important functionary of Jihad. Many of them even enjoyed state government support in different parts and different forms. In many public and private hospitals 'nurses' were specially trained to treat gun-shot wounds. We were able to apprehend a few terrorists with the help of the nursing staff. SIMI, a terrorist organisation has a ladies wing functioning for *jihad*. The concept of "Love Jihad" which started from the state of Kerala has now been adopted by Naxalites and Maoists operating especially in urban areas, cities and townships under the garb of students and information technology professionals. Some of the educated girls are trained to undertake financial operations and information collection. Insurgent organisations such as NSCN (IM), ULFA and NDFB have good number of young girls staying in insurgent camps across the border in Myanmar and Bangladesh and are involved in the smuggling of drugs, weapons, and narcotics and ensuring safe passage of funds and information. It is not easy to identify and apprehend the girl operatives especially in the Indian context. Some of the human rights organisations use these young girls to spread false allegations against state police, government officials and security forces. For *jihadi*/terrorist organisations to survive and succeed they must also include active and passive supporters. These people are not actually members of the group but they are sympathetic and supportive of the espoused credo and objective of the movement. The lady supporters are very useful in covert activities. Many of them are also part of over ground organisations to raise funds for the *jihadi* cause. In some cases, people contributing to these organisations do not know what the funds will actually be used for. Many of the countries in Europe, Middle East and some organisations operating from the USA have been the largest fund raisers and providers for the *jihadi* cause.

It is essential to remember that at the heart of every jihadi and terrorist act there is an ideology, a hidden agenda, a publicised goal or objective, a perceived injustice or denial that is as concrete to the terrorist, jihadi, militant, insurgent and fundamentalist as any political leader's notion of justice or freedom. All over the world, *jihad* or conflicts encompassing *jihadi*/terrorist activities have proliferated, particularly in developing countries like India and our neighbourhood. Democracies like India which permit free expression of ideas, including political protests, communal violence, strikes etc., are particularly vulnerable to *jihadi* violence. The growing number of terrorist attacks, the increasing destructiveness of terrorist's weapons and methodology, connectivity of Jihadi organisation, co-operation and understanding among them and use of information technology are posing new challenges and forcing governments all over the world to adopt preventive measures and precautions. This is resulting in a siege-like atmosphere around government building and institutions, embassy complexes, radio-TV stations, shopping malls, airports, railway stations, the residential areas of political leaders, senior government officials, diplomats and corporate executives, and a constant reminder of the fact that *jihad*/terrorism is neither limited by distance nor by choice of targets.

Networking

A complex web of interaction and relationship between terrorist organisations in different parts of the world is surfacing slowly but surely. Co-operation and connectivity between *jihadi*/terrorist organisations have sustained and been indoctrinated on religious lines and their supporters, sympathisers and sustainers have also been increasing manifold. There is an emerging concept of "techno jihad" and "techno-terrorism". A remote controlled device bomb or explosive mechanism does not recognise or differentiate between class, education, social-status or gender. Anyone can operate any destructive mechanism. The new emerging trend is that many *jihadi*s/terrorist, belong to well-to-do families, they are well educated and thoroughly indoctrinated with misguided religion as their base. This is where the women and girls also get attracted to *jihad*/terrorism.

The financial/fiscal network supporting *jihad*/terrorism is very complex and sophisticated and very difficult to detect. Financial sustenance coupled and connected with smuggling of weapons and drugs, hawala operations, kidnapping for ransom, taking hostages are the means of collection of funds for *jihad*. Many nations finance directly and indirectly. In the Indian context it is almost impossible to bring the culprits of illegal financial transactions to book because of the loopholes in the systems of banking, financing and legal framework. It is only recently that some checks and safeguards have been instituted by government of India.

New Methodologies

One of the concepts of the jihadi organisation is "You (the jihadi) cannot fight them (India-USA) because they have a large army but you can terrorise them by selective killing!" Conditions favourable for any *jihadi* organisation in any part of the world to execute the *jihadi*/terrorist act to obtain their conceived desired results, include:

(a) A proper time, when the wave of terror will be a complete surprise to the targeted society, nation and the world.

(b) Possession of strength sufficient to disrupt even the strongest and most resilient elements among the target group.

(c) Executability in a form that will have the most damaging psychological effect on the target group, society, nation and the entire world.

If examined and analysed correctly it should be clear that in future there will be a shift from "destruction of masses" to "disruption of masses". Disruption will be the key element. There will also be a shift in the focus from "how many killed" to "how quickly killed or destroyed". Therefore, to counter jihad/terrorism there should be shift in our strike and survival capability from "survival of the fittest" to "survival of the fastest". If we do not perfect the concept, mechanism and art of hitting first and hitting fast, we will continue to react and suffer. Individual and collective combat power and war mechanism of superpowers is unable to guarantee against global jihad/terrorism. Conventional wisdom, conventional war mechanism and conventional response alone cannot counter terrorism. We need uncommon commonsense to combat and counter terrorism even in the twenty first century.

Jihadi Concepts of War

The concepts of war which are a product of misinterpreted religious teaching are being redefined and followed by most of the Jihadi/terrorist organisations all over the world. Jihadi concepts are basically based on anger, hate, intolerance, revenge and destruction.

"The resources and energies of the enemy if not preserved intact could add to the power of Islamic state. The identification and application of all elements of national power, the ability to locate and conquer the gravitational centre of war and the judicious and effective application of the military instrument is a perfect strategy. (Syria, Iraq, North African Nations, Yemen are recent examples).

The central idea which must be noted is "identification of all elements of national power and gravitational centre of war". It should be clear as to why and how the terrorist selected the targets for air strike on 9/11! Why do they target American Embassies, Indian Parliament, Red Fort, Akshardham, Mumbai on 26/11 and so on.....

The jihadi war to be planned and waged should be total to the infinite degree. It should be waged on all fronts - internal and external, political and diplomatic, spiritual and psychological, economic and military... Here will be an ideal situation in which the military strategy, operating as integral component of jihad; the total strategy will produce spectacular results. Latest example is ISIS.

The analysis of the above concept will clearly indicate as to why the successive Pakistani government and military rulers have used Kashmir as main issue for the furtherance of concepts of *jihad* against India. "Bringing economic pressure to bear on one's opponent and enemy, we will ceaselessly with long range policy strike at the right moment when the enemy would not dare to offer any resistance and we will achieve our objectives". This is happening in the Middle East and North Africa and will happen in Europe also.

Even the most powerful economy like USA has suffered a great deal of economic and financial setback due to the continuous fighting in Iraq and till now in Afghanistan. USA is likely to suffer in Syria also, if they do not change their strategy and tactics.

It is not easy to achieve victory in this kind of conflict against Jihadis, terrorists and terrorism in short time. The nation/state must show patience in combating *jihad*/terrorism and work thoughtfully and deliberately over extended periods so that *jihadi* groups are weakened through sheer attrition. No fixed or ambitious time limits should be given to ground forces and commanders, or should be even expected, much like in conventional war which is what most of the armed forces are used to because of the peculiarities and limitations of conventional war. The same strategy will not hold good in unconventional warfare to counter terrorism or insurgency.

Counter-Jihad/Terrorism Operations

We must always remember the concept of Mahabharata and the philosophy advocated by Indian philosopher Chanakya: "If you know your adversary and if you can deter him, you will live in peace for hundred years". To achieve this, we must fight the war against *jihad* without losing the lives of our people especially women and children, without loss of our property and above all our "national pride". We must ensure the collapse of Jihadis/ Terrorist, their supporters and sustainers "from within".

Apart from adapting military, political, diplomatic, legal, financial and other means, there is also a need to examine and the analyse following aspects to arrest *jihadi*/terrorist trends:-

(a) What are the motivations of alienation and disaffection which drive men and women- specially the youth towards *jihad*, militancy, terrorism and induce them to take up arms against the established order?

(b) How does a modern lawfully constituted state respond to local rebellions, unrest, terrorism and *jihadi*/terrorist movement?

(c) What are the instruments available to the state to combat/ terrorism, unrest?

(d) What are the aspects of regional and global co-operation to deal with *jihad*/ terrorism? Why has the UN failed even to define terrorism/terrorist till today?

Philosophically we must remember that "Jihad/Terrorism is a weapon of the weak, to take on the powerful. The weak have one weapon, the errors of those who think they are strong"!!

In the given area of responsibility we were successful in combating and arresting terrorism by advocating the philosophy as explained below. To eradicate terrorism we must send a clear message across the world specially to the terrorism sponsoring nations:-

"Do not believe in the alliance of money and machine gun because your children will not get the money, but the machine gun, which will not only kill them but also others including sponsors and advocates of terrorism".

4

The American Withdrawal from Afghanistan 2014: Impact on Strategic Mosaic of South Asia

DILIP MOHITE

Proscenia

Prior to the unfolding of the drama of American withdrawal from Afghanistan in 2014, the South Asian region poses a mysterious and a precarious scenario. There are more than three (India, Pakistan and Afghanistan) regional states directly involved in the issue of Afghanistan from the overall strategic angle; the extra-regional powers like China, USA and Russia have also shown their vital interest in the turmoil ridden state of Afghanistan. Basically, India and Pakistan perceive Afghanistan as their vital security interest. This has led both the states to indulge in a chess-board game while Americans are still holding on to Afghanistan with visible military and political presence. As per the law of nature, everything that begins has to end some day. The year 2014 has been earmarked for the complete or partial American withdrawal. It is not yet ascertained whether it will be a complete withdrawal or the Americans would leave a token military force of seven to eight thousand, giving onus to Afghanistan National Army to control the situation riddled by complete disorder and factional conflicts. According to one source, out of 3,50,000 Afghan security forces only a few troops are well trained, while the rest are illiterate and not capable of performing their role of maintaining peace and stability.[1] It is not only crudely trained but also cannot act effectively. It has to be backed by a strong economy which is going to be a great problem as the American funds would dry up after their withdrawal. Hence, two major hurdles, weak economy and security forces would create a critical strategic, political, economic and a military vacuum in Afghanistan. Who will and who can fill this vacuum? Ideally, it should be Afghanistan itself but it has shown no signs of possessing this capability. The other two direct stake-holders are India and Pakistan. One has to scrutinise their respective capabilities, which would enable us to see whether their ambition matches with their goals in Afghanistan. What India and Pakistan want is a pliant government for which they seek suitable strategic architecture in Afghanistan. What will happen and how it will happen is a matter of conjecture. At the present juncture, the situation is more 'if and but.'

The present strategic scenario is full of concern to the pundits of international relations. Starting with India and Pakistan, the two countries are a part of 'enduring conflict' ever since their birth in 1947. It is not merely restricted to territorial (Kashmir as major and other areas as minor) factors but each claiming for South Asian predominance yet at the same time denying and challenging the other's respective claims. The rivalry is so fierce that most of conceptual idioms like hegemony, balance of power, arms race, militarism, democratic peace, nuclear holocaust, human rights, MAD, war versus peace etc. are applicable to their relationship. Their goals and ambitions are overshadowed by domestic issues like poverty, hunger and starvation, malnutrition, illiteracy, separatism, corruption, caste, religious cultural conflicts. All these make the task of establishing their credentials as influential powers in the region and world at large extremely difficult. Yet circumstantial compulsions are such that it becomes imperative for both India and Pakistan to plunge into the race, with no surety of success. In this context, India has an edge over Pakistan due to its size, better economic and political system, resources, and geo-strategic location. If one recollects, India was called 'jewel in the crown'. Indian ambition of hegemony, if used and understood in its positive sense, is not restricted to the South Asian region but seeks to establish its positive image as 'great power' at the global level. So far as Afghanistan is concerned,

India has done satisfactory developmental work there but under the shadow of American presence in recent times. It is not that Afghanistan–India relation had any problems but it had to break through certain insurmountable geographic limitations and some radical Islamist forces.

For Pakistan, Afghanistan is a life-line-cum obsession. It is more so because under the circumstances, it would try to have a stronger foothold in Afghanistan with a view to keeping India out. Viewing most of the factors, Pakistan's foreign policy is India centric. Ever since joint US-Pakistan operations began in Afghanistan during Soviet invasion of 1979-89 and then again during 2001 till 2014, Pakistan followed a double-edged policy; one supporting USA against Al Qaeda and using American supplied infrastructure against India by initiating low intensity conflict, the acquisition of nuclear capability by Pakistan was also India centric. The direct consequence was that Pakistan transformed the enduring conflict with India into 'low intensity conflict', rather than direct confrontation. Pakistan's NWFP and FATA areas became the recruiting ground for '*jihadi*' elements to strike at India. Pakistan also suffered 'insecurity dilemma', expecting Indian nuclear retaliation. Knowing its geo-strategic limitations, its strategic planners sought strategic depth in a friendly Afghanistan. [2] This made the strategic mosaic of South Asia extremely critical to the extent where nuclear exchange between India and Pakistan was considered a possibility. Pakistan has consistently shown belligerent attitude towards India by supporting several terrorist attacks on various targets which include attacks on Parliament, Mumbai etc. which almost brought the two adversaries to the brink of war.[3] It is reported that "Indian and Pakistani high officials exchanged nuclear threats, whether directly or indirectly, no fewer than 13 times in just five weeks during the Kargil crisis".[4] From the perspective of nuclear capability, Pakistan, though successful in neutralising India's conventional superiority by acquiring nuclear capability, suffered from the inadequacy of 'strategic depth' which its policy-makers sought through a friendly Afghanistan. Initially general Kayani eloquently supported this concept but later quite a few strategic and policy-makers also subscribed to this view.[5] It is this fact which has made Pakistan desperate to step into Afghanistan and this situation makes Pakistan- India competition inevitable. India will get some edge over Pakistan with regard to soft power but Pakistan can involve China to overcome the lacunae. It would also plead to US to give extra military and economic punch to neutralise Indian advantage. Moreover, some Islamic countries are also geared up to support Pakistan. There is one more alarming factor which has caused great concern not only to the region but also at the global level and that is the rise of ISIS (Islamic State of Iraq and Syria). After the American withdrawal, ISIS is likely to enter Afghanistan to fill the political and strategic vacuum.

USA and China are extra regional powers. Both have played their role in shaping the strategic mosaic of South Asia. Both have cleverly exploited Pakistan's psyche to their advantage. Both, US and China have lured Pakistan with money, arms, nuclear capability and often provided 'diplomatic scaffolding', thus saving it from the brink of collapse. In view of their past and present role, US and China would be willing to support Pakistan's urge for favourable Afghanistan. In this context, greater role and presence of US and China would drastically change the strategic mosaic of South Asia.

In view of this, India's strategic location and Indian Ocean and other sea lanes are likely to meet with serious security challenge. The strategic competition between India and Pakistan has already involved USA and China with a view to having strategic edge over India. In the process, Pakistan, Sri Lanka, Myanmar are key players which may facilitate both China and USA, denying India its strategic space in the Indian Ocean.

Thus, the South Asian strategic mosaic reflects a rather gloomy picture for India while the fault line emerging from West Asia and North Africa touches South Asia. The region reflects triad of conflict between India, Pakistan and China namely, low intensity conflict, separatism and insurgency; terrorism; internal political, economic and social squabbles; along with energy and environmental issues. Some issues, either Kashmir or Afghanistan or unforeseen calamity may trigger off larger conflict involving more states, and the worst that can be imagined is the 'nuclear war'.

South Asia's Strategic Mosaic after the American Withdrawal from Afghanistan

William Zartman states that "the Manichaean certainty of the Cold War as a system went when the two super-powers held each other in check.")[6] Zartman expressed a similar extant idea albeit a little differently. The Cold War World Order as a system was managed by the two super-powers, each sharing the responsibility by which conflict and peace was their joint responsibility. The world which was divided into Blue and Red in the twenty first century looks more like 'green' and 'blue'. The American hegemony and preponderance began to be tested soon after the beginning of twenty first century. The North-South divide, conflict based on culture and civilisation, the larger issue of single or multiple polarity and the rise of new powers like China, India and Brazil appeared on the world order staking their claim as important players in world politics.

Simultaneously, the concept of state came under severe challenge. According to Ruthkoff, non-state organisations like religious leaders, mafias, drug dealers etc. have penetrated into the domain of the state undermining its sovereign status.[7] In the 'Third State Debate', similar arguments were made where the non-state actors having financial resources, manpower (followers), their own rules and regulations have posed threat to the western concept of the state.[8] The whole exercise focuses on the creation of a world order based on liberal democratic principles and not on any other ideals; and definitely not on irredentist principles. Going by Manichaean principles, the righteousness of US revolved around oil resources of the West and Central Asia. It is not only US, but the entire old and new Europe's economy which is critically based on West Asian and Central Asian natural resources. According to Donald Rumsfield, nearly 25 per cent to 27 per cent of total oil resources of the world are located in West Asia. This attracted the western capitalist forces to control the region either directly or indirectly; paraphrased as 'neo-colonialism' as Anglo-US consensus on the Iraq war was resisted by France and Germany as Europe as an interest versus Anglo-US as an interest in the Iraq war.[9]

Leaving Iraq war at that level, the paper now would focus on the issue of Afghanistan. It is here that the Anglo-US and the major powers of Europe (France, Germany, Spain etc.) find common cause of 'terrorism' as common security interest. The second reason for intervention in Afghanistan is surely described in this article in phases one and two. In the first phase, the American involvement dates back to Soviet invasion of Afghanistan in 1979. Around this time, Nixon and Ford Administration had cautioned about frequent embargoes on gulf oil due to internal disturbance. Both had insisted on reducing US demand for oil and concentrating on indigenous resources like coal and developing strategic petroleum reserves.[10] During the Jimmy Carter regime, US foreign policy entered realist paradigm by announcing Middle Eastern Oil as vital source of energy. Protecting it became prime goal of US policy. This was eloquently stated by Carter – "An attempt by any outside force to gain control of the Persian Gulf regime will be regarded as an assault on the vital interest of the United States. It will be repelled by the use of any means necessary, including military force".[11]

The Iraqi incursion in 1990 and Soviet invasion in Afghanistan were seen as a threat to the vital American interest. The next step was to make Pakistan as base and prepare Afghan mujahedeen's to fight the Russian Forces in Afghanistan. The American approach to West Asia is a legacy of the British but the USA was keen on collective European approach to this issue. While Barack Obama appealed to European powers to undertake the responsibility of 'dirty work', meaning exercising military option. Europe was reluctantly agreeable to supplement NATO, the United Nations and thereby the United States.[12]

The above paragraph describes a sort of consensus to keep West Asia under their influence as physical control had become out of practice and fashion in the existing world order. Indirect control by instituting favourable governments, making them dependent politically, economically and also taking advantage of regional or internal conflict based on culture and civilisation was seen.

The Americans inherited the divide and rule strategy following the British art of diplomacy. Just one or two examples would suffice to understand this point. Saddam Hussain of Iraq was initially boosted and later turned villain when he attacked Kuwait in 1990. The second example is that of Osama bin Laden. He was boosted to drive Russians out of Afghanistan but later he opposed USA having known Anglo-American diplomacy to install puppet government. His extremism through extremist (religious) ideology culminated in 9/11. Prior to that, several terrorist attacks were registered in Europe, Africa, India and later in Pakistan. The new enemy, in the form of terrorism was born, whose main philosophy was to liberate Muslims from non-Muslims if they possessed their land assets or resources. The Americans attacked under the banner of UNO following Saddam Hussain's attack on Kuwait in 1990, and later under the pretext of possessing or acquiring WMDs. The 9/11 was a shock to the belief that USA was invincible. The primary US task was to mobilise NATO and attack Taliban government in Afghanistan. But the major financial, strategic and military burden was borne by the Americans. The domestic pressure and financial crisis in USA began to occupy centre stage in American Presidential elections. Obama assured that USA would withdraw from Afghanistan by 2014, but not before the installation of a pro-American and pro-west government, so as to continue to enjoy overall strategic advantage. However, it is certain that the American withdrawal is not the end of Afghan crisis. There are political actors (states) from South Asia (India-Pakistan), West Asia, East Asia, Europe and non-state actors (radical Islamic groups) trying to fill the political vacuum created by the American withdrawal. The article deals with two South Asian rivals India and Pakistan, with occasional reference to other stake holders like China, Russia, USA and the EU. There is no doubt that the dilemma before US policy-makers is to determine who should replace in Afghanistan after their withdrawal. Whether, the US has made any choice or not is not clear at this stage but there are more than two aspirants, India and Pakistan, from South Asia and others like Russia, Iran, China and the European Union. Amongst these, the most eager to step in is Pakistan.

PAKISTAN

Afghanistan so far has proved to be the 'grave yard' of great empires. Learning the lessons of history, no power either big or small would venture into Afghanistan with physical presence. The option open for any power is to have influence through friendly government in Afghanistan. From this perspective, throughout history Pakistan has played its diplomatic card quite skilfully. On the one hand Pakistan has kept US happy by collaborating in fighting one group of Taliban while on the other hand it has kept one channel open to Haqqani group with whom ISI has established contacts for their own use. Washington is debating a queer situation due to Pakistan's dual stance as it is realising that one day Islamabad is an indispensable ally; the next (day) it is a back stabbing foundation of Islamist military."[13]

The question is why Pakistan is playing a 'double game'. The answer is that "Pakistan strongly believes that it needs a pliant, anti-Indian regime in Afghanistan as it has done for decades of its foreign policy.[14] The pro-Pakistan government of Taliban can serve best strategic interest of Pakistan and would keep India out. General Kayani's eloquent demand for strategic depth against India, can serve dual purpose of having a 'terrorist sanctuary' which can be transported to liberate Kashmir from India. Secondly, Pakistan is using common Islamic and historic card of occupation of India for almost seven centuries by Islamic rulers. The secular, but Hindu India does not have such an effective card to counter Pakistan's irredentist approach.' Even now, before American withdrawal, Pakistan is engaged in anti-India activities through *jihadi* attacks on Indian installations in Afghanistan. Such a situation would become grave for India if pro-Pakistan Taliban comes to power, which will also be against the US and Russia. The strategic mosaic in South Asia would get affected with pan Islamic group, as Pakistan's goal is adversarial to liberal democratic countries of the West and South Asia. What will be USA's stand since it is overstretched in Iraq and Afghanistan? Would NATO play any role in Afghanistan?[15]

The second advantage which Pakistan has is in the area of trade and commerce. Having common geographical boundary, there has been official and unofficial trade between Afghanistan and Pakistan. Pakistan's agreement with Afghanistan APTTA (Afghanistan, Pakistan Trade, Tariff Agreement) facilitates trade in agricultural products to Pakistan. There is also trade route to Karachi and Gwadar ports from where Afghan goods are exported. There is also a big marijuana trade, which goes to these ports, and also reaches Indian borders. Since Afghanistan is a landlocked country, Pakistan provides access to sizable number of Afghan goods through its sea ports of Karachi and Gwadar. This, in a way creates dependency which would favour Pakistan in future. In fact, Pakistan army uses it as leverage to bend Afghan Government in its favour. These are all hypothetical issues and its actuality would largely depend on the prevailing circumstances, and on which group gains power in Afghanistan. It is all 'pythonic' and divination based on existing facts and situation.

The next advantage that Pakistan has is that of Islam, the common faith in both the countries. A few years back, globalisation, secularism, democratic governance of state and society were the riding principles of statecraft and intra-state relations. One would have ridiculed the absolute role of religion in nation building. No one would have imagined that after the end of Cold War, there would be a spurt in religious or civilisational clash as propounded by Samuel Huntington.[16] The religious radical movement found its root in consolidation of societies and states based on religious principles. In a way it was a decline or retreat of democracy, secularism and globalisation. Afghanistan is a testing ground for this clash, with other states like Iraq, Syria joining the conflict. It's a triangular conflict between the West and within Islamist modern vs. radical groups. A country like Pakistan which was created on the foundation of 'Islam,' failed to cement fissiparous tendencies of culture or regional loyalties. This is evident from the fact that Bangladesh alienated from Pakistan in 1971. The movements of Baluch and Sindh and NWFP have not died down, and quintessentially their direct or indirect contact with Afghanistan is well known. Still for political reasons, a section of Taliban has kept their channel open for Pakistan. ISI, Pakistan's intelligence agency has been able to lure this group with money, arms and future hopes of political power. Their passions are aroused with the hope of not only 'Islamic rule' in Afghanistan but a '*jihad*' against infidels. With these favourable and unfavourable points, Pakistan wants to increase its presence in Afghanistan, including a pliable government. This hope for Pakistan is based on two factors– elimination of Indian influence and expansion of Islamic faith as new nationalism spanning through the Islamic countries where ISIS has challenged pro-West governments in the Gulf and West Asian regions. From the strategic point, Afghanistan occupies a significant place in the geo-politics of the region, as a centre-focal point in the contest.

It is interesting to examine Pakistan's dilemma after its decision to join NATO forces in its war on terror. The USA. opted for Pakistan's support for more than one reason. First, Pakistan-USA relationship is governed by 'dependency' in arms and money. The USA can bend Pakistan to behave according to NATO's war plans. The Pakistan army and ISI had already established cordial relations with Afghan Taliban with a view to using them in Kashmir. ISI's game plan suffered a great set-back, the moment Musharraf was left with no choice but to join the 'war on terror'. The Talibans both of Afghan and Pakistan turned against the state of Pakistan, causing tremendous damage to life and property. The law and order situation became worse, almost unmanageable. Moreover, there was tremendous discontent amongst the Pakistan Army to fight its own Islamic brethren, yet it carried out the operations reluctantly. Right from the time they were recruited, they were indoctrinated with one target (India) but now they are fighting their own people.[17]

The other dilemma is the fear that USA might dump Pakistan after their withdrawal from Afghanistan, resulting in drying up of funds and arms. To meet this possible contingency, Pakistan has begun to promote China, their second mentor. Prime Minister Gilani began to promote China to Afghanistan, the power in ascendency while USA is a declining power. The issue, therefore is whether Pakistan would continue with two masters or one or none?[18]

Pakistan Linkages

Apart from the Islamic card, Pakistan has some advantage in its linkages with extremist organisations like Al Qaeda, Haqqani group and several other groups but on a smaller scale. While acting as 'frontline state' under US auspices, it had established working relationship with major groups. Initially the target was Soviet Union, which enabled Pakistan to organise several 'mujahideen' camps in and around Peshawar. The activity was nurtured by American money, arms and training of 'mujahedeens.' For USA and its Western allies the strategic importance of Afghanistan was crucial. President Jimmy Carter eloquently stated at the time of Soviet invasion that the Middle Eastern oil is crucial to USA and the European powers. Interpreting American interest which includes its interests in European and East Asian allies, mainly Japan, the Middle Eastern Oil continues to hold the key to West's political realism of keeping their economic machine (development) going. The West continues to exercise control over 25-27 per cent oil which is not only their economic lifeline but also caters to American political game plan of global hegemony and unilateralism. Thomas Friedman categorically illustrates the US vision as well as ambition of global leadership by remaining at the top of the world order. Neither Russia nor China nor European Union has developed the capability that the US has. No country can be a substitute for the USA. It is number one in military, economy, human rights and ideals.[19] This statement goes to prove USA's recurring interest in the region and it would look for strategic bases which includes Afghanistan. Apparently, for two reasons, USA would continue to hold Afghanistan as its vital strategic and security interest. First, as stated earlier, the oil and natural gas in the Persian Gulf, Middle East and Central Asia. The second interest is to eradicate vital bases of terrorism which not only affects American security but that of many states of the world. Seen from this angle, the Americans would look for a state which would serve their national interest. Viewing the issue from past experience, Pakistan would be more than eager and enthusiastic to play this role to extract double gain - the natural resources of Afghanistan and access to its sea ports. The second interest is very well known and that is the hindrance to 'strategic depth' and political or any other advantage to India. Pakistan's foreign policy is 'India centric' and that draws the policy-makers and implementers to seek 'hyper-real-politiik path. The approach is juxtaposed between realism and idealism; which one of the two finds operational preference is determined by state capability of hard power and soft power. At least in case of Afghanistan, Pakistan neither has hard power of the capability to hold Afghanistan, nor does it have soft power capability whereby it could venture and buttress into its Afghan policy. The major thrust with which Pakistan wants to deal with Afghanistan is 'Islamic card', which appears to be feeble. So, realistically what sounds as advantage may turn into a nightmare. Under the circumstances, whether USA or China would back up Pakistan in its Afghan policy is a matter of conjecture at least at this juncture. The larger option that Pakistan can exercise is how its two mentors, USA and China would back its game plan in Afghanistan. What price Pakistan would be willing to pay in addition to the price already paid as a 'utility state' or 'rentier state'.[20]

India in Afghanistan

India is another major and direct stake holder in Afghanistan. As seen above, India's keen competitor Pakistan is desperate to diminish existing Indian influence in war-torn Afghanistan. The Indian interest is much broader than Pakistan, though Pakistan's focus remains predominant in its policy options in Afghanistan. India of the past, that is from the time of invasion by Alexander and later by Gazzani and still later by Moghuls in the sixteenth century, had been a victim of several political onslaughts, resulting in a well-established Muslim rule for nearly seven centuries. Afghanistan provided an easy access; anybody who could cross Khyber-pass became master of India. Barring just one man, Kautilya's desperate and passionate appeals to organise a united front against invaders did not succeed. The entire history of India is a history of divided nationalities. A Maratha leader, Chhatrapati Shivaji fought single handed to create an independent kingdom but his major energy was consumed in fighting his own people. But at least, he was the pioneer of freedom movement; unfortunately, his followers could never keep up the spirit and unity of purpose and goal of defending India from foreign invaders. The Third Battle of Panipat in 1761 is a landmark in the history of India from two broad angles. First, as historian R.C. Majumdar states, 'Muslims and Marathas got exhausted in the battle of Panipat, paving way for British supremacy in India'.[21] Second, this time the invaders came through the sea and that too not as invaders but as traders. The political vacuum and disunity was still pervasive in India and that led East India Company to change its posture from trade to political entity and then the new masters of India. Thus, Afghanistan was a base from which India was politically subjugated while the British and other European powers (France, Portugal, Dutch) showed a new entry point which created threat to India's security and still is so.

The Logic of History and Geography

The logic of history and geography is that in present times invasion from the geographically defined territory of the north is a thing of the past. From North, Pakistan remains a security threat to India but it would be imbecility to dream of Muslim reign in India. Another fact is that no Muslim country (involved in invasion of India) has the capacity to enter India, as it did in the past. Today, India ranks amongst six great powers. Any ambition or goal to subjugate India based on past history would be nothing less than living in a fool's paradise. Still, Pakistan is desperately trying to follow and implement a 'seven point' formula of Muslim rule in India.[22]

It is here that the logic of history and geography both has to be taken into account. Historically, Afghanistan was a base for the past attack (invasion) on India while today Pakistan is desperately trying to use Afghanistan as a base to achieve multiple objectives which it has against India, through terrorist activity. Pakistan's inability to defeat India in a conventional war made to it achieve nuclear capability thereby neutralising India's conventional superiority. But, both arch rivals possessing nuclear capability led to the promotion of low intensity conflict (LIC).[23] Pakistan's military and ISI systematically diverted some 'Talibans' to bleed India by a series of terrorist acts which is well documented. For instance, attack on Indian Parliament, several bomb blasts in Mumbai including 26/11, Varanasi, Pune, Ahmedabad, etc. The crux of the discussion is that now India faces security threat from such elements from the North. A pliant group i.e. government in Afghanistan would boost Pakistan's game plan of LIC and keep India on its toes. India therefore also has a strategic interest in Afghanistan and would be keen to deny such advantage to Pakistan. The strategic race between India and Pakistan after the withdrawal of USA, therefore assumes significance for India from the security angle.

India's Soft Power Diplomacy

Historically, India since its independence has a reasonably good record in its official relationship with Afghanistan with some ups and downs. The litmus test came when the Soviets invaded Afghanistan on invitation from the then Afghan government. There was clear cut rift between the Afghan government and Afghan ethnic groups. Later these groups organised themselves as 'mujahideens' to fight against the Russians under US patronage. India faced two crucial political problems and condemned Russian invasion due to its strong strategic and political relationship with the Soviets, thereby inviting Taliban's wrath. Second, Pakistan's acceptance to play the role of 'Frontline State' earned special favours from the Americans. Supply of arms, money and training of Afghan Mujahideens on Pakistani soil encouraged Pakistan to do the same to liberate Kashmir from India. It caused serious security concern as envisaged by the establishment in India. The withdrawal of Russian troops after ten years (1979-89), saw Taliban coming to power and this was a rejoicing event for Pakistan to step in to increase its influence in Afghanistan. India was clearly at a disadvantage, both politically and strategically. The ISI of Pakistan had established strong links with the new Taliban government, almost on the verge of achieving long cherished strategic depth against India. Though, scholars like Ahmed Rashid have called 'the concept of strategic depth 'absurd idea.'[24] However, even if the strategic depth was an absurd and impractical idea, a close contact with one or two Taliban groups could result into joint venture of Afghan-Pakistan Taliban and Pakistan's ISI can cause considerable security concern in India after the American withdrawal. Quintessentially, there would be no check on Pakistan's game plan against India. Indian diplomatic efforts would be based on existing soft power game plan to create goodwill amongst Afghan people if the conditions are conducive.

Post-9/11

The attack on Twin Towers in New York and Washington by the Al Qaeda operatives trained in Pakistan sent shock waves in USA and major countries of the West Europe. The daring act exposed the invincibility of USA. It also showed the strength, determination and faith of Al Qaeda followers under Osama Bin Laden. Recovering from the shock, USA (NATO) declared war on the Taliban government. India reacted favourably to USA's act and offered base facilities but USA preferred to use Pakistan. It is interesting to note that Pakistan was favourably disposed with the Taliban, was forced to fight under US pressure. Musharraf's act surprised everyone in Pakistan and around the world. The state (Pakistan) which was created to protect the cause of all Muslims was compelled to fight 'Taliban warriors' that too on behalf of USA, the arch enemy of Al Qaeda. The act exposed Pakistan's hollowness of commitment to the cause of Islam.[25]

Yet, contact with Haqqani group has been used to disrupt Indian development programme.

India's Development Assistance

India's broad objective in the present and future context is to maintain status quo, especially after the US withdrawal. India desires that Afghanistan be enabled to play its due and independent role in the areas of geo-strategy and geo-politics in the South and the Central Asian region. As it is widely seen and observed, Afghanistan has shown alarming tendencies of fragmentation and internal conflicts between ethnic groups which refuse to accept domination by another group. Violent conflicts within such groups and political exploitation by external forces (Pakistan) make law and order in the society and a unified state a farfetched proposition. Under such circumstances external players have to tread with caution taking all sensitivities of various groups into consideration. Despite such odds, India launched development programme soon after the Taliban government was displaced by American action following 9/11. The purpose is to wash out the negative image which was created after the Soviet invasion. The space for development assistance was provided by the Karzai government which was installed after the 'war on terror.' Indian developmental assistance has been in the areas of (a) infrastructure, (b) road construction, (c) irrigation and power, (d) water supply, and (e) education. The aim is to rebuild Afghan society for the state's stability and consolidation. India has also supplied wheat, medicines, provided experts for police training, clothes, etc. India's investment is to the tune of US $ 650 million. For the first time, Kabul has 24 × 7 days electric supply, portable water and schools educating children. While India's assistance is appreciated by a large number of Afghans[26] there are occasional subversions like bombing of the Indian embassy, attack on construction workers by Pakistani-backed Mujahideens. To protect its personnel, India has deployed a strong contingent of ITBT - a paramilitary force. However, one should also accept the fact that a large American (NATO) military presence has helped India to carry out its development programme. Though this is a fact, yet animosity and hatred for Americans like 'kill American' feeling persists amongst some sections of Taliban. Killing of an American and a British journalist by radical groups is a pointer. Here therefore, India shouldn't be caught in the cross-fire between the anti-American Afghan groups and the Americans, since India is identified with USA in its war on terror. India will have to work hard to sustain its existing positive image so that its involvement and investment is not frittered away after the US withdrawal. Apart from economic assistance, Indian-Afghanistan historic ties, films and above all Indian market for Afghan goods are likely favourable areas but things would depend on rising tide of radical Islamist movement in and around Afghanistan. India will have to be prepared with alternatives to sustain its present position and goodwill.

US Game Plan

Strategic location of Afghanistan and Pakistan is such that any power seeking access to the Middle East and Central Asia cannot afford to let it go to its adversary. Way back in 1947-48, Mohammed Ali Jinnah categorically stated that Pakistan's strategic location is such that US would need Pakistan more than Pakistan needs USA. This has been abundantly proved over a period since the creation of Pakistan. Its sense of insecurity from India and also from Afghanistan reduced its status as 'utility state' or 'rentier state'.[27] During the Cold War it served as utility state against the Soviet Union and covertly against India so as to balance and contain India which was identified as Soviet client state. It is a well known fact that during Soviet occupation, Pakistan was used as 'frontline state', which resulted in the creation of several 'mujahideen camps' in and around Peshawar in Pakistan. Initially, Pakistan was happy that it was able to receive American largesse in the form of weapons and money. Its policy-makers planned to use this against India, especially to liberate Kashmir. The monster was created, initially against India but now it is destroying Pakistan's peaceful existence, and threatering its survival, thanks to its policy-makers who have shown myopic approach to Pakistan's interest as a state gifted with natural strategic location.[28]

The US game plan to exploit Pakistan's strategic location and obsession (insecurity dilemma) with India has been of great success. Right from the time when Pakistan became part of US sponsored military alliances (SEATO, CENTO) it has been a poor loser. It has not achieved anything substantial against India except launching 'low intensity conflict' through terrorist attacks from time to time, and earned a negative reputation in using terrorist acts. But the most alarming issue is that it has become victim of terrorist attacks in which it has been losing sizeable number of lives and incurring damage to property. The price that Pakistan is paying is its submission to American pressure to join the 'war on terror.' Earlier, Pakistan was cultivating Afghan and later Pakistan Taliban in the hope that they would be used against India. Hillary Clinton in an interview to NDTV stated that Pakistan has nurtured poisonous snake in its backyard in the hope that it would bite its adversary (India), but forgot to realise that it can also bite its own creator.[29] Dancing toAmerican tunes, Pakistanis, not only served its (US) interest by using Islamic extremism to pursue its foreign policy agenda in India and Afghanistan but the policy backfired and created internal extremist movement called 'Pakistan Taliban'.[30] Pakistan in its obsession with India has been a victim of American game plan. This has dangerous consequences for Pakistan. First, it has invited severe enmity from group of Afghan Taliban and ethnic groups for fighting fellow 'Islamists.' On American withdrawal, Pakistan is going to find it extremely difficult to fill in the vacuum. Pakistan under pressure from US has played a double game. Earlier, Pakistan was in full support of Afghan Taliban, assuming that in future they would seize power. The ISI has been very active in cultivating Afghan Taliban having established connections during the period after the US withdrew its operations once the Soviets left Afghanistan. US also got busy with the reshaping of post-cold war world order (1989-2000) with a view to maintaining their hegemony. Pakistan got a free hand to establish its influence, establish the much cherished strategic depth against India. While Pakistanis were rejoicing on their diplomatic success, Al Qaeda sponsored terrorist attack on USA (New York, Pennsylvania and Washington 9/11) which changed the entire game plan of Pakistan. George Bush declared war on terror, scrambled all their major allies and attacked Afghanistan, and USA forced Pakistan to join the war on terror. With initial hesitation, Musharraf was left with no choice but to join the fight against Islamist groups with NATO forces. "US pressure to join war on terror was due to two reasons. First was to remain a viable state and the assurance that the West would doubtlessly 'crush' Pakistan's economy if the government (Pakistan) were not cooperative. The second reason was that Musharraf knew that if he did not accede to US demand, Washington had other alternative in South Asia. The new US-India bond, forged by Clinton administration and extended by Bush presidency gave the United States new leverage over Pakistan."[31] This act of Pakistan created tremendous displeasure amongst the Afghan groups as well as amongst Pakistan Army. Some Afghan groups and Pakistan Taliban hate US. This has resulted into number of attacks on US military and Pakistan's civilian and military installations. Federally Administered Tribal Areas (FATA) has large number of refugees where Pakistan or US has no control over their activities. In fact, both are hated to such an extent that 'kill American' concept is very much in vogue. Under the circumstances, US cannot have Pakistan as its proxy. Even for Pakistan, it would be a suicidal move to step in after the American withdrawal. Hence, what options does USA have?

US Options

Obama's election promised that the US's military would be withdrawn from Afghanistan by the end of 2014. The deadline is coming closer by just three months. From 1979 to 2014, US scored two major successes. First, it was largely responsible for the withdrawal of Soviet troops and political control from Afghanistan. Partly Soviet involvement also stretched that country economically resulting in the collapse of Soviet Union. This left US as the only superpower resulting in a 'unipolar world.' The second success was weakening of Afghan Taliban resistance and subsequent killing of Osama bin Laden, the most wanted and dreaded terrorist who was provided shelter in Pakistan. It is strange that US's main target lived in Pakistan, the most trusted ally of US amidst blatant denial by its authorities. Despite Pakistan being the harbinger of terrorist activities against several targets in the world, especially India, the US connived at it most blatantly. Moreover, out of US's pronounced states engaged in terrorist activities, Pakistan does not fall in the list of those countries which have been the seat of terrorist activities."[32] Obviously, Pakistan's willingness to act and serve the American interest amounts to fighting and brutally killing its own Islamist brothers. It should not be forgotten that Pakistan stood for supporting Muslim interest not nationally but globally.[33] This is not for the first time that Pakistan-US cleavage has acted in tandem at the cost of Pakistan's crucial national interest. This behaviour is largely appreciated by the US establishment. Milton Bearden categorically stated, "Never mind, the only country (Pakistan) in South Asia that always did what we (USA) asked was Pakistan.[34] Pakistan's strange behaviour largely stems from anti-India insecurity and fear psychosis from India. One can recall that when war on terror was declared, India offered logistic support to USA which prompted Pakistan to take diagonally opposite turn and offer to join USA in its war on terror. Such USA-Pakistan cleavage in Afghanistan may induce USA to provide it a major role in Afghanistan. Seemingly, US is aware of the fact that Pakistan alone is incapable of sustaining in Afghanistan. Knowing this fully well, the US is also likely to invoke common US and Chinese interest in controlling Islamist terrorism affecting both US and China. US and China both have geo-strategic interest in Afghanistan and natural resource rich Central Asia. From this perspective, "geo-strategically too, a stable, strong and prosperous Pakistan serves Chinese and US (national) interest better than a failing and weak Pakistan."[35] It is also necessary to note that the Chinese clout in South Asia, when India proposed to induct China in SAARC as observer, found India isolated with only Bhutan supporting Indian proposal. The China axis consisting of Pakistan, Nepal and Bangladesh sided with China's move.[36] The incident is cited to show Chinese influence in South Asia where China-Pakistan axis would find favourable disposition from India's three neighbours if Pakistan plans to play major role in Afghanistan as USA's proxy.

US's Compromise Formula

US's war on terror had three specific objectives-first to destroy terror network of Osama Bin Laden, and second to remove the Taliban rule from Afghanistan. The third objective was to establish a pro-West government in Afghanistan with a view to having strategic foothold and also thwart any attempt by rivals to establish their influence in Afghanistan. The issue which would always remain to be answered is whether the Americans succeeded in achieving their objectives? Primarily, they were successful in killing 9/11 mastermind Osama Bin Laden who was hiding in

Pakistan. The second objective was also partially achieved by their establishing pliable government under Karzai. It is a well known fact that the Karzai government was not strong and acceptable to all tribal factions of Afghanistan. Under US sheltered Karzai government, stable and peaceful Afghanistan remained a far fetched objective. Elections were rigged and the Karzai government lacked a strong and honest administration. There were serious loopholes in creating a strong army, police and administrative personnel. Afghanistan lacked infrastructure to provide basic needs like education, health and employment. US aim was to assist Afghan government to enact speedy induction of development process. Indian role in this respect is laudable where power, education, health and roads are being developed by Indian economic assistance.[37] On and oft, pro-Pakistan elements, backed by ISI have indulged in disrupting Indian development activity but India is relentless in its 'soft power' diplomacy. Continuation and zest of Indian activity after the US withdrawal would depend on the type and kind of government formed in Afghanistan.

After Obama made election declaration of withdrawing from Afghanistan, the efforts to negotiate peace with Afghan Taliban and tribal chief began to take shape. German diplomat Michael Steiner and Richard Holbrooke were cleared by Obama to initiate negotiation with Taliban. It was a high level diplomatic interaction where Mullah Omar, Syed Tayyab Agha joined in the talk with a view to finding a peaceful solution to war torn Afghanistan.[38] The Talibans as well as Americans were fagged out by one of the longest wars in history. Both needed a solution which would provide peace to fighting outfits and honourable exit to Americans. It is necessary to note that the Afghan Taliban and tribal heads with their followers were fighting first with Soviets (1979-89) and then with Americans (2001-2014), almost twenty four years with enormous damage to their life and property. The American losses in life and money almost amounted to an average of $ 444 billion. The world financial recession which began in 2008 was affecting US economy adversely. By 2014, the promised (Obama's election promise) improvement of US economy could not be achieved against heavy spending of $ 671 billion in the Afghan war (2011). The urgency of economic recovery was a top priority against the rise of Chinese economy which threatened to overtake American economy in all respects. All these were causal factors for prompting American withdrawal by 2014. The end of 2014 is approaching fast, it is just three months away but there is no sign of final decision on the part of USA to end the Afghan imbroglio. The three major stake holders, present Afghan government, Pakistan and India are in a state of flux. The NATO forces, especially the European powers have not shown willingness to increase their involvement in Afghanistan, especially in the light of historical experience of British, in late nineteenth and early twentieth century. The Russians and now Americans, neither of them can boast of success. Hence, the policy-makers in Washington are examining various alternatives which would keep Afghanistan under the influence of the West.

Analysis and Conclusion

Four continents of the globe, Asia, Europe, America and Africa are found to be involved in Afghanistan for more than one reason. It is historically and strategically proved that Afghanistan is a focal point of interest for major powers, the reason being its geo-strategic location, natural resources (copper deposits, natural gas etc.) and the seat of global terrorism under pan radical Islamic movement. Its land and people have made Afghanistan a hard country. Its people are tough and traditional and possess tremendous resilience. It is possible that the American armed aggression may have loosened up their morale but that is not the end of it. Afghans, after severe blasting from Russians, recouped and are giving a tough time to NATO forces, and are still far from complete defeat.

The American withdrawal does not mean the end of Afghan crisis. While the preparations were on for withdrawal, Washington made serious efforts to involve some major European powers, especially France, Germany and UK. USA being overstretched in Iraq and Afghanistan, expected NATO powers to get actively involved in Afghanistan. This could also mean, not complete withdrawal but maintaining a sizable force to enable the newly elected government of Afghanistan to establish effective control by providing good governance. The proposal was personally taken by Obama but Sarkozy and Merkel had different perspective on the troubled region. Obama received only lip service from these two European powers.[39] If this does not work out, then the US would look to UN to fill the vacuum and maintain status-quo.

Karzai government was not only ineffective but was paralysed by non-action, corruption and inadequate security personnel to maintain peace and order in Afghanistan. In recent times, Karzai hated Americans, Talibans and Pakistanis. It was certain that the Americans would not back Karzai but look for fresh and more acceptable leaders to the people of Afghanistan and the West (Americans). The new leadership of Ashraf Ghani and Abdullah Abdullah had serious differences with each other over power sharing. But several meetings between the two leaders and John Kerry engaged these leaders in a series of negotiations which finally resulted in power sharing agreement between Ghani and Abdullah Abdullah on September 1, 2014. Still, it cannot be said with certainty that both leaders will be able to control their rival groups of Pashtuns and Tajiks effectively. Moreover, one has to view the situation of Pakistan's meddling in the internal affairs of Afghanistan with utmost caution.[40] However, the development provides sufficient relief to the Americans as they plan to leave Afghanistan!

The other stake holders Pakistan-China are clubbed together since both are most likely to team up to fill the political vacuum in Afghanistan. As stated earlier, Pakistan does have economic, political and religious access in Afghanistan, which is its advantage as well as disadvantage. Advantages are that the ISI already has established contacts with Haqqani group which may support Pakistani gesture. The unemployed Afghan youth can be lured into 'jehadi' activities against Indian presence in Afghanistan. Such elements can also be inducted into Kashmir to keep their life time ambition alive. The little advantage that Pakistan has may find political and financial backup from USA and NATO associates. In the existing situation, financial support to sustain Pakistan's support on war is well documented. The disadvantage is that a group of Talibans are extremely angry with Pakistan for having first sided with them and later taking diagonally opposite view to fight side by side with NATO (American) forces. The concept of 'good Taliban and bad Taliban' is floated with an understanding that those who cooperated with USA were identified as 'good Taliban' while those who opposed are called 'bad Taliban.' The latter outfit is not going to make Pakistani presence comfortable. They might hit Pakistan to the hilt along with home grown Pakistan Taliban. Prediction is difficult but one can only contextualise the future.

Chinese-Pakistani Nexus

Pakistan has been a 'utility state.' I have used this term in my earlier articles while T.V. Paul used the term 'rentier state,' this terming has proved to be both lucky and unlucky for Pakistan. It has invited severe criticism from academicians, diplomats, journalists, and its own people for compromising with its sovereignty and national pride. This has stemmed from a sense of insecurity it has suffered from the larger India. Its geo-strategic location has earned many advantages but the same status against India has resulted into earning the title of 'utility' or 'rentier' state. In mid 1950s, Pakistan joined a series of military pacts with the West (US sponsored SEATO, CENTO and recently NATO) with a view to entering into the balance of power game plan. After India's war with China in 1962, it moved closer to PRC which was beneficial to both. Later in 1969, it brokered the opening of China to USA and becoming a facilitator to both (USA and China) against Indian-Soviet axis. After the 1971 Bangladesh war with India, it sought to develop nuclear capability from China and it achieved the status of nuclear state with an unofficial declaration of 'Islamic Bomb,' luring good number of Islamic states and even terrorist outfits. This brief background is given to acknowledge far sightedness of Chinese diplomacy. Amongst multiple goals, China Comprehensive National Plan aims at China becoming the next superpower, much against the wishes of USA and India. China's systematic game plan includes two major steps. The first is to establish its position in East Asia, South Asia and West Asia. In Afghanistan and West Asia it has crucial strategic interest, especially the West Asian and Central Asian oil-gas and other natural resources. In the context of oil, it has been number one consumer displacing Japan. Energy is undoubtedly the means to an end. China wants to ensure smooth and safe passage from above regions to its mainland. In the process Pakistan is a great facilitator by providing land and sea access to West Asia and Afghanistan. China's rise as superpower is meticulously planned with futuristic vision. Pakistan,

Afghanistan and Central Asian states are a part of existing and futuristic Chinese strategic planning. "Chinese firms have invested heavily in natural gas, exploration and pipelines in Turkmenistan and in roads and tunnels in Tajikistan."[41] Moreover, keeping in mind the natural resources in Afghanistan and its Central Asian neighbours, "Chinese companies have secured the rights to oil blocks and what is believed to be the world's largest undeveloped copper deposits in Afghanistan."[42]

Furthering the argument about China's clout, Bill Emmot says US has been able to establish good contacts with bigger powers of Asia (Japan, India, Pakistan etc.) but in case of smaller powers, it is China which, with plenty of capital, can invest in areas like Afghanistan. Chinese owned companies are active in mining especially in the inhospitable terrain where western (or Indian) companies prefer not to tread.

In 2007 November, China's Metallurgical Group (CMG) won the tender for the right to develop potentially huge copper deposits in Afghanistan, world's largest bid of $ 3 billion. This goes with access roads, power stations, as well as (successfully) dealing with unstable politics.[43] The Chinese strategy to engage smaller powers in South Asia (Bangladesh, Sri Lanka, Nepal, Maldives, and Afghanistan) in contrast to USA is paying slow but steady dividends. Dealing with the question of Pakistan's eagerness to step into Afghanistan has Chinese ramifications. Knowing its limitations (military, political and financial), Pakistan is using Chinese boogie. During his visit to Kabul on April 16, 2011, Yousuf Raza Gilani (Pakistan Prime Minister suggested that "Afghanistan needed to look to China, a power in ascendance, rather than to the United States." Reacting to this proposal, an Afghan official knowledgeable about the meeting said "there was a mention of China in the meeting, China as a country, as an emerging economic power, and that maybe we should reach out to a new global economic power." The plea was that Afghanistan and Pakistan should strengthen relations with China.[44]

It is a well known fact that Afghanistan is a landlocked country. Its outlet to the sea and through land is largely dependent on Pakistan, with some clout in Afghanistan. Existing contacts with pro-Pakistan Talibans and some elements in the new Afghan Government of Ashraf Ghani and Abdullah Abdullah cannot ignore the fact of utility of Pakistan-China axis.

Bill Emmot is slightly skeptical. He feels that the Chinese would weigh every step before using Pakistan as stepping stone to Afghanistan. He further argues that China has its own credibility as economic and military power. It would indulge in Afghanistan on its own. However, this argument is not palatable. Chinese Xinjiang province and other borders adjoining Tibet, Pakistan occupied Kashmir are being considered for land route railway and motor transport to Gwadar, the multi-purpose port near Karachi, connecting it to northern provinces of Pakistan bordering North East Afghan. Pakistan can provide logistics while China has capacity for financial investments. By virtue of this, China can access not only Afghanistan but also Central Asia.[45] The other strategic advantage both Pakistan and China would have is to buckle down the common adversary, India. Hence, strategic utility of Pakistan by China is more than a possibility.

Conclusions

The limelight on Afghanistan is episodic, first with Soviet invasion and later by the Americans from 2001 till this date, if one includes the war with the British which predates these other two invasions, then it can be seen that the situation runs into innumerable years of conflict. In recent times, from 1979-89 and 2001 to 2014, a total of twenty four years have shown an unimaginable resilience of Afghan people. The two superpowers, who engaged Afghanistan by no means, claim complete success especially the Americans. With a view to extricating itself from Afghanistan, the consolation that America has is the 'fugal' agreement between Ashraf Ghani and Abdullah Abdullah. No one can predict the future but only suggest conjectures. The reason being, that the region of Afghanistan and its surrounding areas is viewed as an epicentre of terrorism, rather Islamic terrorism. Besides the naivety of the issue, there are deep-rooted factors which are at play. Just the use of brute coercion, latest drones or other modern armaments has not produced pliable results which the world is looking for. In this context, neither the west nor other stakeholders like Pakistan, India, China or some Islamic countries like Saudi Arabia, Iran, Russia etc. can hope to enter the dragon like situation in Afghanistan. The issue of conflict is not only between the west or non-Islamic countries versus radical Islam but something deeper that has enabled

Afghanistan to defy the fury (many times powerful) for more than four decades. Whether the issue is political, economic, socio-anthropological or psychological, apparently, it looks like a conglomeration of all these factors and deep-rooted concerns of Islamic people have given them the strength to sustain the fury of 'great powers.'

The American withdrawal is not an end in itself. USA can only be credited with partial success. Its objective to completely destroy terror network has not met with success. In fact, it would leave Afghanistan in a state of flux. This is because there are many deep-rooted factors which drive the existing currents in a direction that is explosive. The American hegemony (after the end of cold war) was short lived, "Triumphalism as interpreted by American policy-makers in the First Gulf War (1990) and then attack on Saddam Hussain's Iraq (1999) was short lived. Leaving Afghanistan by 2014 is by no means like a successful exit from Berlin after the complete defeat of Hitler and his allies in Germany. In fact, all thc three acts stated above have created the feeling of 'anti-Americanism' which is spreading by leaps and bounds. American zeal for democratic values and tenets of globalisation and free market have created hatred and repulsion. 'Kill America' slogan in its extremity has been in vogue from the fault line starting from Africa to East Asia. World politics, ridden by conflicts, has shifted gears abruptly[46] after 9/11. This time, the involved parties were not the states, but state versus Islamic stake holders within Pakistan to undertake the misadventure. Pakistan Army which is a 'state within the state' is a powerful Islamic entity, which, in its hatred and vengeful attitude towards India may think this to be an attractive alternative.

Samuel Huntington and Francis Fukuyama describe contemporary global politics as the age of Muslim war. "Muslims fight each other (Shia-Sunni, cultural conflict and conflict against the modern state) and the West and the Rest (non-Muslim). These instances of Muslim violence could congeal into one major clash of civilisations between Islam and the rest. That, however, is not inevitable and its more likely that violence involving Muslims will remain (even after American powerful and military presence in Afghanistan, Syria, Iraq and some slave region and Africa) dispersed, varied and frequent."[47] Samuel Huntington outlines four major factors – Muslim identity against modernisation and globalisation; hostility towards the west, tribal, religious, political and cultural divisions within Muslims, high birth rates and bulk of young unemployed, economically deprived youth. Francis Fukuyama has endorsed these factors as the cause of conflict between Islam and the Rest.

Indian ambition to have foothold in Afghanistan seems to have an uncertain future. India has invested in soft power diplomacy while keeping away from hard power approach. Its small and insignificant military presence in Tajikistan (Air Defence Unit and ITBT contingent to protect Indian workers involved in road construction) is not going to be any support to India. The existing 'soft power' diplomacy is effective only if the government in power facilitates it. Existing Karzai government functioned and survived under American protectionism and so Indian development activities were possible. It would not be an exaggeration to say that the Indian presence has, no doubt earned goodwill of common Afghan people but not of all radical Islamic groups of which some are under Pakistan's (ISI) influence. Apart from Afghanistan, the Indian oil and gas blocks interest in Turkmenistan, Kazakhstan is of great importance. But all this would depend on meeting the unforeseen challenges from Taliban forces, and also competitor states like Pakistan and China. Another serious consequence to its security would come from the fanatic radical Muslim mujahideens of Afghanistan and Pakistan. Is India geared to protect against such consequences for its economic and security interest? The answer lies in the future. One may conclude that the American war on terror ends in 2014 but one should not remain under such illusion. American withdrawal is not the end of conflict between 'West-Rest versus radical Islamic non-state actors'. In fact, David Rothkopf has warned that the world is being ruled by a small group of elites, numbering just four to five thousand. This includes religious leaders whose impact is profoundly seen on world politics.[48] This resurgence of new class deeply implicates international politics, economy and global dominance. The American dream of remaining at the apex of the triangular world order has to recoup its energy by relative isolation. The terror world is enlarging with hundreds and thousands of deaths and destruction of humans and their belongings. Would USA, after extricating itself from Afghanistan act like a fire brigade, running into all crises and invite its own downfall? Edward Kennedy, in his phenomenal historical analysis has eloquently proved that the great powers in order to sustain have paid a heavy price in terms of their decline. Soviet downfall is a recent example.[49] For USA, it is wise to create power centres opposed to the rise of radical religious groups, may be under UNO and deal with the crisis in a collective way to sustain as a democratic and liberal power of the world. The other thesis by Joseph Nye, an optimist who lauds American power (also Fareed Zakaria) in his "Bound to Lead", argues that with change of time, the gap between the superpowers/great powers has decreased but believes that the US would remain a dominant power in the world today,[50] much like in Friedman's terminology 'World is Flat'.[51] But the US needs to understand that Afghan like terror centres (ISIS) are on the rise. Will it be imperative for USA to rush in at the cost of losing its top position in the world? Wars have always proved to be fatal to great or superpowers, consuming their political, economic and military energies. Would USA take lessons from UK, Germany and Soviet Union in recent times? Therefore, entering Afghanistan to avenge the attack on USA is not the end but its withdrawal is the beginning of unimaginable threat to the peace and stability of the world at large. Instead taking onus on itself, USA is required to energize UNO and deal with the issue to adopt a broad and universal approach to the issue of terrorism.

Notes

1. Ahmed Rashid, *Pakistan on the Brink*, London: Penguin Books, 2013, p. 91.
2. Saira Khan, *Nuclear Weapons and Conflict Transoformation – The Case of India-Pakistan*, London: Routledge, 2009. Chp 1.
3. Praful Bidwai and Achin Vanaik, *South Asia on Nuclear Fuse*, New Delhi: Oxford University Press, Chp 1.
4. *Ibid.*
5. T.V. Paul, *The Warrior State – Pakistan in the Contemporary World*, New York: Oxford University Press, 2014, pp. 23, 24, 102-3, and 115.
6. William Zartman, (Ed). *Imbalance of power: US Hegemony and International Order*, New Delhi: Viva Press, 2002, pp. 90-92.
7. David Ruthkoff, *Super Class – The Global Power Elite and the World They are Making*, NewYork: Farrar Straus and Giroux, 2008, Chp 1 and 2.
8. Dilip Mohite, *The Third State Debate* In Srikant Paranjape (Ed.). New Delhi: Kalinga Publications, 2009, pp. 24, 30 and 31.

9. William Zartman, op cited. p. 101.
10. Jimmy Carter, *The President's "Proposed Energy Policy*, April 18, 1977, Vital speeches of the say 43, no. 14, May 1977.
11. *Ibid.*
12. Gusfar Schimidt in William Zartman (Ed) op cited, p. 165.
13. Jeff M. Smith, The Washington Times, April 23, 2011.
14. *Ibid.*
15. William Zartman, (Ed). *op cit.*, pp. 164-65.
16. Samuel Huntington, *Clash of Civilisations*, Foreign Affairs (1993).
17. Anatol Lieven, *Pakistan – The Hard Country*, Allen Lane – Penguin Books, London (2011).
18. Reported in The New York Times, April 27, 2011.
19. Thomas Friedman, Paging Uncle Sam, New York Times, Feb. 25, 2009.
20. Dilip Mohite, *Imperatives of Nuclear Non-proliferation in South Asia – A Case of India-Pakistan*, International Journal of South Asian Studies, Vol. 4, January-June 2011, No.1. Also see T.V. Paul, The Warrior State-Pakistan in the contemporary world, New York: Oxford University Press, 2014, pp. 18, 186. .
21. R C Majumdar, *A Modern History of India.*, Macmillan and Co, (Kolkata). p. 533.
22. T.V. Paul op cited. Also see Francis Fukoyama, *Their Target: The Modern World*, News Week Special, Issues 2002.
23. Saira Khan, *op. cit.*
24. Ahmed Rashid, *op. cit.* p. 28.
25. T.V.Paul. op cited, pp. 76 and 121.
26. I P Khosla, *India and Afghanistan: India's Foreign Policy*, New Delhi: Academic Foundation, 2007. pp. 550-552.
27. Mohite, T.V. Paul, *op.cit.*
28. Ahmed Rashid, *Pakistan on the Brink*, *op.cit.*, p. 12.
29. Hillary Clinton to NDTV, July 2014.
30. Ahmed Rashid, *Pakistan on the Brink*, *op.cit.*, p. 12.
31. Stephen P. Cohen, The Washington Quarterly, Summer, 2002, p. 116.
32. United States, Department of State, *Patterns of Global Terrorism*, Executive Summary, 2002, April 2003. State sponsored Terrorism, Cuba, Iran, Iraq, Libya, North Korea, Sudan, and Syria, p. 10.
33. T.V. Paul, *Pakistan- The Warrior State*, *op.cit.*.
34. Milton Bearden, Quoted by Seymor Hersh in New Yorker, January 29, 2002, p. 5.
35. Mohan Malik, *China and India-Great Power Rivals*, New Delhi, Viva Books, 2012, p. 178.
36. *Ibid.*, p. 279.

37. I.P. Khosla, *op.cit.*, pp. 552-553.
38. Ahmed Rashid, *op.cit.*, ch. 6.
39. William Zartman, *Imbalance of Power*, pp. 165-166.
40. Times of India, Ahmedabad, September 22, 2014, p. 9.
41. William Antholis, *Inside Out-India and China*, New Delhi: Viva Books, 2015, pp. 75-76.
42. Erica S. Downs, *China buys into Afghanistan*, SAIS Review 32, No.2, (2012) pp. 65-84. Cited in William Antholis, p. 76.
43. Bill Emmot, Rivals Uralando, Glorida: Mariner Books, 2007, p. 170.
44. Lissa J. Rubin, *Pakistan urged Afghanistan to Distance Itself From the West*, April 27, NY Times.
45. Bill Emmot, *op.cit.*
46. Francis Fukoyama, Issue 2002, p. 54.
47. Samuel Huntington, *The Age of Muslim Wars*, News Week Special Issue, 2002.
48. David Rothkopf, *Super Class*, New York: Farrar Straus and Giroux, 2008, pp. 192-93, see ch. 6.
49. Paul Kennedy, *The Rise and Fall of Great Powers*, New York: Vintage Books, 1989.
50. Thomas L. Friedman's book, The World is Flat, London Pengiuin Books, 2005, chapter 10 describes the changed structure of world order. The hierarchical world order where the gap between the superpower (US) and other powers was huge. Now that this gap has reduced by the rise of powers like China, Japan, Brazil, India and ASEAN states, in terms of their economy, thereby reducing the gap between USA and other powers.
51. Joseph Nye, *Bound to Lead – The Changing Nature of American Power*, New York: 1990.

5

Afghanistan and Regional Peace Building: Myth and Reality

Arpita Basu Roy

Although landlocked and seemingly isolated, Afghanistan has always occupied a position of geopolitical significance and has been the meeting place of four ecological and cultural areas: West Asia, Central Asia, the Indian subcontinent, and even the Far East, for the Pamir Mountains intrude into Chinese Sinkiang.[1] Shared identities and networks span borders and facilitate human activities over which the state has little or no control. Yet, the security concerns upheld by individual states, as they situate themselves within this region, remain crucial to our understanding of Afghanistan. While many of the states in the larger neighbourhood are weak in many respects, they tend to command significant coercive capacity in Afghanistan.[2] Although each neighbouring country has generally tried to stay out of the turmoil within Afghanistan, yet in many cases neighbouring states have felt obligated to support or assist one side or another in order to protect their own internal stability.[3]

Afghanistan's recent history clearly demonstrates that the regional context and external involvement can create or disrupt a peace building process.[4] Afghanistan is situated in a region marked by a range of conflicts, and the interests of different state and non-state actors often run counter to the peace building process in the country. It is being argued in academic and policy circles that it is in the particular interest of regional states to stabilise the volatility within the area and develop a joint approach towards Afghanistan that can secure a more lasting peace.[5] It is more or less accepted that it is not possible to resolve the challenges internal to Afghanistan without addressing the security challenges of its neighbours. Therefore, it has often been reiterated that a regional approach and a regional strategy is required that includes Pakistan, India, the Central Asian States and even China and Russia along with perhaps, at some point, Iran.[6] The objective of this paper is to explore the possible trajectories of a regional approach to peace-building in Afghanistan, the imperatives to promote greater cooperation amongst traditionally competitive states around Afghanistan given the conflicting dynamics of the actors involved and the workable response for India.

Afghanistan in the Region

The area known as Afghanistan has historically been an *in-between land* among all these regions.[7] This uncomfortable status, however, does not mean that Afghanistan was isolated from them. In fact, the exact opposite is true. Afghanistan has been (and continues to be) an overt or proxy 'playing ground' for a variety of outside actors, both near and far. Afghanistan's status as a much intruded upon buffer zone between British India and the Russian Empire, as described by geographer Keith McLachlan, actually helped strengthen the area's sense of itself as an independent nation.[8] More recent foreign intervention, especially since the Soviet intervention in 1979, has yielded more familiar results such as exacerbated ethnic and cultural tensions, rampant warlordism, drug trafficking and so on. In either case, what we see in Afghanistan is a classic geopolitical fault line where at present at least eight external actors are jostling for both influence and position in a twenty first century version of the Great Game.

Contemporary optimists have tried to, and persist in trying to, include Afghanistan into the wider schemes of regional cooperation. These schemes include: (1) making Afghanistan into an 'Energy-Bridge' between energy-rich Central Asia and energy poor South Asia, (2) re-establishing its historical role as a focal point of regional transport and trade, and (3) politically linking its fate to a Greater Middle East, and thereby ending its geopolitical fault line status. It is also generally accepted that the construction of alternative trade and transit routes could contribute positively to regional stability by lessening Afghanistan's dependence on Pakistan. By serving as a land bridge, Afghanistan could not only help strengthen regional interaction, but also provide neighbouring countries with new stakes in its stability. Afghanistan does have the potential to emerge as a major hub of connectivity and energy trade that would encourage constructive engagement from neighbouring countries that have varied security interests.[9] Building economic stakes for these countries in Afghanistan would motivate them to ensure the security and stability of the country and that of the region as a whole. This could recast Afghanistan as a facilitator and convert the zero-sum game being played into mutually beneficial policies. Regional organisations could further enable the three regional security complexes (RSCs) South Asia, Central Asia and the Persian Gulf to interact with each other.

Optimistically speaking, Afghanistan, whose national objectives include achieving internal stability, maintaining friendly relations with neighbouring and regional countries, and acting as a trade and transit hub, a regional approach it is believed, will help it achieve its national objectives. Afghanistan is economically dependent on its neighbours, as the bulk of its trade is with neighbouring and regional countries. In addition, over the past decades, Pakistan and Iran have become home to millions of Afghan refugees, and the return of these Afghans from exile will pose enormous economic, social, and security challenges for the Afghan government.[10] Meanwhile, a number of young Afghans educated in these regional countries can play an important role in the reconstruction and development of their homeland.

Therefore, it is imperative for a consensual approach to emerge in the neighbourhood as stability in Afghanistan is intertwined with the interests of the other countries in the region.[11] Also with increasing Chinese investment and energy network, Afghanistan may transcend its historical status as a landlocked geopolitical 'buffer' state and become part of an entirely different regional security dynamics. In response, India may also intensify its efforts to expand its political and economic cooperation with Afghanistan all this leading to the end of Afghanistan's isolation.

As tempting as these schemes might appear, Kristian Harpviken does not share this optimist vision.[12] He argues that "Afghanistan is an archetypal 'insulator' caught between different regional state systems, each with a strong dynamics of its own". To support his argument McLachan applies the regional security complex approach developed by Barry Buzan and Ole Wæver (see *Regions and Powers: The Structure of International Security*, 2003) to understand these dynamics in South Asia, the Persian Gulf and Central Asia. Unfortunately, this new regional approach has yet to bear substantial fruits because as Harpviken suspects that policy-makers have not used the right form of analysis to form their strategies.

Whether a regional consensus can evolve is a matter of debate and discussion, but it is essential to map the interests and policies of regional states and analyse whether a regional peace building approach is workable in the case of Afghanistan.

Mapping the Concerns and Interests of the Regional States

Apart from the immediate neighbours (Pakistan, Iran, Uzbekistan, Tajikistan, Turkmenistan, China and the disputed neighbour India)[13] several countries wish to have a role in Afghanistan primarily as a function of their relationship (cooperative or antagonistic) with the United States. The non-contiguous states and entities that have significant interests in Afghanistan include the United States, the United Kingdom, NATO, the EU, Russia, Saudi Arabia, Turkey, the UAE, Kazakhstan, Kyrgyzstan, Japan, South Korea, and potentially others. First and foremost, any guarantees would have to address a large range of perceived threats[14]. Mapping these threat perceptions and claims of respective stakeholders, without passing judgment on their validity, may help identify converging interests and disputes that need to be resolved or managed. An attempt has been made to map the most important regional actors below:

Pakistan[15] fears that the regional context is being outweighed by India according to every measure. The Indian presence in Afghanistan, which according to Pakistan, includes the support for anti-Pakistan forces in Kabul, covert action in support of Baluch nationalists, and a base for intelligence and other operations. The Indian-Iranian cooperation which is to open

Afghanistan to trade via the Persian Gulf, thus lessening Afghanistan's dependence on Pakistan is a major concern for the latter. The possibility of a long-term US presence in Afghanistan ultimately allied with India seeking to weaken Pakistan or even deprive it of its nuclear weapons, triggers panic in Pakistan. Moreover, Afghanistan's claim not to recognise the Durand Line as an international border and its past claims on "Pashtunistan" and other policies of the Afghan state that affect the Pashtun population of Pakistan are causes of concern.

A long-term US presence in Afghanistan that may serve as a base for destabilisation of Iran and attempts at "regime change" or attacks on Iran's nuclear programme is Iran's major concern. Moreover, the growth of Sunni extremism (al-Qaeda and Taliban) in both Afghanistan and Pakistan that may threaten Iran, including through Baluch groups such as Jundullah instability and drug trafficking based in Afghanistan have the potential to threaten social order in Iran. US attempts to build oil and gas pipeline and distribution networks that bypass Iran while undermining its energy industry with sanctions, including through Afghanistan, the worsening security in Afghanistan affecting the rate of return of Iran's million-plus population of Afghan refugees[16] are the other major perceived threats by Iran.

India fears Pakistan's use of Sunni extremist groups such as *Lashkar-i-Tayba* (which are in turn linked to Al-Qaeda and the Pakistani Taliban) for terrorist and military attacks against Indian targets and the training and mobilisation of such groups in areas under the control of the Taliban. Moreover there are concerns about nuclear weapons falling into the hands of these groups.[17] A potential US deal with Pakistan to return to "sub-contracting" Afghan policy to the ISI and Pakistan military, under which Pakistan would eliminate or control groups that threaten the United States directly but would continue to support and deploy those that threaten India is a major concern. Continued or increased Afghan dependence on Pakistan for trade and security, increasing Pakistan's leverage and ability to use Afghan land, resources, and personnel as strategic depth against India are issues that keep India worried. Even a limited political comeback of the Taliban will imply a strategic victory for terrorism and Islamic extremism which in turn would radicalise the region and increase geo-political contest.[18]

Russia is concerned about Sunni extremism in Afghanistan, Pakistan, or elsewhere gaining a strategic victory and spreading into Central Asia, the Caucasus, or the Russian Federation itself.[19] The US NATO presence in Afghanistan becoming permanent and providing a rationale for bases in Central Asia, placing NATO and the United States closer to Russia and to Central Asian energy supplies is Russia's apprehension. Russia fears that American presence provides a pole of attraction for some Central Asian states away from Russia. The United States endeavours to dominate Afghanistan through development of pipeline, trade routes and defence arrangements would decrease dependence of Central Asia on Russia. The drug trafficking that emanates from Afghanistan causing a threat to the social order in Russia[20] is also a concern.

China wants Afghanistan should not become or provide sanctuary for Uyghur separatists[21] or help in the recruitment and training of Uyghurs or other separatists in the Jihadi facilities located in the border areas of Afghanistan and Pakistan[22]. China believes that drug trafficking from Afghanistan into China should be curtailed. NATO withdraws following the realisation of a settlement (achieved through a combination of political negotiation and use of military force) in Afghanistan as China feels that NATO's presence is to contain China. The government in Kabul is not antagonistic to China's long-time ally Pakistan as China needs to keep Pakistan as one of its few traditional allies. Chinese economy needs the raw materials available in Afghanistan.

Afghanistan represents both a threat and an opportunity for Central Asian states.[23] Continued instability can be a substantial source of extremism, terrorism, and organised trafficking of drugs and arms. At the same time, stabilisation and reconstruction could lead to an opportunity for cooperation over electricity, gas, roads, pipelines, hydroelectric power, equipment, technology transfer, agriculture know-how and technical support.[24] Trans-border trafficking in narcotics, arms, extremism and terrorism could present an existential threat to their national securities and regime survival. Narco-trafficking along the northern route originating from Afghanistan is another concern that the CA countries share with Russia, which has been accusing USA and NATO of deliberately harming them by not doing enough to curb planting and trafficking. CA countries are concerned that proceeds from narco-trafficking could provide support to groups that seek to destabilise the governments. Another threat that solicits cooperation with Afghanistan is the potential conflict over water sharing. Afghanistan shares river basins of the Amu Darya and the Pyanj with the CA states and is in constant need of water, especially being susceptible to bouts of drought.

Mapping the Policies of the Regional Actors in Afghanistan

The policies of the regional state are varied but converge on certain points and differ on others. Although Pakistan is known to have assisted the Taliban in their early stages of development and subsequent control over Kabul, it has positioned itself in support of US and international objectives, and on September 12, 2001, it officially announced the end of its traditional support for the Taliban. Since then the country has provided some logistical facilities to the United States in the form of bases, and later to the North Atlantic Treaty Organisation (NATO) in the form of transit routes. In practice, however, Pakistan's policy is more ambivalent and complex. On the one hand, Pakistan supports the fight against Al-Qaeda and more generally all groups that are considered as a threat to its own interests. Nevertheless this list of antagonistic groups periodically changes. For example, the Taliban-e-Therik-e-Pakistan (TTP), which Pakistan is currently fighting, was previously one of its protégés until the TTP turned against the Pakistani army following the cycle of attacks and reprisals generated by the Red Mosque incident. Pakistan keeps supporting, training, and funding a number of terrorist groups in pursuit of its foreign policy objectives. Despite tremendous foreign pressure, Pakistan has done virtually nothing against the Afghan Taliban movement present on its territory; the Quetta and Peshawar *shuras* still operate from Pakistani soil. The Pakistani strategy in the area is highly selective and their policies protect, for example, Lashkar-e-Taiba which is a group with an international agenda (as demonstrated by the Headley affair) is always presented by the Pakistani army and intelligence agencies as a local organisation.[25]

Iran's policies in Afghanistan are complex too. While on the one hand, Iran exports "managed chaos" in the form of support to some insurgent groups, on the other hand there is a tendency to invest and also extend its cultural influence. In the interest of stabilisation, Iran has invested heavily—although far less than what it publicly committed—in reconstruction and development Afghanistan. Tehran has helped rebuild schools, provide emergency food assistance, and build libraries throughout Afghanistan. It has funded the development of Afghanistan's power sector, agriculture, and transportation grid. Much of Iranian attention is focused on Herat, a major city on Afghanistan's western border. Iran's largest automobile maker, Iran Khodro, recently announced that it was investing 20 million dollars into a new car manufacturing plant in Herat. Additionally, Iran has opened a chamber of commerce in order to facilitate continued trade ties with Herat province. Culturally, Iran is seeking to strengthen historical ties and extend its influence with many of Afghanistan's Persian-speaking and/or Shiia ethnic and religious minorities such as the Hazaras, Uzbeks, and Tajiks. A branch of Mashad-based Ferdowsi University is soon set to open in Herat, and Iranian textbooks exported to Afghanistan openly praise Iranian-backed militant groups Hizbollah and Hamas. Iran maintains ties to major Shiite clerics in Afghanistan, including Ayatollah Mohammad Asif Mohseni, who oversees a television and radio station and a prominent religious seminary in Kabul.[26] With an estimated two million opiate addicts, Iran has aggressively sought to counter the flow of narcotics from Afghanistan, and has already participated in regional and international efforts to fight the opium trade. It reportedly seized one thousand tons of illegal narcotics in 2008 and spends roughly $500 million per year to combat drug trafficking, much of it is spent on building border walls and training customs officials. Iran's Drug Control Headquarters ambitiously claimed that a concrete wall would separate the country's entire border with Afghanistan by 2010, a goal which, so far, has not been achieved. In contrast to Pakistan, Iran's aid to the Taliban is restrained and ostensibly driven by a desire to foment "managed chaos" in Afghanistan in order to bleed the United States and gain leverage.[27]

India's approach to promoting its interests in Afghanistan has been mainly political and developmental although neighbours like Pakistan would like to view India's role as being strategic and vicious. India backed the Northern Alliance politically against the Taliban when the latter was in power and post-2001 India sought promptly to rebuild its relationship with the Pashtuns and aligned itself with the post-Bonn Agreement government in Afghanistan headed by Karzai. It swiftly revived its ties with all ethnic groups and political formations in Afghanistan through its consulates in Kandahar, Jalalabad, Mazar-i-Sharif, and Herat. India has also embarked on humanitarian, reconstruction, and development projects all over Afghanistan. All the projects are undertaken in partnership with the Afghan Government.[28] It has no interest in deploying troops to Afghanistan, which it feels could affect its good reputation in the country, but concern over the security of its personnel in Afghanistan could necessitate an expanded paramilitary presence. India believes it can contribute best to the goal of stabilising Afghanistan by its ongoing efforts aimed at building institutions, developing businesses and human capital, and strengthening the capacity of the Afghan state to provide for the security and welfare of its own citizens with a view to an independent, pluralistic, democratic, and united Afghanistan. It favours stronger, more Afghan-centric, and more inclusive regional economic and political approaches to the country's problems. Diplomatically, India has a strong interest in forging as broad a coalition as possible against the return of the Taliban. However, it feels the lack of a suitable regional or international forum that can bring together all major stakeholders.

India's economic investments in Afghanistan have been mostly developmental, rather than aimed at the exploitation of Afghanistan's natural resources.[29] It has also made strategic investments in opening sea, road, and rail links through the Iranian port of Chahbahar so as to enhance its access to Afghanistan and Eurasia, as well as reduce Afghan dependence on Pakistan for trade and transit. India's capacity to help Afghanistan, however, is limited by the lack of physical access and international susceptibility to Pakistani sensitivities to India's presence and activities in Afghanistan. As a result, India is not able to contribute to, for example, the training and development of the Afghan security forces and army as much as it could. It also feels that it can do much more in terms of sharing India's experience in nation building (including the evolution of political institutions and the relationship between Islam and the modern state) and development (such as in critically needed areas like agriculture, employment generation, nutrition, curbing illicit cultivation of opium, and so on). The lack of direct land access and transit arrangements between India and Pakistan also deprives Afghanistan of the benefit of India's huge goods and services market.

India is a strong advocate of regional economic cooperation involving all of Afghanistan's neighbours to form transit corridors linking the energy-rich West and Central Asian region with the energy-deficient subcontinent. The primary obstacle to such links within the South Asian Association for Regional Cooperation, which Afghanistan joined in 2005, has been the state of India–Pakistan relations, particularly Pakistan's reluctance to facilitate freer trade and transit between India and Pakistan and beyond.

All of the Central Asian Republics viewed the ISAF operation as positive, and at least at the outset each believed that enhanced security and/or economic advantage would likely accrue from it. Leaders in Uzbekistan, Kyrgyzstan, Tajikistan, and Kazakhstan believed that the destruction of Al-Qaeda camps (which they regarded as a realisable ISAF goal) would improve their security situation. Turkmenistan, however, was much more interested in reviving stalled gas transport projects involving Afghanistan.[30] The Uzbeks and Kyrgyz (in that order) were quick to offer military base access to the United States. The Uzbeks were willing to risk Moscow's ire to cement a steadily improving security relationship between Tashkent and Washington. Till date neither Kazakhstan nor any other Central Asian nation has contributed troops to ISAF. This is partly because their armed forces are "off-springs" of the Soviet forces that battled there in the 1980s, and also because fighting against members of ethnic affinity groups runs the risk of leading to Al-Qaeda or Taliban-inspired attacks within the Central Asian countries.[31] All of these states are eager to participate in regionally-based economic recovery strategies for Afghanistan.

Beijing does not want its Afghanistan policies to strain its long-standing, privileged relationship with Islamabad, undermine the basic stability of the Pakistani state, or harm Pakistan's own national interest's vis-à-vis Afghanistan. A stable, independent, friendly, and regionally influential Pakistan prevents Indian domination of South Asia, weakens Indian influence in Central Asia, and confounds any Indian desire to focus primarily on strategic rivalry with China. A cooperative Pakistan also contributes intelligence and policy support for suppressing domestic Chinese Muslim terrorists, and denying them safe havens in Afghanistan and infiltration routes via the Hindu Kush. Finally, Pakistan offers important opportunities for Chinese trade, investment, and energy supply routes.

China provides significant levels of humanitarian, infrastructure, and financial assistance to Afghanistan. It has also begun developing minerals and energy resources in the country, committed personnel to assist in landmine clearing and police training, and established cooperation on antidrug measures. China's strategy in Afghanistan was mostly focused on business development, and on satiating its vast appetite for energy and minerals. The US Defence Department has valued Afghanistan's untapped mineral deposits at $1 trillion.[32] In December 2012, China's state-owned National Petroleum Corporation signed a deal with the Afghan authorities that would make it the first foreign company to exploit Afghanistan's oil and natural-gas reserves.[33] It has also shown support for the Afghan government on relevant UN resolutions, greater diplomatic contacts, and steady involvement in Shanghai Cooperation Organisation efforts to address the Afghanistan situation (in particular terrorism, drug trafficking, and organised crime).

China has also publicly declared its support for broad US/ international objectives in Afghanistan to fight terrorism, maintain domestic stability and achieve sustainable economic and social development. Beijing has positioned itself as supportive of Afghanistan's long-term stability and prosperity through limited political, economic and diplomatic assistance. It has also been careful to remain on good terms with the Kabul authorities without offending the Pashtuns or their political leadership in the Taliban. It has furthermore tried to support Pakistan's policies, not change them.

Conclusion: Situating India in the Strategic Matrix

From the above-discussion it becomes obvious that there is a range of common objectives such as combating terrorism, narcotics, organised crime, and illegal weapons trafficking which have led to new incentives for regional cooperation on Afghanistan. The rise of terrorism, extremism, and militancy throughout the region, including in China, is a major threat to all regional countries, and the need for a regional mechanism to fight this new phenomenon serves as a new opportunity for cooperation. However, the lack of political will, among many other factors, has complicated the prospects for effective regional cooperation. The countries have yet to look beyond historical differences and open a new chapter of cooperation and collaboration for the benefit of their peoples. Given the current dire political situation in Afghanistan, and growing rivalry among regional countries, it is doubtful that a regional consensus would automatically emerge.

It would be interesting to derive where India would place itself in the complicated matrix involving Afghanistan. It is evident that India-Pakistan rivalry and Pakistan's dual strategies would continue to mar any possibility of India-Pakistan cooperation on Afghanistan. India's interests and policies in Afghanistan converge broadly with those of other key players, such as the US–NATO–International Security Assistance Force coalition, Iran, Russia, the Central Asian Republics and to some degree even China—but diverge fundamentally from Pakistan. India, Iran, Russia, the Central Asian Republics, and China share a common interest in combating the spread of drug trafficking and militant, fundamentalist Islamic ideology out of Afghanistan, though the degree to which these concerns translate into common action varies depending on other competing interests and concerns.

There are also nuances over approaches to Pakistan. India's differences with Iran on Afghanistan relate primarily to the need for US forces to remain in the country at least until the Afghan army and security forces are strong enough to deal with national security threats on their own. Differences with China relate to China's strategic support for Pakistan in relation to India.

Any convergence on the threat posed by militant Islamist separatism and terrorism is presently offset by China's "all-weather friendship" and support for Pakistan, though how China might react in case of the extreme scenario of a radical regime in either Afghanistan or Pakistan remains to be seen. It would seem that there is scope for discreet consultations between the United States, China, and India on this issue. India could also explore possible joint economic approaches with China in Afghanistan. There are no significant differences in interests between India and Russia or the Central Asian Republics over Afghanistan except insofar as they may relate to third countries. In general, India believes that: (1) all these countries have an interest in preventing a return to power of the Taliban; (2) their differences matter less than their points of convergence; and (3) cooperation among these countries could contribute significantly to countering the resurgence of the Taliban and in stabilising Afghanistan.

These points of convergence have not been adequately explored on account of bilateral political differences, regional instability, and the lack of an inclusive forum in which they can be discussed. While not minimising the difficulties of forging a regional consensus on Afghanistan involving the United States, India feels that such a regional approach should be encouraged.

In contrast, Indian and Pakistani interests in Afghanistan are virtually antithetical as mentioned repeatedly. India's clash of political, security, and economic interests with Pakistan over Afghanistan has been elaborated. At heart, India sees Pakistan's entire Afghan policy as predicated on Pakistan's unfinished agenda against India over Kashmir, which it doubts the Pakistani military establishment will ever abandon (even, it appears, at the cost of severe blowback within Pakistan).

Though China has been speaking to India on Afghanistan for the last couple of years, it is unlikely that it would antagonise its all-weather friendship with Islamabad on this. However, with the increasing terrorist threat looming on China, an India-China dialogue/cooperation on terrorism is not far-fetched. The possibility of an India-China-Russia cooperation on Afghanistan is also on the cards and India should not miss any opportunity of such trilateral cooperative initiative. Central Asian countries and India have shared concerns and therefore it is likely to get substantial support from these countries to combat terrorism and drugs. Intelligence-sharing and joint law enforcement efforts for combating terrorism, narcotics, organised crime, and weapons trafficking might become an essential component of effective regional cooperation. India should also be proactive in improving its relation with Iran and leveraging the Iran – Afghanistan-Central Asian connectivity for trade and commerce. The strategic matrix of the quadrangle comprising India- Pakistan – China – Afghanistan will pose interesting dilemmas in the near future.

References

1. *Dupree,Louis.Afghanistan,* Oxford University Press, Oxford, 1973, p. xvii (Introduction).
2. Harpviken,Kristian Berg *.Afghanistan in a Neighbourhood Perspective: General Overview and Conceptualisation,* Peace Research Institute Paper, Oslo, 2010, p. 1.
3. Lohman,Andrew D. "Political Geography", Colonel Eugene J. Palka (ed.). *Afghanistan: A Regional Geography,* Department of Geography and Environmental Engineering, United States Military Academy, West Point, New York, 2001, p.
4. Strand.Ame, Kristian Berg Harpviken and *AstriSuhrke.Afg.lianistan Peacebuilding in a Regional Perspective,* Conference Report, Chr. Michelsen Institute, Development Studies and Human Rights, Norway, September, 2002.
5. lbid.
6. General David Petraeus, "Remarks", Baton Conference, Walter E. Washington Convention Center, Washington, D.C., hosted by the United States Institute of Peace, January 8, 2010.
7. Geopolitical Faultlines- The case of Afghanistan, ISN, Zurich, December, 2011.<http://www.isn.ethz.ch/Digital- Library/ Articles/ Special-Feature/ ... >
8. McLachlan, Keith."Afghanistan: The geopolitics of a buffer state", *Geopolitics and international Boundaries,* Vol. 2, No. 1, 1997, pp. 82-96
9. Pattanaik, Smruti *S.Afghanistan and its Neighbourh od: In search of a Stable Future,* PRIO Paper, Oslo, 2013, p. 5.
10. Mir, Haroun. "Afghanistan", Ashley J Tellis and Aroop Mukharji (eds), *Is a regional strategy viable in Afghanistan,* Carnegie Endowment for International Peace, Washington DC, 20, p. 8.
11. *Ibid*, p. 5.
12. Harpviken, Kristian. *Afghanistan in a Neighbourhood Perspective,* n.2
13. Gilgit-Baltistan, a territory of Pakistan to which India has never relinquished its claim as part of Kashrnir, borders on Afghanistan. Pakistan objects that India is not a "neighbour" of Afghanistan and tries to exclude it from forums dealing with the latter, but India regards Afghanistan as a part of South Asia, a region in which India sees itself as predominant.

14. Gregg *Tom. Is a Regional Pact to Stabilise Afghanistan Possible?,* Center on International Cooperation, New York University, July 2010, p. 4.
15. On the basis of responses to the *Questionnaires* sent out to Pakistani academics and ex-military personnel by the author.
16. Gregg, Tom. *Is a Regional Pact to Stabilise Afghanistan Possible,* op cit, p. 5.
17. Mukhopadhaya,Gautam. "India", Ashley J Tellis and AroopMukharji (eds), *Is a regional strategy viable in Afghanistan,* 'Carnegie Endowment for International Peace, Washington DC, 2010, p. 30.
18. Basu Roy, Arpita. "Afghanistan: India's Strategic and Security Concerns", ShekharAdhikary and Sanjeev Bhadauria (eds), *India's National Security in the 21th century,* Pentagon Press, New Delhi, 2014.
19. Stepanova, *Ekaterina.Russia's Concerns Relating to Afghanistan and the Broader Region in the Context of the US / NATO Withdrawal,* CmOB Policy Research Paper, June 2013.
20. lnformal conversation with Prof Vladimir Boyko and Prof Andrey Medvedev, Moscow
21. Basu Roy, Arpita. "Afghanistan in 2014 and Beyond: The possibilities oflndia -China Cooperation", Paper presented at a seminar on *India and China in the Regional Security Context,* Dept of International Relations, Jadavpur University, February 21, 2014.
22. Sharma,Raghav. "China's Afghan Policy: Slow Recalibration", *China Report,* May 2011.
23. Kucera, *Joshua.Post-Soviet Central Asian National Inter.ests in Afghanistan,* Washington DC: The Century Foundation, 2010, p. 14. See also Martha Brill Olcott, "Central Asian Republics," in Ashley J. Tellis and Aroop Mukharji (Eds.), *Is A Regional Strategy Viable in Afghanistan?,* Washington, D.C.: Carnegie Endowment for International Peace, 2010, p. 53. See also Shahrbanao Tadjbakhsh, Central Asia and Afghanistan: Insulation on the Silk Road, Between Eurasia and the Heart of Asia, PRIO Paper 3, 2012.
24. The author in conversation with scholars of University of World Economy and Diplomacy (UWED) and Institute of History, Tashkent, Uzbekistan, April 2013.
25. Grare, Frederic. "Pakistan", Ashley J Tellis and Aroop Mukharji (eds), *Is a regional strategy viable in Afghanistan,* Carnegie Endowment for International Peace, Washington DC, 2010 pp. 19-20.
26. Zarif, Maseh and Ahmad Majidyar. "Iranian Influence in Afghanistan: Recent Developments", *Iran Tracker,* August 21,2009. < http://www.irantracker.orgianalysis/iranian-influence-afghanistan-recent-developments
27. Sadjadpour, Karim. "Iran", Ashley J Tellis and Aroop Mukharji (eds), op cit, pp. 39-44.

28 Basu Roy, Arpita. “Afghanistan: India’s Strategic and Security Concerns”, *op cit,* p. 237

29 Mukhopadhyaya,Gautam. “India”, Ashley Tellis and AroopMukharji (eds.), *op cit,* pp. 27-38.

30 “Turkmenistan faces challenges in export transportation options”, *Oil and Gas Journal,* 28 October, 2002. < http://www.ogj.com!articles/print/ vo lume-1 OO/iss ue-44/ exp loration-development/turkmenistan - faces-challenges- in- export-transportation>

31 Olcott,Martha Brill. “Central Asian Republics”, in Ashley J Tellis, *op cit,* pp.51-60

32 Peters,Stephen G. and Stephen D. Ludington, Greta J. Orris, David M. Sutphin, James D. Bliss, and James J. Rytuba, eds. *Preliminary Non-Fuel Mineral Resource Assessment of Afghanistan 2007,* U.S. Geological Survey-Afghanistan Ministry of Mines Joint Mineral Resource Assessment, 2007. <www.pubs.usgs.gov/ofl2007>

33 Shlomo Ben-Ami, “China’s Afghan Game Plan”, *Project Syndicate,* July 4, 2012. <http://www.project-syndicate.orgicommentary/china-s-afghan-garne-plan>

6

Russia Returns to Afghanistan-Challenges Persist

R.G. Gidadhubli

The decision of the USA to withdraw from Afghanistan was highly welcomed by Russia, which has been eagerly waiting to reenter Afghanistan. For Vladimir Putin this has been a golden opportunity to return to Afghanistan and also rebuild the relics of the Soviet ties and above all to promote Russia's geopolitical and geo-economic interests. Moreover, for Putin this is an opportunity to showcase Russia's status as an emerging power and, as opined by a western analyst, to demonstrate Moscow's 'political and cultural prowess'. This is reconfirmed from the statement of Stepan Anikeev, who is the spokesman for the Russian Embassy in Kabul, "We want to enlarge our role in the region. It's not only for Afghanistan, but for our own goals." An effort has been made in this paper to analyse Russia's policy priorities and their implementation, Russia-China interests in Afghanistan, responses of Afghans towards Russia and India-Russia cooperation in Afghanistan.

Russia's Policy Priorities

Not to lose an opportunity, the Russian government sent greetings to the Afghan government marking the Persian New Year. To reinforce Russia's interest, Vladimir Putin sent a personal message to Hamid Karzai in Dari language stating, "I am certain that friendly ties and cooperation between Russia and Afghanistan in the future will add to the goodness and welfare of our people".

It is worth recalling Russia's historical roots and connections with Afghanistan. In 1919, the newly formed Russian Federation was the first to recognise independence and sovereignty of Afghanistan. Subsequently, the Soviet Union had been an important foreign partner of Afghanistan except during the decade of 1979-89 when the USSR was embroiled in a festering conflict with that country. In the opinion of some analysts, in the twentieth century, the Soviet Union did manage to become one of the most important foreign partners of the country. However, relations between two countries have not been static and at present for Afghans return of Russia is welcome as Americans leave their country.

Coming to the recent past, 2003-2006 was a period of stagnation when Russia was not able to compete with the growing western influence in Afghanistan. Since 2007, Russia initiated active policy and subsequent to 2009 the Russian government has been actively supporting Karzai government in order to improve relations even as the situation was getting deteriorated in that country. Thus, Russia's policy has been reactive in nature responding to internal developments in the country. Russia analysts opine that peace, security and stability in Afghanistan are in Russia's own interest and in the interest of its southern underbelly.

Russia's Challenges for Policy Implementation

While the Russian government has its roadmap worked out for implementing policies, formidable challenges persist.

Firstly, Russia proposes to facilitate the task of rehabilitation in Afghanistan by compiling a list of 140 Soviet-era projects covering various sectors of economy such as extraction of oil, construction of mini-hydro power plants in three provinces, transport and construction etc. Among various projects priority has been given to the revival of Kabul House-Building Factory which is one of the largest manufacturing facilities. This is going to be a challenging task. Hence in the autumn of 2013, the Russian government earmarked $ 25 million to modernise it and provide it with new equipments. Looking back it needs to be stated that as a part of House building project (prefabricated walls etc), the Soviets developed Microryan in Afghanistan. This Microryan looked like it was transplanted from a small Russian city. Though houses built under this scheme were not luxurious they had all necessary facilities to serve the purpose.

In fact, the Russian policy-makers have reason to be happy that according to Afghan reports even now this project enjoys high popularity among the common people. In fact, the importance of this project lies in the fact that this house-building factory made the prefabricated walls from which Taliban officials, including top leader Mohammad Omar, have built their own homes and offices.

In 2013, this factory produced the walls for one of Afghanistan's biggest prisons. Even as the same old equipments are being used, the new Russian technology is expected to be installed in the coming months. A large section of middle class Afghans seem to have been benefitted by this project which has helped them to build a shelter of their own. Hence, Ahmad who is the head engineer of the house-building factory, has rightly stated that Russia is enjoying long-term benefit of the policy of setting up this house-building factory in Kabul.

Secondly, as economic development assumes great significance for the country, Russia has proposed to modernise bread-making factory set up during the Soviet era which is still producing thousands of loaves every day. As opined by some economists, common Afghan people have nostalgia for this bread-making factory much to the comfort of Russian policy-makers.

Thirdly, having realised that trade and economic relations will play a crucial role for promoting bilateral ties, the Russian leaders have taken necessary steps in that direction during the last few years. For instance, the first meeting of Russian-Afghan inter-governmental commission on trade and economic cooperation took place in March 2011. This meeting has paid off since trade turnover between the two countries has increased by about 12 times between 2004 and 2011 when it amounted to about $ 985 million. The challenge facing Russian leaders is that bilateral trade is highly fluctuating. Apart from that Russia has huge trade surplus with Afghanistan which has a huge debt to pay to Russia and which is exporting lubricants, metals and machinery and pharmaceutical products to Russia.

Fourthly, the Russian government is keen to revive its cultural linkages and for that it has decided to spend $20 million to renovate the Soviet House of Science and Culture, which was constructed in 1982. It is appreciable that Hamid Karzai's government has shown its readiness to cooperate and has ordered to build a Russian Cultural Centre in Kabul. This will strengthen Russia's activity in Afghanistan apart from promoting teaching of Russian language and cultural programmes.

Fifthly, there is valid speculation that geopolitical angle persists in Russia's interest in Afghanistan, which is a part of Central Asian region. Russia's Great Game in the Central Asian region is being played by adopting strong multi-vectored regional policy priority by reviving close socio-economic and political relations with Afghanistan, which enjoys common border with three Central Asian states, namely Tajikistan, Uzbekistan and Turkmenistan with which Russia has close ties. Hence Russia wants to consolidate its own dominance and interest in the region.

Sixthly, education is an important field that can help Afghanistan's economy. As a result the number of students studying Russian at Kabul University has doubled in the past two years. Russia, in turn, has doubled the number of scholarships it offers to Afghan students. In the opinion of a British scholar specialising on Central Asia, the Russians invested a lot of money and human resources into development of countries they "occupied", and that includes Afghanistan.

Seventh, some Russian analysts have tried to compare Soviet development activities with those of the American. It is contended that even many Afghan scholars have opined that many US aided projects have been wasteful and misguided. On the other hand, many Afghans, including President Hamid Karzai have praised the Soviet model even though they fought a bloody 10-year war against the country's army. In the opinion of Russian Ambassador Andrey Avetisyan, who was also based in Kabul as a young diplomat in the 1980s, the financial assistance to Afghanistan by the USA lacked proper strategy. In contrast with this, in his interview to the *Washington Post*-Karzai was candid in stating "the Soviet money went to the right place. They were efficient in spending their money and doing it through the Afghan government".

Eighth, Russia and China have certain common interest in Afghanistan. In the present context, by 2012 with the prospect of a decline in US influence in the region in sight, Russia and China were reaching out to Pakistan and Afghanistan in a bid to improve economic ties and to secure their southern borders against the spread of Islamic fundamentalism. At the same time, both China and Russia will be happy to see US troops leave Afghanistan, but they are equally worried about the Taliban and other extremist groups penetrating Xinjiang province in southern China and the Central Asian republics, whose national security is very much in the hands of Russia.

Equally important is the fact that Afghanistan enjoying observer status in the Shanghai Cooperation Organisation (SCO), which is led by China and Russia, has taken a new lease of life. Russia, both through the SCO and bilaterally, is willing to offer major help to Afghanistan such as improving the Salang Tunnel highway, the critical link road between Kabul and the north which the Soviets built in the 1970s.

Problems Persist

Notwithstanding several factors that bring Russia close to Afghanistan, there are problems such as threats to security, Islamic fundamentalism, terrorism, drug trafficking etc. which are of concern to Moscow.

Firstly, Afghanistan continues to be a major source of narcotics that pour into Russia through Central Asia. Illegal production of drugs has been a major problem and production has increased.

Secondly, thousands of youth have become victims of drugs. It should be a matter of concern for Russia to combat drug trafficking which, according to some critics, has increased hundreds of times during the stay of NATO troops. As stated by Lyuba Lulko, in 2001 which was the last year of Taliban rule in Afghanistan, 185 tons of opium was collected which increased to 12,000 tons. During the last seven years, opium production has increased by 44 times. It is beyond comprehension as to how and why NATO forces allowed such increase in opium production and drug problem to escalate to this extent. While drug trafficking has become a major problem, there is strong expectation that a Russian-funded counternarcotics programme could curb that illicit trade.

Thirdly, as opined by some analysts, Russia has major concern about security as threats emanate from terrorist organisations such as the Islamic Movement for Uzbekistan and Islamic Jihad etc. who according to some Russian analysts, take shelter in tribal areas of Pakistan. The Central Asian States of Uzbekistan and Tajikistan have been the victims of the terrorist acts by these organisations during the last two decades. Russia has been a guarantor of Central Asia's stability. Russia has bases in Tajikistan and Kyrgyz Republic to support and ensure security in the Central Asian region. The CAS, with the exception of Turkmenistan which has opted for positive neutrality, are members of regional organisations such as CSTO in which Russia has been a major player. Hence developments in Afghanistan after 2014 have direct relevance for CAS. For Russia peace and security is a priority in its southern underbelly, it being a strong supporter of security in the region through CSTO, SCO etc. Moreover, Russia has legitimate concern for the spill over effect of terrorism in Central Asia for its own security.

Fourthly, there are persistent differences between Russia and the West so far as Afghan issue is concerned. On the one hand Russia has extended support to the West on certain issues including transportation of goods etc. through Russia. Russia strongly supported UN Security Council resolution for setting up International Security Assistance Force in Afghanistan in 2001. Russia supported Joint EU-Russia Joint Agency to fight against drug trafficking in Eurasian region emanating from Afghanistan, which was certainly in Russia's own interest. At the same time Russia has differences with the West which is evident from the fact that Russian leaders strongly objected to US bases in Central Asia. Hence in 2009, under pressure from Moscow, the Kyrgyz Republic was to terminate agreement with the USA forcing it to close down its Manas Base for military operations.

Fifthly, Russia is aware of the fact it will not be easy for it to carry its programmes if Taliban comes to power in the future, the possibility of Northern Alliance being active in Afghanistan would also cause concern for Russian leaders.

India-Russia

India has been playing an active role on issues concerning socio-economic developments in Afghanistan. Having contributed close to $2 billion in aid over the past decade, India is the fifth largest donor nation to Afghanistan. India did finance the construction of a road from Chabahar to Delaram, a town in the west of Afghanistan that is situated on its Ring Road, to transport goods into the country. Even as India has depended on Iran to facilitate its trade with Afghanistan but that country's port facilities at Chabahar may not be able to support larger volumes of shipments. Both India and Iran need to work out strategy to overcome this constraint.

Peace and security in Afghanistan is a common policy priority for both India and Russia. Similarly, India and Russia can cooperate in the development activities in Afghanistan on issues concerning security and economy. There are some positive signals in this regard. According to some reports, while not committing troops on the ground, India has agreed to pay Russia to deliver small arms, such as light artillery and mortars, to Afghanistan. To strengthen Afghan military, India is reported to transfer heavy artillery, tanks and possibly attack helicopters.

Russia has been supporting Turkmenistan-Afghanistan-Pakistan-India (TAPI) project which is intended to bring Central Asian hydrocarbon resources to all three states, namely Afghanistan, Pakistan and India. The total length of pipeline will be 1,735 km going through 200 km in Turkmenistan, 735 km in Afghanistan and 800 km in Pakistan till the pipeline reaches the Fazilka settlement on Pakistan-India border. The annual capacity of the pipeline is 30 billion cubic metres of gas. The projects participants include Turkmengaz, the Afghan Gas Corporation and the Pakistani Interstate Gas Systems and India's GAIL. As per Russian reports Russian companies are also interested in participating in the TAPI project which should be in India's interest considering the fact that this project is highly contentious and ambitious even amidst the volatile situation that persists in both Afghanistan and Pakistan apart from the high cost factor. However, as and when this project materialises, it will certainly bring both the Central Asian and South Asian regions closer. It needs to be added that both China and West have been making considerable progress to reach out to energy resources of Central Asia.

In lieu of conclusion it may be stated that Russia has been looking forward to return to Afghanistan. The Russian leaders have drawn up a roadmap to undertake policy measures to ensure their growing presence in Afghanistan which is a part of its soft southern underbelly. However, problems and challenges persist making the task formidable to the Russian leaders. India and Russia have no conflict of interest and have common interest in ensuring that Afghanistan emerges as a stable, neutral and independent state to facilitate security in the region.

7

The Afghan Crisis: An Appraisal of UN's Role in Combating Taliban Insurgency

B.N. Mehrish

The paper analyses and examines UN's Role in the security and development of Afghanistan since 9/11. Afghanistan is one of the world's most embattled countries. The US invasion of Afghanistan in 2001 became a strategic priority for the US and its allies. The credibility of President Karzai's regime was challenged by the war lords in the North and the Taliban militants in the South. The US bypassed the UN and used NATO for its strategic interests in Southwest Asia.

American's war in Afghanistan, the longest and costliest in its history, is drawing to a close. How this shapes Afghanistan's future will have a significant bearing on India's security. Will the fate of Afghanistan be different from Iraq and Libya where the US intervened militarily? Iraq has been partitioned into Shia, Sunni and Kurdish sections, while Libya seems heading towards a similar three-way but tribal-based partition. Afghanistan's large ethnic minorities enjoy '*defacto*' autonomy. The rupturing of Karzai's political alliance with minority leaders had also added ethnic polarisation. Sujatha Singh, India's foreign secretary has advocated a cautious approach towards initiatives for bringing peace to war-ravaged Afghanistan. The US-Afghanistan talks over the bilateral security agreement were deadlocked which would allow some US troops to stay in Afghanistan beyond 2014.

Major Players and Factions

The major players in the Afghanistan crisis are Mullah Fazlullah, Pakistan's General Kayani, Imran Khan and other Right Wing groups and Pakistani Prime Minister Nawaz Sharif. There are various factions, namely, Mehsud and Mohmand factions (Tehreek-e-Taliban) which are included under an umbrella group of the various militant groups in the Pakistan-Afghanistan region. There are at least two other Taliban groups, the Afghan Taliban and the Haqqani Network. SWAT faction is headed by Fazlullah, this is a weaker faction of the TTP and was responsible for the attack on Malala Yousafzai. Punjabi Taliban is a loose knit group which includes Sipah-e-Sahaba and the Jaish-e-Muhammad. Many of these groups have offered to fight with the Afghan Taliban. Post-US troop withdrawal in 2014, they are focused on fighting the Shia community and religious minorities in Pakistan. There are breakaway factions like the Jundu Uah group and these factions have been disowned by the TTP because they have conducted operations without the approval of the TTP leadership.

India's Role and Perspectives

President Hamid Karzai allayed India's concerns over the situation in Afghanistan after the scheduled US troops pull out and he reassured Salman Khurshid, India's External Affairs Minister, and the Indian Government agreed to provide three military choppers and appreciated Karzai for his efforts to establish a genuine Afghan controlled reconciliation process in Afghanistan. India called upon the international community to fulfil its pledges of rebuilding the Afghan National Army and the Afghan National Police, India's concern is mainly threat to Afghanistan's security and its internal stability due to terrorism and extremism. Qari Yousef Ahmadi, a spokesman of the Taliban, observed that, "US faces the same fate as the Soviets on the occasion of the twentyfifth anniversary of the Soviet troops' withdrawal from Afghanistan in line with the so-called Geneva accords".

FACTIONS Tehreek-e-Taliban is an umbrella group of the various militant groups in the Pakistan-Afghanistan region. There are at least two other Taliban groups: the Afghan Taliban and the Haqqani Network

▪ TTP's former chief Hakimullah Mehsud (center) with other militants in South Waziristan. REUTERS FILE

TTP is seen as a loose alliance of like-minded militants and less as a central structure. However, there are groups that work from within TTP while others work with it when interests converge

MEHSUD AND MOHMAND factions: These are the central TTP groups. The Mehsud group has held to the mantle of the TTP's leadership but this has now gone to the Swat Taliban, which is seen as an outsider to the central groups. There is a tribal rivalry between the Mehsud and Mohmand groups, as was seen with the rise of Wali ur Rehman, who considered himself as the alternate leader to TTP during the time of Hakimullah Mehsud.

SWAT faction: Headed by Fazlullah, this is a weaker faction of the TTP but one that was empowered following the takeover of Swat by the Taliban and the subsequent military operation in the valley in 2011. Swat faction of the TTP was responsible for the attack on Malala Yousafzai.

PUNJABI Taliban: This is a loose knit of groups which even include the Sipah-e-Sahaba Pakistan, the Lashkar-e-Jhangvi and the Jaish-e-Muhammad. The Punjabi Taliban is seen more close to the Afghan Taliban and many of these groups have offered to fight with the Afghan Taliban post US troop withdrawal in 2014. Primarily the Punjabi Taliban are focused on fighting the Shia community and religious minorities in Pakistan. Unlike the TTP, the Punjabi Taliban are seen close to the country's intelligence agencies and have been used in the insurgency in Balochistan.

BREAKAWAY factions: These include groups like the Jundullah Group. Many such factions have been disowned by the TTP because they have conducted operations without the approval of the TTP leadership. Some groups have broken away on matters of money while others have parted ways on TTP's initial stance to talk peace with government

Major Players

MULLAH FAZLULLAH: the new leader of the TTP. Fazlullah is charged with heading an outfit that is currently in a state of uncertainty. There is speculation that consistent drone attacks may bring them to the negotiation table. Fazlullah is an outsider so he has a more challenging job. Traditionally, the TTP is headed by someone from the Mehsud tribe

GENERAL KAYANI: Soon to retire, General Kayani has spearheaded the military campaign against the TTP. Kayani is expected to be replaced by another hardliner who sees talks with the TTP as a waste of time and pushes for a military solution. The military silently supports US drone strikes

IMRAN KHAN and other RIGHT WING groups: Imran Khan and other right wing leaders vociferously support talks with the TTP. The demand that drone strikes end so that peace talks can start. Khan insists that the TTP can be brought to the negotiation table if the Americans end their drone strikes and the government gives some major concessions to the TTP

PRIME MINISTER NAWAZ SHARIF: Sharif's government has made progress over talks with slain TTP leader Hakimullah Mehsud. However there is a limit to what government can offer the TTP and one of the most important demands, the end to drone strikes, is something that is not on the table. Sharif claims that the US has said it will end drone strikes but there is no time frame and no clear indication of this happening soon. Sharif's government is being pressurized by right wing parties to hold talks so suicide bombing and attacks on govt installations end

Recent Developments and Challenges Ahead

Afghans voted on 5 April 2014 in large numbers to choose a successor to President Hamid Karzai in the country's first democratic transfer of power as US-led forces ended their 13 year war. In the Southern Afghan city of Kandahar voters lined up in huge numbers in stark contrast to the violent 2009 election. Kandahar emerged in the early 1990s as the city of much insurgent unrest since 2001. Obama threatened Karzai with complete withdrawal of US troops. The new government in post-2014 scenario will require training and anti-terror missions. Pakistan shifted policy on tackling terror and vowed retaliation. After a year spent in waging war on terror in Afghanistan and Iraq the Western public feels it has learned a hard lesson, almost $1.5 trillion direct costs was incurred and thousands of lives were lost.

A smaller US force in Afghanistan indeed, as has been aptly observed, would only increase US's imperative for Pakistan and perpetuation of US's dichotomous Af-Pak policy will bring the Afghan, Indian and regional security under strain.

The world after 9/11 and 26/11 faced many challenges. Iraq was invaded by George Bush J., former President of the US.

There were futurologists galore. Francis Fukuyama, a contemporary historian, known for his book *The End of History* expressed the view that Islamic terrorism is posing a challenge in the twenty first century like Communism during the Cold War era. The terrorist attacks have been described as "a conspiracy" of religious prejudices.

On October 20, 2010, the UN General Assembly passed a resolution declaring the first week of February of every year the *World Interfaith Harmony Week* to help stem the growing inter-religious intolerance. The resolution was proposed by King Abdullah II of Jordan.

The Bush administration deliberately marginalised the United Nations, preparing to operate on its own or with a few allies rather than going through the long drawn-out process of building international consensus. This was repeated in Afghanistan.

Afghanistan is one of the poorest and most ravaged countries in the world. The United States waged a war against militants in Afghanistan by every possible means. The US-led coalition in Afghanistan failed in ousting the Taliban and after the Soviet withdrawal there has been no progress in democratic governance in Afghanistan.

Obama's Afghan Policy

The US President Barack Obama had sent US troops to fight in Afghanistan. The US policy in Afghanistan was "dominated by the military surge, though couched in terms of protecting Afghans."[1]

Foreign ministers from 44 countries in the US – NATO led mission in Afghanistan met on December 7, 2009 to discuss the strategy to combat the narco-terrorism which has been responsible for the continuing war against US-led NATO coalition force. Helmand is Afghanistan's main opium growing province and the most violent front in the Afghan war. There is a very strong link between opium growers and the Taliban. According to the United Nations, a hectare planted with opium in Afghanistan produced three times as much cash value as the same land planted with wheat in 2009. The farmers of Afghanistan have been forced by the Taliban to grow poppy, according to British military experts.

Bombing with tons of 'precision' bombs, US/NATO forces killed about 10 times more Afghan civilians than they killed Serbs in 1999.[2] In June 2011, President Obama announced phased pullout of 100,000 US troops from Afghanistan to end a costly war launched after 9/11 attacks. But the Taliban dismissed Obama's announcement as symbolic and rejected any talks with the government in Afghanistan.[3]

Afghanistan President Hamid Karzai welcomed the US President Obama's announcement on a limited withdrawal of US troops from Afghanistan which created a heated debate among the US decision makers. They argued that Obama's announcement "will mean little unless accompanied by a clear statement that he intends to negotiate an end to conflict, just as Lyndon Johnson eventually promised during the Vietnam War, though it took the efforts of the Republican Richard Nixon to carry the talks through."[4]

A phased out reduction of the US troops from Afghanistan might not result in a zero-sum game. The US military presence in Afghanistan after the Soviet withdrawal has resulted in turbulence in Afghanistan. In southern Afghanistan, the absence of an overt US presence, Islamic fundamentalism "could also be channelled towards the creation of a Pashutan territory that straddles the Durand Line. This cross–border Pashtunistan, largely autonomous of Islamabad, is already a reality."[5]

The US was not interested in such divisions. Analysts of the Obama administration have spoken of the need "To keep using Afghanistan as the base for incursions into Pakistan."[6] The US also made serious investments and has air bases in Afghanistan, as US Vice-President Joe Biden spoke on the feasibility of such a strategy.[7]

The Obama administration had escalated the fight against the Taliban, as a large number of US soldiers lost their lives in action. In 2010 alone, 701 foreign defence personnel were killed, among them 496 were Americans.[8] The confidential UN maps published in the *Wall Street Journal* in December 2010 showed a clear deterioration of security in Afghanistan. Year 2010 was the most lethal year for non-combatants in the Afghanistan war.

The biggest challenge to end Afghanistan's civil war has been the interference by its neighbours, particularly Pakistan. At a summit in June 2011, Russia, China and the four Central Asian states of the Shanghai Cooperation Organisation came out with a suggestion for a 'Neutral' Afghanistan – This has also been the position of India and Iran.

The assassination of Burhanuddin Rabbani, former Afghan President and head of the High Peace Council on September 20, 2011 hurt the peace process and shattered Afghanistan's tenuous stability. Northern Alliance leaders, most of whom are ethnic Tajiks and Hazaras also denounced the peace process.

The inability of most governments to take tough and timely decisions also stands in the way of preventive diplomacy in crisis management and conflict resolution. The media also has inordinate influence in shaping perceptions of the success or failure of international action. Former US President George W Bush was under Congressional pressure to withdraw US troops from Iraq.

The world community relies on an 'ad hoc' system of international security that is driven by political consideration, as it is perceived by the major powers. These problems make preventive action by the United Nations difficult.

Taliban's Doha Delegates Blacklisted by the UN

When the Taliban opened their political office in Qatar stepping into the halogen glare of TV cameras, it was the first time in a dozen years that the world got to see members of the insurgents' inner circle– and they seemed different. Urbane and educated, they conducted interviews in English, Arabic, French and German with easy fluency, passed out and received phone numbers and, most strikingly, talked about peace!

Back in Afghanistan, though, it has been the same old Taliban. Fighters have waged suicide attacks that have taken an increasing toll on civilians, and militants staged a deadly strike right at the heart of the heavily secured government district in Kabul.

For officials watching the talks, those contradictions offer a picture of a top Taliban leadership taking advantage of two different tracks-orchestrating the fighting element even while setting up a new international diplomatic foothold in Doha. This complicates efforts to pin down the insurgents' true goals.

At the Taliban office, it quickly became clear that the contingent's members had all been carefully vetted for their diplomatic credentials. Though many were officials in the old Taliban government, often sent abroad, none are known as fighters. And they all are considered loyalists to the Taliban's reclusive leader in exile, Mullah Omar.

Further, while the delegates claimed to be there to talk peace with the Afghan government and US officials, on closer examination, what they did was essentially to set up a virtual embassy which sent what many saw as the reverse message, raising serious questions about the insurgent movement's real motives in going to Qatar in the first place.

"From minute one, the Taliban didn't play this by the book," said a Western official who has tracked the Taliban for a number of years. "They overstepped pretty well agreed upon guidelines."[9]

The identities and backgrounds of the delegation's key members – and thus some of the Taliban leadership's aims in choosing them can now be detailed based on interviews with four disparate officials and on public appearances by the group in Qatar. The sources include a member of the Quetta Shura, the Taliban's leadership council in Pakistan, a Taliban military commander from eastern Afghanistan, a former Taliban official and a Western official in Kabul who is close to the Doha talks and spoke about the delegation's general approach.

Every single member has been picked by the Taliban leadership after a long series of lengthy discussions.

1. **Tayeb Agha:** The apparent leader of the delegation. Omar's secretary and chief of staff.
2. **Hafiz Aziz Rahman Ahadi:** Son of Omar's teacher at his madarsa in Quetta.
3. **Sohail Shaheen:** A former second secretary in the Taliban's embassy in Islamabad.
4. **Mohammad Naim Wardak:** Embassy official of former Taliban govt.
5. **Mualavi Nik Mohammad:** A former minister for agriculture and commerce.

6. **Khalifa Sayid Rasul Nangnarhari:** A former low-level diplomat of the Taliban govt.

Pakistan's Game Plan

The bombing of an Indian consulate in Jalalabad and the killing of jawans on the LOC were all part of Pakistan's attempts to exploit the US withdrawal from Afghanistan and undo its strategic reverses of past two decades. US intelligence had confirmed to India that Lashkar-e-Taiba cadres were being moved into the provinces of Kunar and Nuristan in expectation of the US troop withdrawal from Afghanistan in 2014.

Pakistan similarly transferred militant cadre recruited from its Khyber Paktunkhwa province to boost military ranks in the Kashmir valley. Lashkar chief Hafiz Sayeed declared in an interview with *India Today* saying "Full-scale armed *jihad* will begin in Kashmir after American forces withdraw from Afghanistan."[10]

The Pakistani game plan is quite clear which is to infiltrate militants eastward and westward across the Durand and Radcliffe lines.

Prospects for Democratic Transition

Afghanistan's presidential election in 2014 will mark the first peaceful transition of power in Afghan history."[11] Afghanistan has been ravaged by endless wars since 1979 and peaceful democratic transition "can come only if Afghanistan frees itself from the external albatross that has turned it into a cursed nation."[12]

Afghanistan's political and security transition hinges considerably on two factors, firstly, the level of interference by Pakistan which still harbours militant sanctuaries and the command and control structure for Afghan insurgency and secondly, the likely post-2014 role of US-led NATO forces. Indeed, US, President Barack Obama's U-turn on NATO military presence in Afghanistan will keep Afghan insurgency alive."[13]

Obama had declared in Cairo in 2009, "We do not want to keep our troops in Afghanistan and seek no military bases...." But in a change of heat, Obama now seeks bases in Afghanistan for a virtually unlimited period to house fairly sizeable US-led NATO forces armed with authority to "conduct combat operations."[14]

Terrorism and insurgency as has been aptly observed, "have never been defeated in any country without choking Trans-boundary sustenance and support." Perpetuation of US's dichotomous Af-Pak policy will bring Afghan, Indian and regional security under strain. In the State of Union address presented to a joint session of US Congress Obama said "Wind down war in Afghanistan by removing most troops and completing mission by the end of 2014."

Afghan's Election (2014)

Afghans voted in large numbers as has been the case of 2014 General Election in India. It is the first democratic transfer of power as US-led forces end their 13-year war despite Taliban threats, voting was reported largely peaceful. Around 13.5 million people were eligible to vote. In 2009 election only around one third of voters had cast their votes. The Taliban has rejected the election as a foreign plot.[15]

The extraordinary turnout of 58 per cent in Presidential election sent "a message of steely determination from a nation wracked by war and state failure."[16] For a demographically youthful nation like Afghanistan, where 75 per cent of the population is below the age of 25, "revolutionary shifts in attitudes towards politics within a short and rapid timeframe are not inconceivable."[17]

Western opinion-makers claim that contemporary Afghan youth are from "Generation America." However, the influences of successful democracies like India, which is much beloved among people of various hues of Afghan and Turkey, where Islam and democracy which have found "a harmonious co-existence via media", are also quite strong on the Afghan psyche.[18] After one decade of pouring in blood to stabilise Afghanistan most Afghan youth are conflicted in their minds about the American and European roles in their country. It is aptly observed, "Youth power for democratising Afghanistan cannot be exaggerated at the present juncture of political evolution where accountable government is still "an aspiration."[19]

Recent Developments in Afghanistan: India's Concerns

Despite a renewed push from Afghanistan's President Hamid Karzai for deepening defence ties, India is extremely cautious of the issue of the supply of lethal weapons which is to be overseen by the Cabinet Committee on Security (CCS). According to senior officials of the Ministry of External Affairs, India is treading a cautious path even as Kabul raised the pitch for deeper military ties. The Afghan President met former Indian Prime Minister Manmohan Singh on December 13, 2013 and discussed wide ranging topics including bilateral security pact and cooperation on the Chabahar port in Iran with the US[20] India expressed its willingness to send more military technicians, provide training to personnel and supply key elements including supporting equipments, transportation vehicles like trucks and jeeps.[21] Afghanistan has been urging that India should take a more active role to clamp down on the extremists. India has been playing an active role in the reconstruction of war-torn Afghanistan.[22]

The US is expected to withdraw its forces from Afghanistan towards the close of 2014; it is argued that a fresh batch of warlords could come up in Afghanistan, as was seen between 1992 and 1996 before the Taliban came to power.

Two things stand out, despite the threat of the Taliban's return to power after the US pullout. One is that the Americans do not approve of their soldiers remaining in Afghanistan; and second, the situation in Afghanistan has improved dramatically. Surveys have shown that more than 75 per cent of the people voted and debates on television contributed to people's enthusiasm. Under the Taliban regime there was hardly any television in Afghanistan. As for India, 2014 election is of enormous significance because India must have the confidence of whoever becomes the successor of Hamid Karzai, a friendly government in Kabul will act as a check on the activities of terror groups."[23]

Afghanistan's poll will undergo the first autonomous democratic transfer of power in its history. Despite a spate of terror attacks, including kidnappings and murder of election staff in the provinces, Afghans displayed a certain resilience and desire to have their voices heard. Abbas Farasoo, a Kabul-based regional analyst and the Chairman of a policy and strategy focused think-tank 'A 3' (Afghanistan Analysis and Awareness), told *Hindustan Times* correspondent that 2014 election and its implications will be far-reaching for India and Pakistan and hold the key to regional stability in the Central South Asia region. It is in India's interest to have democratic nations on its doorstep.

Frustrated by Hamid Karzai's refusal to sign a security pact, the US special representative for Afghanistan and Pakistan, James Dobbins expressed the hope that India would be able to use its influence to persuade Karzai to sign the agreement. Afghan Ambassador to India, Shaida Abdali told *Hindustan Times* reporters that Karzai refused to sign the agreement demanding that the US should negotiate through Pakistan's government. The outlawed Tehreek-i-Taliban Pakistan (TTP) rejected the Nawaz Sharif government's call for an unconditional ceasefire.[24]

India and Russia worked on an understanding by which India would be able to meet Afghanistan's defence wish list. Both India and Russia decided to revive a weapons maintenance factory in Afghanistan. With Afghanistan's future becoming uncertain after US-NATO pullout, India and Russia expressed the willingness to revive their 1990s' cooperation with the avowed intention of keeping the Taliban out.[25]

Preliminary Results of Afghanistan President Election

As no candidate registered an absolute majority, second round runoff between former foreign minister Abdullah and Ex-World Bank economist Ashraf Ghani is necessary and second round tentatively has been scheduled for June 7, 2014. According to the Independent Election Commission (IEC) Abdullah secured 44.9 per cent, followed by Ghani with 31.5 per cent and Zalmay Rassoul secured 11.5 per cent. Hamid Karzai was constitutionally bound to step down as President after more than 12 years in power.[26]

The Election Commission will probe as authorities (investigation) found half a million votes suspected to be fraudulent. Nearly seven million people had voted in April 5, 2014 presidential election, out of an estimated electorate of 13.5 million.[27]

Abbas Farasoo, a regional analyst based in Kabul and the chairman of a policy focused think-tank, 'Afghanistan Analysts and Awareness' told *Hindustan Times* that neither of the two front runners was particularly different in terms of policy from India's perspective, Farasoo indicated that the key concern for

India "is the success of the broader political process, ensuring that Afghanistan's first ever democratic transition of presidential power is legitimately elected and accepted by the people."[28]

Opium Trade and its Impact after US Withdrawal

The opium from Marjah, a district in southern Helmad province will make its way to drug addicts as US troops leave Afghanistan. The US has spent $ 7.5 billion trying to eradicate opium in Afghanistan which represents one of the most tangible and visible failures as the American-led military force prepares to withdraw by the end of 2014 and with Afghanistan's emerging anti-narcotics forces vastly outnumbered both by Taliban brokers and corrupt officials involved in the trade, the opium trade likely will only grow.[29]

According to Ashita Mittal, acting country director for the United Nations Office on Drugs and Crime in Kabul, opium trade is going to impact the whole economy of Afghanistan. The UN drug agency stated that in coming years, opium will grab even larger share of Afghanistan's troubled economy as money from US military contracts and aid work dries up.[30] Throughout its mission in Afghanistan, the US worked with Afghan forces to try to store opium – a major source of funding for the Taliban insurgency.[31]

Conclusion

Whatever the final outcome, voters in Afghanistan's presidential election have delivered "a powerful mandate" although Abdullah Abdullah, who emerged in the lead, has raised serious concerns about fraud. Abdullah is a veteran of anti-Taliban Northern Alliance. The purpose of the 2014 election was to allow Afghans to choose a legitimate successor to Karzai. Afghanistan has four main ethnic groups namely the Pashtuns, Tajiks, Hazaras and Uzbeks and all of these major groups want to be represented in the Afghan political system. They rejected the insurgents' authoritarian alternative and showed little interest in the hard line Islamists who stood in the election. They want to keep Afghanistan's link to the West.

The front runner in 2014 Afghanistan's presidential election picked up ahead of a second round of polling in May 2014. Former Foreign Minister Abdullah Abdullah came out on top according to a preliminary tally in the first round of voting on April 5, 2014. Zalmai Rassoul, another foreign minister, backed Abdullah on grounds of "national unity, stability, peace and prosperity of Afghanistan." According to *Reuters* Abdullah had garnered 44.9 per cent of the first round vote.

India's new government headed by Shri Narendra Modi will face "a rapidly changing and dangerous challenge in Afghanistan, similar in some ways to the crisis in the late 1980s, when the Soviets withdrew from Kabul."[32]

Pakistan tried hard to disrupt the Afghan election, and also tried to disrupt with blasts Modi's election rallies. But Pakistan underestimated the Afghan's desire for freedom. Abdullah Abdullah is the ISI's "worst nightmare", a twenty first century Ahmad Shah Masoud, an Afghan leader who would not take orders from Rawalpindi."[33] The ISI-backed Taliban, Al Qaeda, Lashkar-e-Taiba and other *jihadis* will join in the effort to make Afghanistan their sphere of influence.

India backed the losing side in 1989, as has been observed by Late Indira Gandhi and late Rajiv Gandhi "stuck with Moscow and its communist warlord Najibullah."[34] In 1992, India's Afghan policy collapsed. Under Modi's leadership, India hopefully may be a much stronger state and will face many foreign policy challenges to curb the Pakistani proxy war in Afghanistan.

Militancy has been on the rise since the Taliban launched the so called spring offensive on May 12, 2014 in Afghanistan. Insurgents are seeking to take advantage of the full withdrawal of foreign combat troops in an effort to overthrow the Hamid Karzai led government of Afghanistan and regain territory lost in nearly 14 years of war.

There is the Al-Qaeda-Taliban nexus and their various branches have been targeting western troops.[35] There is no disputing that the gravest security problem that international community and especially India faces is the *jihadi* terrorism for which the epicentre is Pakistan. After 26/11, India has been persuading the United States to put pressure on Pakistan to act against terror groups.

The Conference of 23 countries hosted by the UN Security Council in 2010 attempted to create a framework towards finding solutions to challenges faced by India after the 26/11 terrorist attack.

The United States plans to keep a residual force of 9,800 in Afghanistan after the conclusion of its combat mission at the end of 2014. This residual force will be tasked only to aid and train Afghan forces and take part in anti-terrorism operations to prevent Al-Qaeda from regaining lost ground. President Hamid Karzai has refused to sign a bilateral security agreement (BSA) with the US despite the approval of a Loya Jirga (congregation of elders) demanding US intervention to get the Taliban to agree to a peace deal. The Obama administration is hopeful of clinching a BSA with Karzai's successor.

India has watched with mounting concern Hamid Karzai's refusal to sign the BSA. India fears that without US troops in Afghanistan, it will slide back into pre-2001 chaos under the influence of Pakistan. India even tried to use its leverage with Afghanistan to persuade Karzai to sign the BSA, without any success though. Both Afghan presidential candidates Abdullah Abdullah and Ashraf Ghani have reiterated their intention to sign the bilateral security agreement with the US, if elected.

Prime Minister Narendra Modi and Afghan President Hamid Karzai discussed various ways to deepen bilateral ties, including security cooperation and the fight against terrorism. Modi reiterated India's commitment to development and reconstruction of Afghanistan and the reconciliation process, according to foreign secretary Sujatha Singh, "Afghanistan would be Afghan-led, Afghan owned and Afghan controlled".

A ruling PML–N legislator and an ISI official were allegedly kidnapped by the Taliban, from Pakistan's Punjab province near Pindi Bhattian, some 150 km from Lahore, Upto 200 militants from across the border attacked Pakistan posts. The attack took place in the Bajaur tribal district bordering Afghanistan. Pakistani forces along the border took offence against the Taliban militants for killing civilians.

On a visit to Afghanistan, US Defence Secretary Chuck Hagel expressed the hope that the release of US Army sergeant Bowe Bergdahl would lead to direct talks with the Taliban as a "reintegration process." Republican lawmakers have criticised the Obama administration's move as it will set a bad precedent and endanger US soldiers still in Afghanistan.[36]

Taliban insurgents had launched a major offensive in southern Afghanistan to gain territory vacated by US troops. The assault highlighted the challenges facing Afghan security forces battling the Taliban as US-led NATO forces pull out. The US troops pulled out of Sangin, Nowzad and Musa Qala districts.[37]

The political crisis threatened the presidential elections of Afghanistan in 2014. Both the presidential candidates, Abdullah Abdullah and Ashraf Ghani had agreed to an audit of all the votes cast to form a unity government under the victor. There has been optimism about the possibility of a smooth political transition in Afghanistan. However, a number of challenges still remain. The most immediate is the auditing process itself and the lack of consensus between the candidates regarding the audit methodology.[38]

A more pressing challenge will be the nature of the power-sharing agreement. How will powers be divided? Reports suggest that the losing candidate will assume the role of chief of the Executive Council under the new President, and following constitutional amendments in 2016 the post-of a Prime Minister will be created. The endurance of the new system would depend largely on the division of powers between the President and the Prime Minister. This is not the first power-sharing agreement in Afghanistan. The 1992 Peshawar Accords and the 1993 Islamabad Accords had provided for a coalition government, but these accords were short lived.

Finally, a more irreconcilable problem is likely to be the peace talks with the Taliban. The Hamid Karzai government has been persistently denounced and considered as unrepresentative and termed as a 'stooge' of the West by its opposition. The best way to cope with the crisis of political transition in Afghanistan is that Hamid Karzai should deal with his successors. Most Americans believe that the war in Afghanistan has achieved little.

For decades the United Nations has been unable to agree upon a definition of terrorism. The stumbling block has been that member states of the Western bloc want States and State agents to be exempt from any definition as observed by Glies Fraser in his article published in the *Guardian*. A number of Islamic countries want some national liberation movements exempted.

Notes

1. *Associate Press*, November 30, 2006.
2. Marc W Herold, "Matrix of Death," *Frontline*, October 24, 2008.
3. Jonathan Steele, "Listen to the Taliban", *Hindustan Times* (New Delhi), June, 2011, p.12.
4. *Ibid.*
5. Ashok Malik, "Withdrawal Symptoms," *Hindustan Times* (New Delhi), June 28, 2011, p.12.
6. *Ibid.*
7. *Ibid.*
8. *Frontline,* April 22, 2011, p. 60.
9. Rod Nordland and Allisa J Rubin, "Taliban's divided tactics raise doubts over Doha talks, "*Hindustan Times* (New Delhi), June 27, 2013, p.17.
10. *Hindustan Times* (New Delhi), August 8, 2013, p. 19.
11. Brahma Chellaney, "A Curse, Not A Cure," *The Times of India* (New Delhi), April 9, 2014, p. 20
12. *Ibid.*
13. *Ibid.*
14. *Ibid.*
15. *Asian Age* (New Delhi), 6 April 2014, p. 8.
16. Sreeram Chaulia, "A vote for Afghanistan," *Asian Age* (New Delhi), p. 6.
17. *Ibid.*
18. *Ibid.*
19. Nazes Afroz, "There's a palpable sense of change." *Hindustan Times* (New Delhi), April 6, 2014, p. 14.
20. Jayanth Jacob, "Karzai's push for lethal weapons worries India," *Hindustan Time*s (New Delhi), December 10, 2013, p.10.
21. *Ibid.*
22. B.N. Mehrish, "Security and Development of Afghanistan: An Appraisal of India's Role and Strategy, *The IUP Journal of International Relations,* Vol. VII, No. 2, 2013, pp. 29-37.
23. Editorial, "There is a lot at stake," *Hindustan Times* (New Delhi) April 6, 2014, p. 14.
24. *Hindustan Times* (New Delhi) February 27, 2014, p. 20.
25. Indrani Baghchi," India, Russia work to meet Af' weapons wish list," *The Times of India* (New Delhi) January 24, 2014, p.18.
26. *Hindustan Times* (New Delhi), April 27, 2014.
27. *Ibid.*
28. *Ibid.*

29. Abdul Khaliq and Kay Johnson, "As US leaves, Afghan opium yield thrives," *The Asian Age,* (New Delhi) 2 May 2014, p.14.
30. *Ibid.*
31. *Ibid.*
32. Bruce Riedel, "Islamabad will not give Modi time for pleasantries," *Hindustan Times* (New Delhi), May 21, 2014, p. 14.
33. *Ibid.*
34. *Ibid.*
35. Abdel Bari Atwan, "Militancy is now a familiar Concept", *Gulf News*, May 16, 2010, p.12.
36. *Hindustan Times* (New Delhi), June 2, 2014, p. 18.
37. *Agence France – Prese.*
38. Aryaman Bhatnagar, "Power shaming holds the Afghan peace process; *Hindustan Times* (New Delhi), July 28, 2014, p.14.

8

State of Afghanistan after 2014 and the Policy Options for India and China

SUBHADEEP BHATTACHARYA

The defeat of the Americans in the Vietnam War was the biggest event of the Cold War era when a Super Power with all its might was routed by the guerrilla fighters of a Third World country with its comparatively 'unsophisticated' weapons. It was undoubtedly the most significant event of the last century. Some compare the American missions in Iraq and Afghanistan with Vietnam War saying that history is repeating itself. Today, on the eve of the withdrawal of US-led NATO forces, the question of the future of Afghanistan post-2014 is haunting policy-makers around the globe. The question is more nightmarish for the neighbours of Afghanistan, especially India and China. Both have had century old relations with Afghanistan and they are well aware of the consequences of Afghanistan relapsing to the post-1989 period. The paper tries to analyse two things - firstly, the international mission to establish a 'modern state of democratic Afghanistan' and secondly, the policy options for its big neighbours, India and China.

Afghanistan: a Conflict Ridden but Invincible Territory

Afghanistan has had a strategic importance since the early period of history. It is the connecting point of several regions between Asia and Europe. It is located in the east of the Iranian Plateau where the frontiers of the ancient empires of

Central Asia, West Asia (Middle East) and the Indian subcontinent met at the borders of this land-locked terrain. At the same time this region has been the route of invasion since the early period of history. From the Greeks, Huns, Persians of ancient time to the Soviets and Americans of modern days, Afghanistan bears the footprints of all the big powers of human history. Afghanistan has suffered and sustained foreign invasions and has also been ripped with severe internal ethnic conflicts. The freedom loving tribes of Afghanistan have clashed with each other time and again to ensure their respective liberty and territorial sovereignty. Their obsession with this independence has undoubtedly helped Afghanistan to remain free from any colonial domination during the era of European colonialism. No external power was successful in subjugating the Afghan tribes since, whenever there was a foreign invasion, these groups fought together, while left to themselves they would resume their bloody internal strife. As Stephen Tanner said, "*...evidence indicates that Afghanistan is capable of unity only when its people respond to a foreign threat. Left to their own devices, Afghans engage in internecine battles, or simply enjoy freedom-not the kind enforceable by a Magna Carta, Bill of Rights or Communist Manifesto, but of more ancient derivation-unbothered by a government at all.*"[1] Afghanistan is a crisis-ridden society. The main demerit of the country is that it has miserably failed to emerge as a united state. Afghanistan has sustained a feudal structure torn apart by the internecine tribal conflicts, It holds the image of a 'barbarian failed state' populated by 'wild tribesmen' and the asylum of international terrorists.[2]

As mentioned earlier, the Afghan territory was never subdued by any foreign power due to gallant opposition of the tribal communities. The Afghans were the most formidable warrior class of the region who defended their tribal territorial belts and the vast Afghan territory from invaders. One of the reasons why Afghanistan never sustained a strong central authority commanding the entire Afghan territory is its free tribal factions who could never be united under any ruler for long. These tribes could remain independent of the central jurisdiction due to the terrains which helped them to survive independently among inaccessible mountains. At the same time, they could easily descend from the mountain tops to join forces for collective defence. Moreover, with the passage of time, the Afghan route became less important in global commerce which eventually pushed the territory to isolation. The Afghan tribes also started living in isolation within an isolated enclave. They were a warrior class living a secluded existence, and who spent time fighting among themselves when no outside challenge was there. So when the world was moving towards economic progress, the Afghans became a threat to the civilisation outside.[3]

Afghanistan, however unruly and medieval in character, still holds strategic importance due to its location. It was the 'crossroad of Empires' and the route to both East and West. From Alexander the Great to American the Super Power, the big players who wished to safeguard their regional interests in adjacent Asia, could hardly overlook Afghanistan. Afghanistan became the subject of the *Great Game* between the British India and the Tzarist Russia/Soviet Russia till the conclusion of the Second World War. Then for long the duel between rival gangs of Cold War remained subdued due to shrewd diplomacy of the Afghan King Zahir Shah but the Cold War crept inside Afghanistan with the Soviet intervention in 1979 to 1989 and the simultaneous foundation and arming of the *Mujahedeen* from among the Afghan tribes by US in Pakistan. In the post-1989 era, when the Soviet withdrew, the Americans left them without enemy and with sophisticated weapons. Now, free of foreign occupation, when Afghanistan again returned to the era of eternal ethnic conflicts, a new warrior class was born to fight against the 'enemies of Islam and Muslims' around the world. With the Taliban being triumphant in 1990-96 Afghan tribal conflict, the war ravaged territory became the haven of '*jihadi*sts', fighting against the West, including USA, and other 'enemies of Islam'. Al Qaeda chief, Osama Bin Laden spearheaded the *jihad* against USA resulting in 9/11 which again brought back the Americans to Afghanistan.

History repeated itself. Afghanistan again came under foreign intervention with the Americans hunting the country length and breadth to smash the Taliban, the way the Soviets did in the concluding phase of the last century. This time, however, the Americans had another job to perform, to construct this war ravaged crisis ridden wild territory into a modern state system by rooting the pillars of democracy deep inside its infertile soil and to ascribe the lessons of Western political thinking in the minds of the 'unruly' populace of this territory. But today when they are packing their bags to return, the question of security of Afghanistan and its neighbours is prevailing over the analysis of the success and failure of the American mission.

Afghanistan and the Associated Fear

Taliban became a household name only after the 9/11 massacre. Before this tragedy occurred, the world, especially the West, remained ignorant about this horrendous faction of the Afghan tribes and their day to day atrocities in Afghanistan. 9/11 made them realise the impending threat from this Islamic extremist group to the world, mainly the 'non-Muslim civilised' West. The Americans could now see their mistake of leaving Afghanistan to its own in the aftermath of the Soviet intervention. The evil nexus between Al Qaeda and Taliban got exposed while Afghanistan was unveiled as the breeding ground of Islamic extremism and associated terrorism. It was a new realisation for the world that this wild, secluded territory populated by the 'most unruly and wilder' tribal communities who have converted the land into the labour room of terrorism cannot be left to its own.

During its long seven years of reign of terror, the Taliban converted Afghanistan into a hell. Afghanistan remained obscured from the outside world and was governed in the cruellest manner. In these years of obscurity, Afghanistan became the hub of Islamic extremism. Not only this, extensive murders of ethnic Afghans and especially women, became a regular event in the country. If on the one hand, the Taliban tried to unite entire Afghanistan under its supreme command, on the other hand, their mission of purging the non-Pashtun Afghan tribes and imposition of medieval rules and conducts on the Afghan women tormented Afghan society.

The world was however, not very concerned with the internal developments of Afghanistan. They played their part only by refusing any official recognition to the Taliban regime of Kabul, exception being UAE, Saudi Arabia and Pakistan. The world concentrated seriously on Afghanistan only after Osama Bin Laden and his Al Qaeda conducted the 9/11 as a consequence of which the USA waged the 'War on Terror' against Al Qaeda. Their initial target was not Taliban but Osama. When Taliban refused to hand over Osama to US as demanded, they became the enemy number one of Washington. It was only then that the Americans and the West could see the devil in Taliban and their atrocities in Afghanistan. Piles of research were conducted and numerous books written on Taliban, their fanaticism and the 'mistakes' of the Americans who left Afghanistan to the fighting tribal factions after the Soviet withdrawal. Afghanistan was 'rediscovered' by the West. The US-led 'Operation Enduring Freedom' in Afghanistan in 2001, had the double mission of freeing the land from Taliban grip and stabilising it via democratisation. It was an attempt to correct the mistake the West committed twenty years back by leaving Afghanistan to its own means.

To ensure that Afghanistan does not become the haven of the Taliban or similar fanatic faction who can pose challenge to the global and regional security is the prime concern of the international community. If Afghanistan is left to itself again with its bloody ethnic strife, there is a full chance of the return of Taliban. Thus, after the fall of Taliban in 2001, the global community launched 'Humanitarian Intervention' mission in Afghanistan. It was meant to reshape Afghanistan in a democratic form with a modern state structure. In other words, the international community wants to create a modern state of Afghanistan bearing all the necessary characters of such system. The restructuring of the Afghan National Army (ANA) with proper training and sophisticated weapons (supplied by the West) and framing of a constitution are the motives behind such mission. The foremost job for reconstructing Afghanistan is an end to the fratricidal conflict. This was mentioned in '*Agreement on Provincial Arrangements in Afghanistan Pending the Re-establishment of Permanent Government Institutions*' popularly known as the Bonn Agreement 2001 (between the non-Taliban groups and the international community) which expressed determination to end the tragic conflict in Afghanistan and promote national reconciliation.[4]

The Bonn Agreement was meant to make provisional arrangements in Afghanistan under the United Nations supervision. The insistence on the national reconciliation was significant since to convert a territory into a modern state, the intra state ethnic conflicts should be eradicated otherwise the territory cannot be brought under one ruling entity. The agreement also mentioned an interim administration with Chairman and his deputies along with the several departments including defence, finance, foreign and interior affairs. All these arrangements were made to establish a modern *state-based* system in Afghanistan. This was a significant move in a country which never produced a 'national entity' transcending the individual tribal identity. It was a difficult task to introduce the 'rule of law' with state based rules in Afghanistan in the post-Taliban era since the territory had different bodies of law resonating differing religious or traditional cultures. The Bonn Agreement underlined the efforts to establish a political authority in the country which led to the adoption of the 2004 constitution reflecting the international human rights standard and resolving to hold elections for Presidentship and Parliament memberships of Afghanistan in 2004 and 2005 respectively.[5]

The recognition and reflection of the international human rights standard in the legal framework of Afghanistan was natural after emerging from the days of Taliban atrocities while the resolution to select the administration of the country via election was significant.[6] It was an attempt to make the new administration of the country gain popular legitimacy so as to make it acceptable to the international community. Democratisation of Afghanistan was criticised by many as a Western (or American) attempt which eventually would prove to be a failure. True, it is difficult to make a system work if the factors making it workable do not internalise it due to lack of experience. Afghanistan never experienced a Western style democracy[7] and so such apprehension was understandable. However it won't be proper to conclude that the democratisation mission has failed completely in Afghanistan as gradually Afghan democracy is also becoming popular; nevertheless it is not comparable with other working democracies in the West or in India . There is an impartial Independent Election Commission which supervises the elections. Voter turnout of the 2014 Presidential elections is an important indicator of the growing acceptability of the 'Western system' among larger sections of Afghan society. Some seven million people turned out to vote in the first round of elections defying the Taliban threat. The percentage of women voters was almost thirty five per cent (thirty eight per cent according to the Independent Election Commission). They came out to vote because they thought it was their 'duty' to vote.[8] This sense of 'duty' arising among the Afghans, especially women, is undoubtedly a significant change in the Afghan mindset which signifies the growing acceptability of the democratic system among the Afghan population, who have never experienced such practices before. This is certainly the victory of the mission to convert Afghanistan into a modern democratic state. The election was so popular among the Afghans that they turned out in high numbers in some places which made three hundred polling stations run out of ballot papers.[9] These developments are important in a country like Afghanistan which knew only bloody power struggles and ethnic conflicts, the common Afghans were not involved in government formation and were the subject of the whims of the ruling administrators. The modern state system with Western style of governance is a new experience for Afghanistan which seems to be gaining in popularity.

The Afghan National Army

Another important aspect of a modern state foundation is the creation of a strong 'national' army. Afghanistan is the land of warriors. The Afghan people are born fighters but still one of the priorities of the reconstruction plan of post-Taliban Afghanistan is the formation of the Afghan National Army (ANA) which the country lacked seriously. A national army is the prime character of a state, ancient, medieval or modern, which defends the sovereignty and integrity of the state. Creating a working national army was a tough job in a country like Afghanistan, known for its strong ethnic divisions and conflicts. However, the international community found it necessary to build a national army for Afghanistan which subsequently takes up the charge of defence of the territory, especially against the Taliban resurgence. This was another step of building a modern state of Afghanistan.[10] To make the army truly national, the international community at the Bonn Conference in 2002 decided to create a new Afghan army that should be 'ethnically balanced'.[11] Also, to reconstruct a country like Afghanistan, ethnic divisions have to be overcome and that is important towards building a modern national army. The US took the main charge of constructing the ANA. Although it is debatable whether ANA is fully ready to take charge of Afghan security, the attempt to build a national army for Afghanistan is an important endeavour to convert the territory into a modern state.

Afghanistan: the Great Game between India and China

The two rising neighbours of Afghanistan, India and China, have their respective stakes in the country. Afghanistan is important for both of them. An unstable neighbour, ridden with internal conflicts is absolutely undesirable for any country. Afghanistan holds strategic, security and economic significance for both India and China. Therefore, the future of Afghanistan in the post-2014 period is a matter that concerns both India and China. Moreover, being the rising economic powers, hungry for resources, India and China eye Afghanistan's huge untapped raw material resources like coal, copper, lithium, gold, rare earth materials etc., having an estimated overall worth of $ 1 trillion. On the other hand, the internal security of both the countries is linked with Afghanistan. Kashmir and Xinxiang are neighbours of Afghanistan and both are serious security concerns for India and China respectively. The ammunition of the Afghan War of late last century got diverted to Kashmir along with the Islamic radicalism while the Uighur separatists of Xinjiang found Afghanistan as a place for both taking refuge and conducting training. Thus, an unstable Afghanistan, ruled by extremist elements, is a nightmare for both.

Therefore, we see points of convergence on security issue between India and China in the Afghan context. Yet, it should not be forgotten that India and China are strategic rivals.

Ruling the neighbourhood is the prime condition for any rising power. Given the strategic and economic importance of Afghanistan, China wants to play significant role there and given her rivalry with India, it is obvious that Beijing will disapprove similar role for India. In this case, China relies on her strongest South Asian ally, Pakistan. It was with Pakistan that China colluded (along with USA) to fight the Soviets during the latter's intervention in Afghanistan. The *Daily Telegraph* reported that "China is flying arms and ammunition to the insurgents in Afghanistan."[12] The objective behind the Chinese mission in Afghanistan was to ward off the 'Soviet threat'. Today, the Chinese are undoubtedly in a difficult position. The secured

Afghanistan is important for China to deal with the Uighur separatists of Xinjiang who have connections with the extremists of Afghanistan who hide in the chaotic North Waziristan at the Af-Pak border, and there are also some 250 Uighur separatists present in the Nuristan and Kurnur provinces of Afghanistan, according to the Afghan Taliban sources.[13] China blames the Uighur 'terrorists' for the recent bloodshed in the Kunming province where 29 people were killed, who, according to Beijing, run terrorist camps along the rugged border near Afghanistan and Pakistan.[14] Thus, if Afghanistan slips into the hands of Islamists again then China has reason to fear. Also, China wants her economic security in Afghanistan where she has invested $3 billion and also she eyes the country's unexplored resources China does not want to involve directly in Afghan affairs but would prefer the Western powers, especially USA, to continue to bear the security responsibility and so insists on the US to bring stability to Afghanistan.[15] In the aftermath of the American withdrawal, Beijing insists on the international community to playing a bigger role.[16]

India's concern in Afghanistan is Pakistan. In the aftermath of the Afghan War of 1989, Pakistan initiated a proxy war against India in Kashmir and for that Afghanistan became an important tool. As Zalmay Khalilzad, former US Ambassador in Afghanistan said, "With regard to Afghanistan it (Pakistan) would like to count on the use of Afghan territory and other assets in any confrontation with India. Already Islamabad is using Afghanistan in its confrontation with India in Kashmir. Many Kashmiri militants are being trained in Taliban regions of Afghanistan and some members of the Taliban have fought in Kashmir."[17] India, very logically, sees Pakistan's shadow in Afghanistan. The occasional attacks on the Indian Embassies in Afghanistan are orchestrated by Pakistan's notorious Inter Service Intelligence (ISI), according to India. Thus, the prime objective of India is to keep Afghanistan free of Pak influence. Also, India invested $2 billion in Afghanistan and is interested in exploiting its resources and also wants to use Afghanistan to reach Central Asia, bypassing Pakistan. Thus, Afghanistan is important for India in every respect.

In the possible Great Game between India and China in Afghanistan both sides will want to curb the influence of the other and in this case, Pakistan will be the major factor helpful in the Chinese mission of thwarting growing influence of India in Afghanistan and containing the anti-China elements from prospering there. Between 2008 and 2013, Pakistan seized 20 Uighur separatists and handed them over to China.[18] Yet, too much dependence on Pakistan can be dangerous for China. Moreover, given Beijing's assertive policy in the Xinjiang province, the Uighur separatists can draw sympathy of the Muslim fanatics in Af-Pak region against China who can hardly be controlled by Islamabad. Therefore dependence on Pakistan will not be beneficial for China in the long run. The Americans, who once were the darling of these extremists, are their number one enemy today. Also, the ISI needs to push forward its anti-India mission both inside Afghanistan and outside. Referring to the terror attack on Indian Consulate in Herat province of Afghanistan, the Afghan President Hamid Karzai told the newly appointed Indian Prime Minister Narendra Modi at the latter's swearing in ceremony this May that, "According to the information that we have available to us – the one given to us by a Western intelligence agency – is that the perpetrators were of Lashkar-i-Taiba."[19] This anti-India mission of Pakistan in Afghanistan is undoubtedly exacerbating the internal situation of the country which is against the interests of those (including China) who want stable Afghanistan for their economic and strategic benefit. China also does not want to depend on Pakistan solely in post-US situation of Afghanistan. This is evident from the appeal of Beijing to international community for strong support for Afghanistan at the UN Security Council meeting in June this year where the Chinese representative expressed his country's concern over "unabated civilian casualties as a result of terrorist and violent attacks in Afghanistan."[20] Like India, China also wants stability, both social and economic, in Afghanistan and Pakistan is an impediment in this context.

Pakistan is a major factor in India's Afghan policy whose main objective is to counter Islamabad's influence over the Afghan extremists. China can be helpful for India in reining in Pak mission in Afghanistan if New Delhi can coax Beijing to put pressure on Islamabad. At the end, marginalising the extremists is beneficial for China also. That India is giving due importance to China in Afghan affairs is clear from the statement of

Prime Minister Modi who said, on the occasion of the recent visit of Chinese President Xi Jinping to India, that, "We agreed that there is a need for a peaceful, stable and prosperous Afghanistan."[21] He also added that both the countries want to cooperate to fight extremism and terrorism.[22] India can be hopeful that the Chinese will agree with India to rein in Pakistan to ensure security to Chinese investments in Afghanistan including the thirty year leases for copper mining in the country.[23] Both the Indians and the Chinese are looking for options to deal with the Afghan issue in the post-NATO era. For that India, China and Russia held trilateral talks in January 2014 in Beijing.[24]

Compared to Pakistan, Russia is undoubtedly a better choice but unlike Russia, Pakistan is more knowledgeable of Afghan affairs. Therefore, Pakistan can hardly be kept out. Reining in the extremists is also important for Pakistan who claims to be the victim of terrorism like India but its anti-India obsession is compelling it to nurture the terrorists there. Therefore, when China cannot overlook Pakistan, India may have to depend on China to influence Islamabad. However, since India and China are strategic rivals, the Chinese may not allow too much Indian influence in Afghanistan where Pakistan can be useful for them. So, Pakistan is an obligation for Beijing. India however will dislike too much Chinese influence on Afghanistan.

Both India and China are concerned about the future of Afghanistan since both have their investments at stake in that country. There is scope for both to jointly contribute into the infrastructural projects of the country. Also, the country is strategically very important for both. The case of Afghanistan is serious for both and for the rest since Afghanistan is yet to be a modern state with a working government. More than half of Afghanistan is still vulnerable to Taliban seizure. Thus, both India and China will look for elements who can push their respective interests in the country which can trigger contests between them in future. Much will depend on how India and China wish to deal with Afghanistan in future.

Notes

1. Stephen Tanner, *Afghanistan : A Military History from Alexander the Great to the Fall of Taliban*, New York, Da Capo Press, 2002, p. 4.
2. B.D. Hopkins, *The Making of Modern Afghanistan*, Great Britain, Palgrave McMillan, 2008, p. 1.

3. Stephen Tanner, op cit, pp. 123-124.
4. Agreement on Provincial Arrangements in Afghanistan pending the re-establishment of permanent government institutions, www.un.org/news/dh/latest/afghan/afghan-aree.htm
5. William Maley, 'The rule of law and the weight of politics' in Whit Mason (ed), *The Rule of Law in Afghanistan: Missing in Inaction*, Cambridge, Cambridge University Press, 2011, p. 69.
6. It is no doubt the imposition of a Western notion on a society run by primitive tribal norms, but it is an important step.
7. However, attempts were made previously to gain public legitimacy for the administration via limited reforms introduced by Amanullah and Zahir Shah regimes. But election via adult franchise is a brand new introduction in Afghanistan.
8. 'High turnout in Afghan runoff election', DW, June 14, 2014, http://www.dw.de/high-turnout-in-afghan-runoff-election/a-17707498
9. *Ibid.*
10. Afghanistan did have strong national army earlier but reconstruction of the armed forces (and the police force) in the crises ridden Afghan society in the post-Taliban period was undoubtedly a formidable challenge.
11. See *Summary of Afghan National Army (ANA)* Programme for Culture and Conflict Studies, www.nps.edu/programs/ccs/Docs/Pubs/ANA_Summary_Web.pdf
12. Quoted in Raghav Sharma, *China's Afghanistan policy'*, China Report 2010,Institute of Chinese Studies, http://chr.sagepub.com/content/46/3/201.full.pdf+html
13. Saud Mehsud, Maria Golovnina, 'From his Pakistan hideout, Uighur leader vows revenge on China', http://in.reuters.com/article/2014/03/14/pakistan-uighurs-idINDEEA2D08U20140314
14. *Ibid.*
15. Read 'US troops in Afghanistan must bring stability: China', www.chinadaily.com.cn/china/2014-05/29/content_17552400.htm
16. 'China calls on support for Afghanistan', 26.06.2014, www.chainadaily.com.cn/china/2014-06/26/content_17616440.html
17. Quoted in K. Warikoo, 'Afghanistan factor in Kashmir crisis' in K. Warikoo (ed) *Afghanistan : The Challenge,* New Delhi, Pentagon press, 2007, p. 202.
18. Saud Mehsud, Maria Golovnina, *op cit.*
19. *Karzai Blames Lakshar-e-Toiba for Indian consulate attack*, May 26, 2014, http://www.dawn.com/news/1108704
20. See 'China calls on support for Afghanistan', China daily, http://usa.chinadaily.com.cn/china/2014-06/26/content_17616490.htm
21. 'Stable Afghanistan important for India and China says PM Modi', The Economic Times, 18.09.2014, http://economictimes.

indiatimes.com/news/politics-and-nation/stable-afghanistan-important-for-india-and-china-says-pm-narendra-modi/articleshow/42806868.cms

22. *Ibid.*
23. Prathapan Bhaskaran, 'China the key to India's Afghan puzzle', Asia Times, 01.07.2013, http://www.atimes.com/atimes/South_Asia/SOU-02-010713.html
24. China, Russia, India hold talks on Afghanistan, China Daily, 16.01.2014, http://www.chinadaily.com.cn/china/2014-01/16/content_17240254.htm

9

NATO Troops Withdrawal from Afghanistan and Its Implications for Regional Peace and Stability

ARVIND KUMAR

The continuing challenges in Afghanistan emanating from the current situation where peace and stability seem to be a distant dream have renewed interest among the members of the strategic and academic community to debate and discuss the probable future of Afghanistan in the emerging regional security environment especially after the NATO troop withdrawal. It is a well known fact that the intensity and the degree at which the levels of insurgency and terrorism have been growing in Afghanistan reflect major concerns among the members of the international community in general and the United States and India in particular.

The internal fabric and architecture of Afghanistan's security have been threatened especially in the context of the growing influence of Taliban in Afghanistan. The ongoing war on terrorism (since its launch in October 2001) has so far not been able to produce desired results. It is generally believed among the members of strategic and academic community that the ongoing global war on terrorism cannot eliminate or eradicate terrorism unless and until the root cause is properly addressed. The killing of Osama Bin Laden by the United States has, to a great extent aggravated the situation. The vulnerability has been increased. How best the nation states across the globe can make a concerted effort in terms of seeing that the existing vulnerabilities get decreased remains a real challenge.

The debate on the future of Afghanistan affecting the regional security environment has again gained salience. There are conflicting perspectives on these debates. Some feel that the situation in Afghanistan is going to stabilise after the NATO troop withdrawal. Others argue that Afghanistan will continue to be a very highly volatile place and peace and stability would be too difficult to realise. The paper will make a modest attempt to assess and analyse the probable and possible emerging situation after the troop withdrawal. It will also analyse the probable scenario especially with focus on the peace and stability in the region.

Critical Analysis on the US Drawdown Strategy

The declaration of drawdown strategy and the time table announced by the United States in the year 2011 raised a fundamental question whether it would be drawing down from a position of strength. The other related issue was whether the United States has been able to accomplish the enshrined task when it launched the global war on terrorism in October 2001. When President Obama announced in June 2011 his plans to begin the withdrawal of US troops from Afghanistan, the assessment on peace and stability seemed to be missing. An announcement was made that 10,000 troops would be removed by the end of the summer of 2011 and 23,000 additional troops will be leaving at the end of the summer of 2012. At the height of the United States' involvement in 2011, the United States had 101,000 troops in Afghanistan. There was an anticipation that the Afghan security forces will move into the lead and ultimately Afghan people will be responsible for their own security. It must be highlighted here that the United States in the time span of more than the last decade has not been able to bring normalcy and stability in the region. In fact, the problems in Afghanistan have been compounded and many times have gone beyond control. It must be reiterated that the United States' does not seem to have gained significantly in maintaining security in the region.

More recently, President Obama's Afghanistan announcement ignited a broader debate about the military strategy and the probability of the most effective way to wind down a war. The troop withdrawal decisions should realistically be based on an assessment of the conditions on the ground. Under the new time table outlined by the President of the United States', the 32,000 American troops in Afghanistan will virtually be reduced to 9,800 troops after 2014. It has been planned that by the end of 2015, 9,800 troops would be further cut to half and by the end of 2016 only be a very limited force will be assigned for the sole purpose of providing protection to the US embassy in Kabul and also helping the Afghans with military purchases and other security matters.

In the current situation, the United States will continue to have troops engaged in lethal counter terrorism operations in Afghanistan for at least two more years. There is a growing acknowledgement and recognition that Afghanistan will not be a perfect place and whether the United States even shall attempt and take the responsibility to make it one remains a very important question for the deliberations. The emerging precarious situation in Afghanistan and its neighbourhood provided impetus to the military commanders to recommend that a sizeable amount of troops roughly 10,000 in numbers would be left in Afghanistan for several years after the formal end of the combat mission in 2014. These troops will finally train Afghanistan security forces. It seems ironical that the US troops have not been able to train the Afghan security forces in the last 13 years.

It must be emphasised here that from 2015 onwards, the United States' troops are expected to be stationed at Bagram airfield and in Kabul. The US has never signed up for having a permanent security force in Afghanistan to fight against the Taliban. The Alliance members are likely to follow US lead in pulling out by the end of 2016. The US mission will change from combat to support.

The US drawdown strategy of the United States is in transition. The rough calculation suggests that nearly 14,000 US, NATO and other international troops will remain in Afghanistan after the withdrawal of combat forces at the end of this year. After nearly 13 years of intervention by the

United States and the NATO, the security situation in Afghanistan is still a major concern for the international community.

It is assumed that the United States had a desire to move Afghanistan from an economy shaped by war to one that can sustain a lasting peace, but somehow such desire so far has not culminated into peace and development in the region. Whether good governance, which was envisaged by the United States has been achieved remains a part of the discussion. It must be emphasised here that the US has not been drawing down from a position of strength, but only because the larger complexities of the region remain unresolved.

Implications of the US Draw Down for the Regional Peace and Stability

Afghanistan has by and large been always plagued by insecurity, insurgency, impunity and corruption. It has also been confronting a number of problems including terrorism and warlordism. Such problems have always undermined the potential for progress on all the other fronts. The lack of competent security institutions in Afghanistan became the main reason for the continuing crisis. It must be pointed out here that within the international coalition, the goal of establishing internal Afghan-focused security achieved less primacy than the goal of destroying the international terrorist networks. It should have been the other way around because stable Afghan governance and security forces are required to create a viable long-term alternative to the Taliban. The challenge has always been to create a capable and effective government in Afghanistan. Another challenge has been to develop effective Afghan security forces, which can help in administering and maintaining law and order.

The future of Afghanistan depends upon the legitimacy of the Afghan government and its will and capacity to implement the rule of law. It would be crucial for effectiveness and the delivery of governance. In the past, the *Amir* in Afghanistan established a centralised administration and *sharia* courts to assure security and for justice respectively, the authorities and responsibilities for local governance and dispute settlements were left to the tribes and communities. Currently, the central government continues to ensure security and justice on the national level. The central government has been showing signs of its seriousness in terms of adherence to the rule of law within the communities. The civil society in Afghanistan has to become more mature and help the government in maintaining and adhering to the rule of law. The participation of civil society in framing and evolving state's policies might be a good way forward in terms of legitimising the government.

The current scenario in Afghanistan undermines the potential for progress on all other fronts. Al Qaeda's strategy of global *jihadi*sm and the rise of Talibanism have kept Afghanistan in perpetual tension. The complete Talibanisation of the region will somehow see how best they can dominate and serve their interests. The ongoing reconciliation process has indicated that the role of Pakistan has become significant in terms of dealing with the Taliban.

There is no denying the fact that Pakistan has a central role to play in the stabilisation of Afghanistan. India too will remain important for the overall reconstruction of Afghanistan. Pakistan has become a victim of its own state policy. Hence, the Talibanisation of the regional security environment has lots of negative implications for Pakistan's national security. The wider ramification of such Talibanisation will also impact India and its national security. The United States certainly becomes highly vulnerable if the Taliban becomes stronger day by day. The back-channel diplomacy with the Taliban in all the reconciliation process so far has failed. It has not been able to garner the confidence and support of the Talibans. Such back-channel diplomacy had never included India. However, there is certainly a much greater acceptance among influential Pakistani civilians of India's presence in Afghanistan. India remains the most popular foreign country at the local level in Afghanistan.

The probable return of Taliban in a dominant role in the foreseeable future will have negative consequences for India and the region. However, India has been supporting a reconciliation policy targeting foot soldiers and field commanders. The London conference on reconciliation saw lots of changes in India's approach towards Afghanistan. The current position of India has been, by and large, in consonance with its policy towards domestic insurgent groups, in which rehabilitation and reintegration commonly offered to militants who wish to give up all violent methods and adopt constitutional means.

The basic tenet of counter-insurgency has been to evolve an integrated civilian and military effort and see how assistance would win hearts and minds and which, in turn ultimately would lead to peace. However, such peace will not be attainable unless and until the vicious cycle of insecurity, insurgency and corruption is duly addressed. The ongoing violence in Afghanistan must be brought under control.

Progress towards achieving peace and stability is still below satisfactory level. The goal of establishing internal Afghan focused security was subordinate to the goal of destroying the international terrorist networks. So far, stable Afghan governance and security forces have not been achieved and hence the question of peace and stability gains salience. The efforts to create a capable and legitimate government including the development of Afghan security forces seem to be poorly organised. The will and the capacity to implement the rule of law in Afghanistan seem to be missing.

It seems very unfortunate that the international community and the Afghan government have not engaged the capacity of the broader Afghan society. Afghan society should have been made the engine of progress, but, it still remains the unwilling subject of rapid change. It is largely because of regional competition which continues to undermine Afghanistan's long term prospects. Regional cooperation is necessary and significant to provide a significant security and economic boost in Afghanistan, Pakistan and the region as a whole. Peace and stability can be achieved through this process. However, there are stumbling blocks in this regard because of certain inherent contradictions in Pakistan's policies.

On the part of Afghanistan, it will be important to evolve a coherent strategy that can bridge the gap between conflict and democracy and also between tribal councils and Supreme Court. The next decade must be spent in building those bridges. The rise of Talibanism and Al Qaeda's global *jihadi*sm has been the major impeding factor for these bridges.

Conclusion

Over the past three and half decades, half of the population in Afghanistan has been displaced – with one-third leaving the country altogether. The rough estimate suggests that more than a million Afghans were killed and millions more traumatised or died prematurely due to the lack of sufficient food, clean water or basic medical care. The decades of turmoil in Afghanistan have ruined the path of progress and prosperity.

There seems to be a growing need and reasonable expectation for sustainable change in Afghanistan over the next 10 years. There is an urgent requirement for having a long-term vision for forming a liberal democratic political system with an emphasis on individual rights and a free market economy.

The primary goal of Afghanistan would be to enjoy a secure environment with sufficient food and basic elements of justice. Afghanistan must be prevented from becoming a safe haven for international terrorist networks. The onus lies on the collective responsibility of the international community in general and the United States and Pakistan in particular. Despite the fact that the United States national security concerns have largely dictated the direction of countering terrorism, nothing tangible is visible. A large part of Afghanistan's territory is still being exploited by terrorists and traffickers. Hence, instability has accrued most of the time.

Undoubtedly, security is the '*sine qua non*' of the stabilisation and reconstruction process. Without maintaining security, nothing can be expected. There is an immediate need to legitimise the institutions to transform or eliminate both the roots and perpetrators of conflict.

It is high time the international community and the Afghan government engage the capacity of the broader Afghan society making them the engine of progress rather than unwilling subjects of rapid change. India must work to create a regional environment which would be conducive to Afghanistan's success. The ongoing global competition in terms of endeavour of each nation to enhance its own sphere of influence in Afghanistan has to a great extent become a stumbling block in the overall stability of the region.

Societies which are transitioning from war to peace have to struggle with a very difficult balance of establishing security, stability and democratic governance. The development of security institutions must be done in close alignment with the broad goals of state building. The role of Afghan society will be dominant in the transition process. The process of negotiation and the likely fall-out is not going to be conclusive without the participation of the inclusive Afghan society. The Afghan National Army (ANA) and the Afghan Police were supposed to take the responsibility to independently take over the security function and completely train the ANA.

India certainly can help Afghanistan in evolving a coherent and systematic strategy, which would help in bridging the gap between conflict and democracy and between tribal councils and a Supreme Court. The responsibility of India in the region will increase after the complete implementation of the United States' drawdown strategy. The primary goal of India should be to help Afghanistan secure an environment with sufficient necessities and basic elements of justice. Afghanistan should also be saved from the tentacles of terrorist networks. The security of a nation is an essential ingredient of the stabilisation and reconstruction process. The challenge of creating rule of law and legitimate institutions in Afghanistan to transform or eliminate both the roots and perpetrators of conflict can be addressed only when the role of civil society becomes dominant and becomes a part of larger decision-making process. The drawdown strategy of the United States might help civil society in Afghanistan in regaining confidence. It is high time Afghanistan resumed its responsibility of maintaining security and developing bilateral relations so as to promote economic cooperation and reconstruction.

The regional players must desist from the temptation to carve Afghanistan into local spheres of influence. Instead, these players should help Afghanistan to make the region more peaceful, secure and prosperous. Pakistan, in particular, should play a very positive role in building peace and stability in the region. Without Pakistan's commitment to peace and stability, normalcy in the region will not be attainable.

Pakistan has become the victim of its own state policies. The cross-border terrorism as an element in Pakistan's foreign policy needs to be abandoned completely and must support the cause for peace and stability. If there is not going to be a complete withdrawal of the US and NATO troops, there is bound to be a contest and competition among major powers. The regional solution to the regional problem very much depends upon the actors of the regional system. It is high time the United States understood the ground reality and took steps conducive for peace and stability.

10

The Future of Democracy in Afghanistan

MOHAMMAD ATTA ROSHANGAR

Democracy and democratisation have been the dominant discourse in the post-9/11 Afghanistan. During the past ten years plenty of books, articles and journals have been written about democracy and its related issues both inside and outside the country, but there are some problems with these. Most Afghan writers who are well aware of the ground realities and complexities of Afghan society have written in Persian or Pashtu. It is impossible for the English audience who don't know these two languages to understand their views. Foreign writers, who have written in English or other languages don't know much about ethnic structure, tribal culture, and traditional values and their effects and influence on the democratisation process in this highly conflicted and conservative society. This, in my view, gives rise to the misrepresentation of Afghan society in general.

Such a scenario makes it very difficult for non-Afghans to know the ground realities and facts of this country. In my paper, I will try to demonstrate the facts about democracy in my country from the perspective of not an academic or student of political science, but as an ordinary citizen. I have experienced both the difficulties and hardships of living under the Taliban authoritarian regime, as well as the privileges and advantages of living under a relatively democratic government.

In the post-9/11 era, Afghanistan has seen the emergence of a middle class youth population, which is considered a driving force for the success of democracy after the pull back of foreign troops. As a member of this middle class population, I will try to explain how democratic values, free media, higher education, freedom of speech and expression and so on, have affected the life and world views of my generation. Even though, in comparison to the total population of Afghanistan the middle class comprises a small chunk of population, its their willingness and determination for preserving what it has achieved in the past couple of years is a source of hope and inspiration for the survival of democracy post-2014.

I have divided the paper into two parts; in the first part, I will give an overview of the achievements and challenges of democracy and democratisation process in the last one decade in Afghanistan. The second part will focus on the way ahead and future prospects of democracy in Afghanistan, which is going to be the main focus of the topic.

Without any doubt, in the past decade a military, diplomatic and economic support of international community in general and the United States of America in particular were the main guarantors of relative success of democracy in Afghanistan. While American troops are preparing themselves for withdrawal by the end of 2014, and international aid is decreasing, people are worried about the future of their country and the fate of democracy.

A Brief History of Democratisation Efforts in Afghanistan

Afghanistan provides a remarkable example of the history of democratic struggle and the subjugation of Islamic reform movements to external powers. Afghanistan was the first country in the Islamic world that introduced "constitutional government" and heralded many social reforms in the early twentieth century. During the reign of the reformist Afghan King Amnanullah Khan, the first Afghan constitution called "Nezamnama" was adopted in 1923.

The constitution incorporated equal rights and individual freedoms. Afghanistan's second democratisation attempt lasted almost a decade (1964-73) where the country adopted a kind of constitutional monarchy based on the region's most enlightened constitution.

Afghanistan's first and second democratisation attempts were, however, derailed by a combination of factionalised elites and external interference, and not by its ancient tribal nature or Islamic identity. In fact, Afghanistan's colourful cultural heritage and its approach to religion helped promote universal values and inclusive politics.

Afghanistan's third wave of democratisation started shortly after the fall of the Taliban in 2001. In December 2001, delegations of all Afghan ethnic groups, under the leadership of United Nations and direct support of the United States of America, reached an agreement which later became known as "Bonn Agreement". In fact this agreement paved the way for third attempt of democratisation followed by ratification and implementation of new constitution and the first fair and free presidential elections in the history of the country.

Afghanistan's third democratisation attempt confronts two formidable challenges that derailed the previous two efforts, however, the current endeavour is owned by millions of citizens who came to vote on April 5 despite the Taliban's army of suicide bombers, their profound disappointment with the Afghan government, and the cloud of uncertainty over the future of the country.

Social and Economic Changes and Achievements in the Post-9/11 Era

In order to provide a better perspective and richer understanding about the future of democracy in Afghanistan, it would be essential to know about the social, demographics and economic changes which have happened, since the collapse of the Taliban regime following the US-led military intervention.

Afghanistan's demographics and economy have changed in significant ways over the past decade. Rather than being mired in a perpetual feudal twilight, Afghanistan is actually becoming a modern country. The statistical evidence of change, gathered from sources including data from the US Agency for International Development, is overwhelming. The urbanisation and economic development that have reshaped Afghanistan do not mean that the country will have a bright political future or that the Taliban won't regain a measure of power after US troops leave in 2014. But the future won't simply be a replay of the past. The Afghanistan movie won't just restart where it left off when the Taliban were driven out from power. Afghanistan has seen the most obvious change in urbanisation. Close to half the population now lives in cities and towns. Kabul is a city of five million people, and the populations of Herat, Jalalabad and Kandahar have all tripled in the past decade. This urbanisation weakens ethnic and tribal affiliations and helps women get access to jobs and education. While still primitive in some rural areas, the country is also getting plugged into the global grid.

More than 20 million people, or two-thirds of the country, now have access to mobile phones, up from none a decade ago. Based on some estimates, around 60 per cent of population watches some television and nearly 95 per cent of population has access to radio. During the Taliban regime Afghanistan had one public radio station and television was banned; now there are 75 active TV channels, more than 175 radio stations, including several hundred print media and dozens of websites.

Gross domestic product per capita has increased nearly fivefold since 2002, with an annual growth rate of about nine per cent. Only 18 per cent of the population has access to reliable electrical power, but that's triple what it was a decade ago. The improvements in health are striking, even after a decade of war. Access to basic health services is available to more than 60 per cent of Afghans today, up from nine per cent in 2001.

Life expectancy has increased from 44 years to 60 in the past decade; the maternal mortality rate has declined 80 per cent; the under five mortality rate has dropped 44 per cent. The number of primary health-care facilities has increased nearly fourfold. Afghanistan has rebuilt an education system that had nearly stopped functioning. In 2002, only 900,000 students were in primary school, nearly all boys. Today, 10 million students are in school, more than a third of them girls. University enrollment jumped from 8,000 in 2001 to more than 200,000 in 2014, and about 20 per cent of these higher-education students are women. Higher education institutions have increased from seven governmental universities to 34 public and 82 private universities.

Literacy is currently about 35per cent, but it's expected to grow to 55 per cent in 10 years and 80 per cent in 20, unless disaster strikes. The gains women have made are an especially visible index of change, but they are also a reminder that progress is fragile and could be reversed by the Taliban. In addition to the vastly larger number of female students, women now hold 28 per cent of the seats in Parliament, three Cabinet posts and 120 judicial positions. By the end of this year, at least 30 per cent of government employees will be women.

Challenges Towards Democratisation

Despite these entire significant social, political and economic changes and progressive achievements in the country, Afghanistan's young and fragile democracy faces tremendous challenges and debacles. Prolonged insurgency, highly corrupt and centralised government (poor-governance), economic dependency, lawlessness, and unemployment would be at the top of the list even after more than a decade of war against violence and brutal insurgency. Taliban and other terrorist groups are the main source of threat to stability of the country and the region, based on the New York Time report of recent months, "Afghanistan National Security Forces (ANSF) are leading 97 per cent of all operations against the Taliban insurgents independently. There is no doubt that Afghanistan National Security Forces are strong, well-experienced than ever before, but they have many problems as well, high illiteracy, addiction, involvement in drug trafficking, ill equipment are among other challenges".

Corruption and poor governance are other challenges in Afghanistan; *Transparency International*, a watchdog group, says Afghanistan is among the world's most corrupt countries and getting worse. The group says at least $1 billion donated over the past eight years has been siphoned off. Wide spread corruption has decreased the functionality of the government and reduced the trust of the people in governmental institutions. Some experts believe that highly centralised nature of the Afghanistan government is one of the main reasons behind snowballing corruption in this country, they say, in the past decade President Karzai has tried to concentrate all the power in Kabul in his hand, it has weakened the functionality of the local governments and paved the way for bribe and systematic corruption. Beside these challenges a dependent economy seems another obstacle in the post-2014 era.

Over the past decade Afghanistan's economy has been almost exclusively dependent on outside assistance. The numbers are staggering. According to the World Bank, an estimated 97 per cent of Afghanistan's roughly $15.7 billion gross domestic product comes from international military and development aid and spending in the country by foreign troops. The economy is already contracting as troops leave, and future growth will be slower, especially in urban areas and areas of conflict. Even though the United States and other nations have promised that they will not abandon Afghanistan, which happened in 1989 after the Soviet Union was pushed out. The World Bank has warned that an abrupt aid cut-off could provoke a collapse of political authority, civil war and a greater reliance on opium production.

Post-Withdrawal Perspectives and Consequences

As the withdrawal of US and NATO forces from Afghanistan approaches, anxieties about the future of the country have increased. Thinking about the Afghan situation *post*-West withdrawal is characterised by a palpable sense of pessimism which is being felt by Afghanistan as well as its neighbours. What will happen in Afghanistan and the region when foreign troops leave Afghanistan? How will the domestic situation evolve? How will the regional powers position themselves? What is the role of international community especially the big powers? These questions and others loom large while considering the future of Afghanistan and its potential impact on regional and international dynamics. There are no simple answers to these questions; mapping the future of Afghanistan is indeed a complex task. The number of Afghan and non-Afghan actors, their competing interests and fluctuating alliances, and the lack of a cohesive vision for the country's political future make it difficult if not impossible to predict clear scenarios beyond a certain level of generality.

Based on this generalisation, two broad scenarios are predictable; optimistic and pessimistic:

As per the optimistic perception Afghanistan's government succeeds in maintaining power and keeping relative stability in the country, which is supported by a number of factors. The current situation is often compared to that of 1989, when the Soviet troops left Afghanistan after ten years of unsuccessful war. Afghanistan's Najebullah government that was supported by the Soviet Union was overthrown after three years by the opposition forces. This history is frequently recalled with hints that the United States withdrawal could face the same fate. Also, a widely held opinion is that all the empires that invaded Afghanistan failed, the latest examples being Great Britain in the nineteenth century and the Soviet Union in the twentieth century—making Afghanistan the 'graveyard' of great powers. This image casts a pessimistic shadow over the draw-down plan of American and other international forces from Afghanistan.

However, the situation in Afghanistan today is quite different from that of the 1980s, not to say the nineteenth century. The most significant difference is that all the great powers in the world support the Afghan government and no single country stands by the Taliban and in spite of their shortcomings, the secular political institutions are preferred by a significant part of the population over an extreme religious regime. Further, the pullout of foreign troops will have a positive impact, removing a major invitation factor used by the Taliban for their benefit.

Finally, the Afghan government has much stronger military forces than the Taliban has. All Afghan National Security Forces (ANSF) will reach 360,000 by the end of this year. The success of this scenario depends, though, on many 'ifs' including a capable government, successful national reconciliation, necessary international aid, international solidarity, and improvement of the economy. All of these conditions are vital, as the failure of any of them could lead to failure of the overall mission in this war torn country.

As per the pessimistic view along with optimistic expectations, there are pessimistic scenarios as well. One of them is that the Afghan government maintains only limited control over the country, with the Taliban unable to seize national power either. The country would be torn up not only politically, but also administratively and geographically. In the worst such case, the country would be divided, with two or more governments. Another scenario is that the Afghan government loses control of the country and falls into a new civil war and chaos; some experts believe that civil war is inevitable in Afghanistan after 2014. Yet another possible scenario is that a new national power forms, but with a different balance of power and political basis, and with a new political structure and different ideological orientation.

A recent article in the *Foreign Affairs* magazine predicts the possibility of a military coup in the absence of foreign troops. As the writer argues, "Over the past ten years, we have been witnessing the emergence of a relatively professional and strong army in Afghanistan, along with a weak and corrupted government, which has been losing its credibility in the eyes of its people. If the situation continues like this, some high ranking officers may think of handling the crisis, by launching a military coup and seizing political power by force." Finally, one outcome entails the return of the Taliban, which is almost certain to occur; the question is more about the role the Taliban will play. One possibility is that the Taliban returns as a participant within the Afghanistan government, inside the framework of existing political institutions, which would constitute a legal return. Another possibility is that the Taliban returns as a political body equal to the Afghan government, based on a balance of power but beyond the existing political framework. This possibility would also be considered legal, especially if reached through negotiations. The first of these possible outcomes is the most desirable for both the Afghan government and the United States. Although the second outcome is unfavourable to the Afghan government and the United States, it is not at all impossible. The essence of the ongoing talks of the Afghan government and the United States with the Taliban is to safeguard a legal return of the Taliban by power sharing. Some believe that the Taliban has undergone a transformation in recent years and has become more practical-minded and 'soft'. If this is true then there is room for optimism that the negotiations will end successfully and that the political dynamics within Afghanistan will change.

To the extent that this is a real policy shift by the Taliban and not a temporary expedient, steps in this direction would be welcome. All that said, a third kind of Taliban return—an illegal return—entails the Taliban's overthrowing the Afghan government and seizing control of the country after US and ISAF forces leave, a scenario widely predicted in academic circles. Although this outcome should not be excluded, it cannot be totally overlooked. The Taliban is strong enough to persist in fighting a guerrilla war, resorting to such tactics as the use of improvised explosive devices (IEDs), but such an approach will not be enough to take back national power.

The outcome will depend more on factors related to the Afghan government itself, the Afghan National Army (ANA), and the Afghan National Police (ANP) as well as international support to them. As Hekmat Karzai, director of the Centre for Conflict and Peace Studies in Kabul, says, "the problem is not that the insurgency is strong, but that Afghan institutions are weak".

Conclusion

As it has been mentioned many times through this paper, in the past decade international diplomatic, economic and political support has been the main guarantor and preserver of democracy in Afghanistan.

While, foreign troops prepare to leave the country by the end of this year, the fate of political transition is not clear; still no one knows who will be the next president?! What would be his policy towards the Taliban and other insurgent groups?? A more important question arises – whether Afghanistan will survive as a democracy or again fall into a horrible civil war???

Over the past ten years Afghans have well understood, that for having a strong, united and prosperous country they have no better option than democracy, which gives them respect, freedom, dignity and provide them with social and economic opportunity to fulfil their desires and pursue happiness in their lives. Now Afghans have the right to take part in their national and local politics through elections and other democratic and legal channels, to choose their favourite political party and select their president or their representatives in the local and national assemblies. These are unprecedented achievements in the history of the country; these accomplishments have not been achieved easily, all Afghan citizens have paid a huge price and been victims to attain them. Forecasting Afghanistan's *post*-withdrawal situation is very difficult, because there are many factors which determine the developments in this country.

References

Persian sources

1. 8 subh daily newspaper.
2. Afghanistan daily newspaper.
3. Afghanistan's ministry of higher education website (http://www.mohe.gov.af/)
4. Afghanistan 's ministry of education 2013 report(http://moe.gov.af/en)
5. http://www.shafaqnet.com/
6. http://urozgan.org/

7. http://dailyopensociety.com/fa/
8. http://www.mandegardaily.com/

English

1. Afghanistan daily outlook newspaper.
2. Khamapress.com (challenges of democracy in Afghanistan).
3. Kabultimes.com

11

Pakistan's Perspective in Afghanistan: Policy Options for India

TEJ PRATAP SINGH

Afghanistan is the graveyard of empires. Since time immemorial all the empires which at the peak of their power tried to vanquish Afghanistan met with stiff resistance from the Afghan people and had to retreat without accomplishing their mission and in the process weakening and undermining the empires themselves. It happened with Alexander the Great, who could not conquer and move beyond the area presently called Afghanistan and had to beat a hasty retreat. History repeated itself in the nineteenth century, when Britain at the height of its imperial power, invaded Afghanistan and was humbled, marking the beginning of the end of the British Empire. The Soviet Union, one of the two superpowers of the cold war era, intervened in Afghanistan and met with the same fate. It was a disastrous intervention, a blatant case of imperial overreach. Afghan misadventure eventually led to the collapse of Soviet empire. The sole superpower, the US committed the mistakes earlier committed by other empires, that is, to invade Afghanistan. Its initial decisive victory and regime change created the impression for a while that historical trend has been reversed but soon it became evident that the US like other empires, cannot change the course of history.[1] After more than a decade of fighting, the longest and costliest war in US history[2], the US, like other imperial powers, came to the conclusion that Afghan war is unwinnable and so drew a plan of drawdown of troops that is going to be completed by the end of 2014.[3]

During his election campaign, President Barak Obama criticised Iraq war as a 'war of choice' and so 'unnecessary war' but termed Afghanistan as 'war of necessity', and so the US must aim to win Afghan War at any cost. He reiterated it later also, while addressing war veterans on August 16, 2009, "We must not forget. This (Afghanistan War) is not a war of choice. This is a war of necessity. Those who attacked America on 9/11 are plotting to do so again. If left unchecked, the Taliban insurgency will mean even a larger safe haven from which Al Qaeda would plot to kill more Americans."[4]

Both Afghan and Iraq wars turned into war of attrition sapping US energy, will power and raised the prospect of a new Vietnam in the making. This fear first compelled the US to wrap up its military mission in Iraq and then Obama shifted his focus to Afghanistan. Despite spending trillion dollars, the US could not achieve the desired result either in Iraq or Afghanistan. The US succeeded in regime change but could not put in its place a functioning government either in Iraq or Afghanistan. Elections were held to elect a democratic government but these elections were marred by various controversies and deeply divided the societies on ethnic and sectarian grounds. The result was anarchy in both Iraq and Afghanistan. The US failed miserably in its nation-state building mission in Iraq and Afghanistan. Both turned out to be costly American misadventures, reviving the memory of the Vietnam fiasco and exposing 'the limits of American power and exceptionality'.[5]

Pakistan is a critical player in the Afghan end game. Without Pak support and acquiescence no Afghan solution is possible. The international community, regional stakeholders and Pakistan itself are aware of the centrality of Pakistan in the Afghan imbroglio. Pakistan wants to exploit this favourable situation in Afghanistan to its strategic advantage even at the cost of regional and global peace, security and stability. Withdrawal of Soviet troops and end of cold war had diminished the strategic significance of Pakistan, but 9/11 and subsequent US 'war on terror' and 'operation enduring freedom' revived the fortunes of Pakistan, a country that had harboured Al-Qaeda Islamic extremists including its chief Osama-Bin-Laden responsible for 9/11 and other Jihadi attacks on American installations, emerged again as the frontline state in the US war against the Taliban regime of Afghanistan. Pakistan offered logistical support to US and its allies in their military operation against the Taliban regime of Afghanistan. The US, because of its hostility to Iran was left with no option but to accept the Pak offer, who had earlier during cold war period offered the same facility to the US and its cold war allies against the Soviet intervention in Afghanistan. India had also offered all possible assistance to the US in its 'war on terror' and 'Operation Enduring Freedom' but because of Pak concerns and sensitivities, the US politely declined the Indian offer particularly in its Afghan mission.

Strategic Objectives of Pakistan in Afghanistan

Afghanistan is a landlocked country and has access to sea only either through Pakistan or Iran. This geographical factor makes Pakistan and Iran very critical in the geopolitics of Afghanistan. Pakistan shares not only border with Afghanistan but also ethnicity, religion and culture. Afghanistan, Pakistan and India in fact have shared history, geography, culture that goes back to the millennia. Afghanistan was part of many Indian empires and Buddhism flourished before the advent of Islam in Afghanistan. Bamiyan Buddha and Gandhara art are the testimony of this shared past and culture. Pakistan till the recent past was part of India. Thus, all the three have a shared past and are destined to have shared present and future. They have common destiny. If one nation is destabilised the whole region will be affected. India and Pakistan cannot insulate themselves against turmoil in Afghanistan. Therefore, like Pakistan, India too has high stake in the peace, security and stability of Afghanistan. However, Pakistan wants to keep India out of Afghanistan and has made this its foremost strategic objective in Afghanistan.

Pakistan is conducting its foreign policy in Afghanistan as a zero-sum-game, as per which any gain for India in Afghanistan is treated as loss for Pakistan. This zero-sum-game strategy of Pakistan has vitiated the whole security scenario in Afghanistan. Pakistan does not recognise that India too has vital interest in Afghanistan. Pakistan is opposed to friendly relation between

India and Afghanistan. Pakistan not only wants a friendly government in Afghanistan but also wants that Afghan government must be hostile to India.[6] Taliban government in Afghanistan from 1996 to 2001 was such type of government, which was not only friendly to Pakistan but also hostile to India. But because of 9/11 and the US 'War on Terror', Taliban were ousted from power and Hamid Karzai government, friendly to India, assumed power in Afghanistan. This is not to the liking of Pakistan and from day one Pakistan wants to see Karzai thrown out of power because of his proximity to India.

Pakistan and Afghanistan are divided by Durand line.[7] This is a disputed border which was never accepted by Afghanistan, which treats it as imperial border imposed on it by British India disregarding ethnicity, language and culture. It divides proud Pakhtun tribe into Pakistan and Afghanistan. Even friendly Taliban regime dependent on Pak moral and material support refused to recognise Durand Line as legitimate border between Afghanistan and Pakistan. Pakistan is afraid that any strong government in Kabul will try to unite all Pashtun people into one state and this will lead to further shrinkage of Pakistan territory after the heavy territorial loss suffered by the independence of Bangladesh from Pakistan. Defending Durand Line and securing Afghan recognition of this line are one of the most significant objectives of Pakistan in Afghanistan. Pakistan is apprehensive of rising soft power of India in Afghanistan and believes that India wants to dismember it further and eventually to wipe out Pakistan from the global map. Pakistan is of the firm opinion that India still is not reconciled to the partition and creation of Pakistan. It is because of this Pak paranoia, Pak policy towards Afghanistan is India-centric. Pak feels India is promoting irredentism in Afghanistan and instigating Kabul government to claim North West Frontier Province (NWFP) of Pakistan, inhabited by Pakhtun tribe, who constitute almost half of the Afghan population. NWFP has been renamed recently as Khyber-Pakhtunkhwa.[8]

Afghanistan has granted permission to India to run four consulates in different parts of the country at Kandahar, Herat, Jalalabad, and Majar-e-Sharif apart from embassy at Kabul because of close India-Afghanistan relations. Pakistan is opposed to these Indian consulates and wants Afghanistan to close it down. Pakistan is accusing India of using these consulates to support secessionist movement in Baluchistan, to spy against Pakistan and to destabilise and if possible dismember Pakistan. India denies all these baseless Pakistan allegations and affirms that consulates are only providing consular services to the people and promoting bilateral, cultural, political and economic relations. Problem of Baluchistan is the creation of Pakistan. Instead of addressing the problem, Pakistan is unnecessarily dragging India and holding India responsible for its internal problems.

Pak Quest for Strategic Depth in Afghanistan

Pakistan's strategic policy is Indo-centric. India is the arch enemy, rival and existential threat. To meet existential threat posed by India, Pak is seeking strategic parity with India since its creation in 1947. Pakistan has not abandoned its goal of strategic parity, despite bifurcation of Pakistan and transformation of East Pakistan as a new nation-state of Bangladesh and the halving of Pak population and territory. Pak strategic policy is conceived, designed, articulated and pursued keeping India in mind. India provides the context for the Pak strategic policy. Unending Pak quest for parity with India is the most significant determinant of Pak's strategic policy. However, this quest for parity so far has proved to be an elusive goal. This excessive Pak obsession of parity with India has precluded any possibility of Pakistan's pursuit of the enlightened national interest vis-à-vis its neighbours.[9]

Pakistan is obsessed with its security, territorial unity and integrity. It feels that east-west depth of Pakistan is very narrow in comparison to north-south and so it wants to compensate this strategic weakness by having a friendly and if possible pliant government in Afghanistan. So that in case of need, it can shift its valuable military asset to Afghanistan for its safety and later use and also to retreat if need arises so as to lure the enemy inside and fight back later when it is advantageous to Pakistan. Pliant/friendly government in Afghanistan will provide a kind of cushion to safeguard strategic interests of Pakistan. For Pakistan, India is the only enemy threatening to its national security. Therefore, eastern border with India has to be secured by Pakistan for its unity, integrity and survival. East-west depth being narrow, Pakistan wants to bring Afghanistan in its security ambit by creating a wider strategic depth encompassing Pakistan and Afghanistan so as to deal effectively with any security threat emanating from its eastern neighbour India.

The concept of strategic depth[10] is very controversial and Pak quest for it so far has been illusory. Only during the brief period of ISI created Taliban regime in Afghanistan, Pakistan enjoyed much sought after strategic depth. However, Pak quest for strategic depth has deeply divided Afghan polity and society on ethnic-sectarian grounds. Pak quest for strategic depth has not only destabilised Afghanistan but the whole region of South Asia, Central Asia and West Asia as well. Even Pak strategic analysts have also questioned the concept of strategic depth. Sartaz Aziz, advisor to PM Nawaz Sharif on national security and foreign affairs called strategic depth an 'outdated policy.'[11] Seeking strategic depth in Afghanistan has turned out to be like digging one's own grave.[12] Noted Pakistani Journalist Kamran Shafi in his write up in Pak popular newspaper *Dawn* has argued that in case of war between India and Pakistan, Pak army has to fight Indian army at its eastern border itself and resist its onward movement in Pakistan towards west. It is absurd to argue that Pak army with its weapons will retreat to west and if need arises to Afghanistan to avoid fighting Indian army. Will Pak Generals instead of fighting Indian army, pack up and take refuge in Afghanistan?[13] If Indian attack has to be repulsed, it has to be repulsed at the eastern border itself and should be prevented from overrunning the whole of Pakistan and fight it on western border from Afghanistan.

Pakistan's search for strategic depth revolves around army's threat perceptions. Earlier, in the 1980s the Soviet Union was considered as a security threat along with India, but now as per Pak perception, security threat emerges only from India. When former army Chief General Kayani argued in favour of western borders being secure he meant that strategic depth provides Pakistan the ability to concentrate on Indian borders. A friendly and subservient Afghanistan can help it shift its military assets to Afghanistan in the event of conflict with India.[14]

However, whatever the merit/demerit of the concept of strategic depth, it has fascinated the Pak security establishment and ISI has pursued it with all sincerity. This single-minded pursuit of strategic depth in Afghanistan by Pakistan has vitiated the security environment in Afghanistan, Pakistan and India.

Pak Strategic Ambitions in Afghanistan and its Fallout

Pak strategic ambitions in Afghanistan have led to excessive interference by Pakistan in the internal affairs of Afghanistan. Pakistan wants to control Afghan politics through its proxies. Taliban was created by Pak ISI for this very purpose. In the past, many imperial powers tried to control and rule Afghanistan but they failed miserably. The recent example is of Soviet Union, who through different proxies tried to control and rule Afghanistan but eventually was humbled. To prop up its proxies Babrak Karmal and then Najibullah regime in Afghanistan, the Soviet Union intervened militarily but had to pull back its troops because of stiff resistance from the Afghan people, in the process losing money, material and men. ISAF (International Security Assistance Force in Afghanistan) led by the NATO and the US is facing the same fate, which the Soviet Union faced in 1980s.

Like earlier imperial powers, Pakistan also cannot succeed in its mission of installing its proxies such as Gulubudin Hekmetyar of Hizb-e-Islami, Haqani Network or Quetta Shura. If past history is any guide, then it can be safely predicted that like earlier imperial missions in Afghanistan, Pak imperial mission/ design in Afghanistan too is bound to fail and its efforts might boomerang, jeopardising its own national security. Like for the British, Soviet and Americans, Afghanistan will be graveyard for Pak imperial ambition too.

Pakistan: Part of Solution or Problem

Pakistan has played a dubious role in Afghanistan. Instead of stabilising Afghanistan, Pakistan has been the main factor for Afghan instability. Pakistan is a major spoiler in Afghanistan. Pakistan, instead of being part of solution has itself become a problem in Afghanistan. Pak and Afghan problem are so intertwined that separation of the two is not possible. Even Afghan President Hamid Karzai went to the extent of saying that two are tied to one umbilical cord. During his visit to Pakistan in March, 2011, Karzai observed, "India is a close friend of Afghanistan but Pakistan is a twin brother of Afghanistan. We are more than twins, we are conjoined twins. There is no separation, there cannot be a separation."[15] To address Afghan problem, Pak problem has also to be addressed. That is why, US has clubbed Pakistan and Afghanistan together and created a new acronym AfPak and appointed a special representative to address jointly the problems of Afghanistan and Pakistan.

Pak Double Game in Afghanistan

Pakistan on the one hand has joined the US in its 'war on terror' and 'operation enduring freedom' in Afghanistan and on the other hand is providing safe haven to the fleeing terrorists and *jihadi*sts from Afghanistan, thereby undermining the US efforts in Afghanistan and the world at large in ridding it of the scourge of terrorism and religious extremism. Killing of Osama Bin Laden, the global face/symbol of terrorism and Islamic Jihadism, in Abbotabad, Pakistan, near an army cantonment by the US, is the testimony of Pak complicity with Taliban, Al Qaeda and other *jihadi*sts. Investigations in global terror strikes have always led its trail to Pakistan. Over the years, Pakistan has emerged as an epicentre of global terrorism. All global terrorists head to Pakistan for training, motivation and indoctrination. Pakistan has turned a blind eye towards terrorist training camps being run in different parts of its territory. In the process, Pakistan has lost control over FATA (Federally Administered Tribal Area) to the terrorists, who have even begun tormenting its master Pakistan itself. Pak intelligence agency ISI is actively involved in running some training camps for terrorists to be used against India and these are treated by Pakistan as 'strategic assets'[16].

Pak double game of running with the hare and hunting with the hound has been exposed to the international community in the wake of killing of Osama Bin Laden. On the one hand, Pakistan claims to be the victim of terrorism and is helping the West in its war on terrorism and on the other hand has given shelter to terrorists. All top Al Qaeda and Taliban leaders including Mullah Omar are hiding in Pakistan. How long Pakistan will succeed in its double game of helping and undermining US war efforts in Afghanistan is difficult to say. Due to Pak centrality in Afghan imbroglio and the US hostility to Iran, the US is left with no option but to depend on Pak to continue its logistical support to its troops based in Afghanistan.

The only other available northern route passing through Russia and Central Asian Republics is also not very reliable as Russia has only permitted non-lethal supply to Afghanistan. Deteriorating US-Russia relations over Ukraine crisis, resumption of cold-war and intensifying US-Russia rivalry has further reduced the significance of the Northern route. This northern logistical route compared to Pak route is very lengthy too. Therefore, even after knowing the Pak double game, the US has exercised restraint and silence because of its dependence on Pak for its military supply to Afghanistan. Pakistan seems to be a lesser evil in comparison to hostile Iran and unreliable Russia.

Terrorists: Strategic Asset or Liability

Pak double game is backfiring as terrorists, nurtured as strategic assets by its intelligence agency ISI to be used against India, are turning their guns against Pakistan itself. Tahrik-e-Taliban Pakistan (TTP) popularly known as Pak Taliban has begun targeting Pak security forces, civilian leaders and military-civil assets. Some of their attacks such as on military headquarters in Rawalpindi, Karachi airport, Naval station, Marriot Hotel and numerous mosques have been audacious and daring. This also shows that these terrorist groups are no longer in the control of Pak ISI and the latter has created a Frankenstein. Jihadi atmosphere created by these religious extremists has radicalised Muslim community in Pakistan. Radicalisation of Muslim community has not only created animosity against other minority religious groups but has also widened the sectarian fault-lines within the Muslim community. Increasing Saudi Wahabi influence has pitted majority Sunni Muslims against the minority Shia Muslims and Muslim sects like Ahmadia, Vohra, etc. These Islamic groups are being repeatedly targeted by Sunni Jihadists and these terrorist attacks have vitiated the whole atmosphere in Pakistan.

The International community is now scared of the future of Pakistan. When it was created in 1947 on the basis of religion, the international community was of opinion that Pakistan is more homogeneous and religion will bind the new state together. Whereas the international community was sceptical of Indian territorial unity and integrity, because of its vast heterogeneity based on religion, race, region, language, caste, etc. Doomsayers in case of India and soothsayers in case of Pakistan have been proved wrong. India has maintained its territorial unity, social peace and political democracy whereas in case of Pakistan, it has been balkanised and is facing deep social and religious divisions, democracy is still shaky and it is on the verge of becoming a failed state. Prospect of Pak failure as a state is horrifying to the whole world as Pakistan is not an ordinary state like Somalia or Yugoslavia but a nuclear weapon state. Pak failure will result in falling of its nuclear assets in the hands of non-state actors probably Islamic Jihadists. If this happens, nobody knows, how will Pak Jihadists behave? The US has made some contingency plan to secure Pak nuclear weapons in case of Jihadist takeover of Pakistan, but sometimes, even the best plan may fail. Nuclear weapon equipped Islamic Jihadists will be a frightening proposition for the international community.

Pak intelligence agency ISI created and nurtured various terrorist outfits as 'strategic assets' to further its foreign policy objectives which is mainly to target India in Afghanistan and to oust it from there and to target India within Kashmir and other parts of the country, to disturb social peace, communal harmony and weaken and undermine its sovereignty, territorial unity and integrity. However, this 'strategic asset' has been transformed into strategic liability as these terrorist outfits apart from targeting India, US and Western interests, sometimes target their master Pakistan itself. Pak retaliation and effort to control and manage these Jihadi groups have further alienated these Jihadists from Pakistan and these Jihadists are now increasingly targeting Pakistani strategic interests. The whole Pak effort to use Jihadists against India has boomeranged on Pakistan.

Regional Implication of Pak Interference in Afghanistan

Pak quest for 'strategic depth' in Afghanistan against India and sponsoring and nurturing terrorists as 'strategic asset' to be used against India and blackmailing the international community to bail out Pak from the social, political, economic and financial mess created by it, has serious regional and global implications. India is the worst affected by Pak short-sighted policy of strategic depth in Afghanistan and treating Jihadists as strategic assets. Iran, Central Asian Republics (CARs), China, Russia are other regional powers apart from India have also been affected in various degrees by Pak interference in Afghanistan. Globally the US is the major country affected by the dubious Pak role in Afghanistan. AfPak has emerged as the epicentre of global terrorism and so there is hardly any region or country which is not affected by global terrorism having its root in Afghanistan and Pakistan.

Among the regional powers, after India, Iran comes next in the list of regional countries affected by Pak effort to manage Afghanistan through its proxies. Taliban created and nurtured by Pakistan are Pakhtun Sunni Jihadists, who are opposed to Shia and non-Pashtun ethnic groups in multi-ethnic Afghan society. Iran treats itself as saviour of Shia Muslims and their interests and this self-assumed role of Iran has pitted it against the Pashtun Sunni Taliban, sponsored and sustained by Pakistan. In the Afghan civil war, Iran is siding with 'Northern Alliance', a conglomerate of non-Pashtun ethnic groups consisting of Tajiks, Uzbeks, Hazara Shias, etc. based in the northern part of Afghanistan. Iran being the western neighbour of Afghanistan, is immediately faced with the possibility of heavy influx of Afghan refugees in case of any turmoil in Afghanistan, which is a recurrent phenomenon.

The Central Asian Republics on the northern border of Afghanistan are affected by any turmoil in Afghanistan as Central Asia has shared ethnicity with Afghanistan. Due to ethnic ties, CAR are extending support to Northern Alliance against Pak supported Taliban. Any Afghan turmoil has spill over effects in CAR. It not only destabilises Afghanistan but its fallout is felt in CAR too. Jihadists have radicalised CAR also and all the CAR governments are threatened by the rising Islamic extremism. These Islamists have taken refuge in AfPak region and from there are targeting their governments in Central Asia. Drug trafficking emanating from Afghanistan under the patronage of Taliban is another threat to the CAR.

Russia though not immediate neighbour of Afghanistan, has also been affected by the Talibanisation of AfPak as it has significant minority Islamic groups within its border, particularly in Chechnya. Under the influence of radicalisation of AfPak, Chechen Muslims have also been radicalised and are fighting against the Russian government for the establishment of Islamic

Republic of Chechnya. Drugs originating from Afghanistan are another trouble for Russia.

Like Russia, China is also facing the fallout of Islamic radicalism in AfPak. Islamic extremists from Xinjiang, who are called Uyghur, have taken refuge in Pakistan and Afghanistan and from there have launched movement for independence of Xinjiang, which they call East Turkistan. Despite Pakistan being 'all weather friend' of China, the former has not been able to rein in Uyghur militants operating from tribal area of Pakistan and Afghanistan. Uyghur Islamic extremists have joined hand with Taliban extremists and are helping each other in targeting their enemies.

Thus, there is hardly any country in the immediate or extended neighbourhood of AfPak which is not feeling the heat of raging Islamic terrorism and extremism. Islamic extremism in AfPak has global implications too. Globally these radicalised Islamic youth are targeting Western interests in general and American interests in particular. All Islamic terror attacks in different parts of the world have their roots in AfPak region including 9/11. Without stabilising Afghanistan-Pakistan, the global menace of terrorism cannot be dealt with.

Conclusions: The Way Out

What is the way out of this Afghan crisis created mainly by Pakistan perspectives in Afghanistan, which is primarily anchored in its policy of 'strategic depth' and 'strategic asset' conceptualised against India? Since Afghan crisis has regional and global implications any solution of it must have all regional and global stakeholders on board. Any effort to exclude any important stakeholder from the resolution of Afghan crisis will not produce desired result and the Afghan wound will continue to fester, exacting heavy toll from the international community. Pakistan and the US are trying to exclude India and Iran respectively from any regional or global efforts for the resolution of Afghanistan crisis. Both India and Iran are significant stakeholders in Afghanistan with vital interests in Afghanistan and any effort to exclude them will undermine and weaken global efforts for the resolution of Afghanistan.

It is ironical that American interests are closer to the countries, which are not very friendly with the US. For America, Iran is still a rogue State, part of the evil empire, which has to be contained and isolated. Russia is still not trustworthy and India, though friendly cannot be befriended at the cost of Pakistan. America knows that it is mainly because of Pakistan that its 'War on Terror' and 'Operation Enduring Freedom' has not succeeded in its mission of stabilising Afghanistan, despite American troops being there for more than a decade. Iran might be an adversary of the US in Middle East and its nuclear weapon programme has created grave threat to the security of the US and its allies but in Afghanistan, there is complete convergence of the US-Iranian interests.[17] Any solution of Afghan crisis has to be as broad based as possible for its successful resolution.

Following policy options can be suggested;

1. Pakistan has to surrender its policy of 'strategic depth' in Afghanistan against India. It is a flawed strategy and can never be achieved.
2. Pakistan must stop nurturing terrorist outfits like Lashkar-e-Toiba (LeT), Hizb-e-Islami, Haqqani Network, Quetta Shura, and treating terrorists and extremists as 'strategic asset' to be used against India and blackmailing international community to bail it out from its economic and financial mess.
3. Pakistan and United States must be persuaded to allow India and Iran to be involved in any negotiation for the resolution of Afghan tangle. If no resolution to Afghan problem is possible without the full consent of Pakistan and United States then, without active involvement of India and Iran no Afghan solution can succeed. Pakistan and the US must give up their reservations for India and Iran respectively in the larger interests of regional and global peace, security and stability.
4. Afghan security forces and police must be strengthened to take care of their internal and external security. Eventually it is going to be Afghan armed forces and police, who will provide security to Afghan people and not international assistance forces.

5. The withdrawal of NATO led forces has to be gradual. Any sudden pull out of western forces will enable Taliban to stage a comeback and whole exercise of ousting Taliban from power in the wake of 9/11 will be negated in one stroke.
6. Afghan government must agree to allow a limited number of western/US troops to remain in Afghanistan in the post-2014 period to avoid any Iraq type of situation created by ISIS (Islamic State of Iraq and Syria) in Afghanistan. Even a small number of troops will keep the US committed to future security of Afghanistan from any ISIS type of threat to its security.
7. Some kind of rapprochement between different ethnic groups of Afghanistan has to be brokered by the international community for lasting peace in Afghanistan. Multi-ethnic character of Afghan society must be respected and must be given due recognition while reaching any solution. Any Afghan regime must give representation to all ethnic groups of Afghanistan. Exclusion of any ethnic group will be recipe for disaster.
8. Since Afghanistan problem has become a regional and global problem and so its solution has also to be regional and global. A broader regional and global approach must be adopted while addressing Afghan crisis.
9. Afghanistan should be developed as a bridge between South Asia and West Asia and South Asia and Central Asia. Afghanistan has the potential to emerge as energy hub and corridor between energy deficient South Asia and energy surplus west and central Asia.
10. Afghanistan's vast natural resources can fuel industrial growth in the region. China, India and other nations interested in Afghan natural resources must form a consortium to harness the Afghan resources for the benefit of all.
11. Afghanistan has the potential to emerge as a trading hub. This will create trade linkages between the countries of the region and it will help a great deal in stabilising Afghanistan.

12. Pakistan has to abandon its zero-sum-game approach in Afghanistan vis-à-vis India. Without allowing India due role in Afghanistan, the latter cannot be stabilised. India enjoys enormous soft power in Afghanistan much more than any other country of the world and this fact cannot be brushed aside.

These policy options must be adopted for the stabilisation of Afghanistan post-2014, after the withdrawal of US troops from Afghanistan. Without peace, security and stability in Afghanistan, global peace, security and stability cannot be achieved. Afghan peace is linked to global peace. In view of this fact, Pakistan has to rise above its narrow selfish national interests and bring desired change in its perspectives in Afghanistan. This will also be in the larger interests of Pakistan as any instability in Afghanistan will destabilise Pakistan also. So the need of the hour is that Pakistan must join hands with the US and India and other regional and global stakeholders in stabilising Afghanistan.

Notes

1. Seth G. Jones, *In the Graveyard of Empires: America's War in Afghanistan*, W.W. Norton and Company, 2010; Stephen Tanner, Afghanistan: A Military History from Alexander the Great to the War against the Taliban, Da Capo Press, 2009.
2. Afghanistan is by far the longest and costliest American war. It has overtaken Vietnam War both in terms of duration and money spent. The cost of maintaining an American soldier in Afghanistan for a year is $ 1 million. http://www.globalresearch.ca/the-most-expensive-war-in-world-history-costs-of-iraq-afghanistan-wars-could-rise-to-6-trillion/5329432 Afghanistan aid has also overtaken largest American aid programme called Marshal Plan for European reconstruction, $ 103.4 billion. http://blog.foreignpolicy.com /posts/2014/07/30/ the_united_states _has_outspent_the_marshall_plan_to_ rebuild_ afghanistan The US wars in Afghanistan and Iraq will cost $ 4 to 6 trillion. Stephen Friedman a senior US official has to resign in 2002, when he estimated the cost of Afghan-Iraq Wars can go up to $ 200 billion. http://www.washingtonpost.com/world/national-security/study-iraq-afghan-war-costs-to-top-4-trillion/2013/03/28/b82a5dce-97ed-11e2-814b-063623d80a60_story.html
3. The US intends to keep 9800 troops in Afghanistan even after 2014 for training and bolstering nascent Afghan National Army and Police. The US is suspending only combat operation in post-2014. The US needs its troops and bases to launch drone attacks in Pakistan against

terrorists hiding there. However, the future of the US troops depends on the signing of US-Afghan Strategic Partnership by the new Afghan Govt. assuming power after 2014 election. http://www.theguardian.com/world/2014/may/27/obama-us-afghanistan-force-2014

4. The New York Times, August 17, 2009, http://www.nytimes.com/2009/08/18/ cus/politics/18vets.html?_r=0
5. Andrew J. Bacevich, *The Limits of Power: The end of American exceptionalism*, Metropolitan Books, New York, 2008.
6. Aparna Pande, "Pakistan's Nightmare", *The Friday Times*, (Lahore), July 04, 2014, http://www. thefridaytimes.com /tft/pakistans-nightmare/
7. Durand Line was demarcated by British India and signed into a treaty in 1893 by Afghan ruler Amir Abdur Rahman Khan. The treaty was for 100 years and has expired in 1993. Since then all Afghan rulers has refused to renew Durand treaty including Taliban regime, despite Pak efforts and pressure. http://www.afghanistans.com/information/history/durandline.htm
8. In 2010 North West Frontier Province (NWFP) was officially renamed as Khyber Pakhtunkhwa. It is one of the four province of Pakistan and only one which was not named after the dominant ethnic group of the region such as Punjabi, Sindhi and Baluch. With the renaming of NWFP this anomaly has been addressed. http://www.khyberpakhtunkhwa.gov.pk/aboutus/
9. Tej Pratap Singh, "Unending Quest for Parity", Defence and Security Alert, vol. 2, issue 7, April 2011, pp. 71-73.
10. The concept of strategic depth was conceptualized by former Pak Army Chief Mirza Aslam Beg in 1980s.
11. The News, December 19, 2013. http://www.thenews.com.pk/Todays-News-13-27399-Strategic-depth-an-outdated-policy,-Sartaj-tells-Senate
12. Imtiaj Gul, *The Friday Times*, July 11, 2014, http://www.thefriday times.com/tft/is-this-the-end-of-the-strategic-depth-doctrine/
13. Kamran Shafi, "Defining 'Strategic Depth'," *Dawn*, 19 January, 2010. http://www.dawn.com/wps/wcm/ connect/dawn-content-library/dawn/the-newspaper/columnists/14-defining-strategic-depth-910
14. P.M. Kamath, "Pakistan's Strategy after Osama", Defence and Security Alert, vol. 2, issue 11, August, 2011, p. 32.
15. The Times of India, March 11, 2010. http://timesofindia.indiatimes.com/world/south-asia/India-close-friend-but-Pak-conjoined-twin-says-Afghanistan/articleshow/5672129.cms
16. "Terrorists as Strategic Assets", *Pakistan Today*, May 12, 2014. http://www.pakistantoday.com. pk/2014/05/12/ comment/terrorists-as-strategic-assets/
17. Tej Pratap Singh, "Stabilisation of Afghanistan", *Defence and Security Alert*, vol. 2, issue 11, August 2011, p. 75.

12

Pakistan's Search for Strategic Depth in Afghanistan

P.M. KAMATH

Since the birth of Pakistan in 1947, it has considered India as the number one enemy. Earlier in the 1970s and the 1980s, the Soviet Union was also considered as a national security threat along with India. Now it has improved its relations with the successor state of the Soviet Union—the Russian Federation. Hence, now security threat is seen to emerge only from India. This feeling has been compounded since Pakistan's division in 1971, with what was earlier East Pakistan, becoming an independent state of Bangladesh.

Prior to that, East Pakistan, separated from West Pakistan, almost by 10,000 miles of territory of India, was a national security strength multiplier for Pakistan, as it saw eastern wing as a dagger held at the heart of India. Hence the loss of East Pakistan was considered by military authorities, entirely because of the manoeuvres by India, though in reality, India only acted as a midwife. The original cause for the Bengali nationalist rebellion in East Pakistan and emergence of Bengali nationalism was because of despicable atrocities conducted by the West Pakistan's then military rulers on the helpless people of their own eastern wing! It also served a notice to Pakistan that religion alone cannot help a nation to hold together.[1] However, Indian involvement in the liberation of the Bengali people only further contributed to Pakistan damning India as the permanent enemy.

Army that has ruled Pakistan for a longer period than democratic governments, has very well succeeded in creating the perception within the majority of their countrymen that India is an enemy of Pakistan. A recent survey confirmed that fifty-four per cent of Pakistanis see India as the greatest threat to its security.[2] Since the US invasion of Afghanistan in 2001, it is an open secret that the American administration has tried, so far unsuccessfully, to drive the point to Pakistani Army that it is not India but Pakistan-bred internal terrorist groups and Al Qaeda, which are the greatest threat to Pakistan's survival as a moderate Islamic state.

President Obama had tried to convince the democratically elected Government of President Asif Zardari and Prime Minister Syed Yusuf Raza Gilani that if Pakistan accepts that point of view, he could help it to settle political differences with India. Hillary Clinton, former Secretary of State while addressing a joint press conference in October 2011 with the then Pakistani Foreign Minister, Hina Rabbani Khar, had put it very succinctly when she said: "You can't keep snakes in your backyard and expect them to bite only your neighbour." [3] She had left the term 'neighbour' undefined but it applied to India as well as to Afghanistan.

Strategic Depth

It is an old saying that a State has neither permanent friends nor permanent enemies but only permanent interests. Applying this yardstick since 1971 more obviously—because of the loss of its Eastern wing, Pakistan has been in search of finding a 'Strategic Depth' against a perceived threat from India for its survival as an Islamic state and that has been its lasting national interest.

What is meant by 'Strategic Depth'? It generally refers to geographical distance between a nation's frontlines and its civil and military assets. Primarily it is a geopolitical concept. Pakistan is geographically narrow and Indian Army can cut through and divide it into two halves. Even during the 1965 War against India, undivided Pakistan under the then military Dictator, Ayub Khan, had chosen to move Pakistani aircrafts to Iran—using its closeness to the Shah of Iran; as then both—Iran and Pakistan, were military alliance partners of the United States (US). Sense of securing a 'Strategic Depth' increases if a state is able to move its frontlines farther away from its civil and military assets; the farther it is able to take them the greater is the sense of security. In military literature, Strategic Depth as per the Wikipedia is a term which "broadly refers to the distances between the front lines or battle sectors and the combatants' industrial core areas, capital cities, heartlands, and other key centres of population and/or military production."[4]

General Zia's Search of Strategic Depth

Pakistan's search for strategic depth has been a military concern which revolves around Army's threat perceptions. Army Chief, General Zia-ul Haq (1979-1988), who also enjoyed political power as the military dictator, in addition to military power, focused on India's province of Punjab bordering Pakistan to create a buffer state between itself and India. Success of the project would have not only healed hurt ego of Army for its defeat in Bangladesh War in 1971;[5] but it would have also provided Strategic Depth to Pakistan.

However, Pakistani scholars credit General Mirza Aslam Beg (1988-1991) with the creation of the concept of Strategic Depth in the context of Pakistan. He had argued that "Pakistani Army can now in conventional Pak-India military conflict, retreat to mainland Afghanistan, regroup and launch a counter offensive against India."

Thus, having failed in the mission to force a secession of Punjab from India, subsequent military generals focused on Kashmir and Afghanistan. While Kashmir is an ongoing project of Pakistan to bleed India, after the victory of its protégé Taliban in capturing power in 1996 in Afghanistan post-Soviet withdrawal Pakistan looked at Afghanistan as the ideal choice to provide it with the much needed Strategic Depth. Another military dictator, General Pervez Musharraf, the one who was dragged by former US President George W. Bush in the war against Afghanistan after 9/11, also considered Afghanistan as the apt location that can provide Strategic Depth to Pakistan in the event of a conflict with India.

Afghanistan

Though the Afghanistan policy followed by every military dictator of Pakistan had an element of Strategic Depth concept as well, yet no one articulated it so well as the former Army Chief of Pakistan, General Pervez Ashfaq Kayani. During his interactions with correspondents of foreign media in Islamabad on 1 February 2013, he said, "We want Afghanistan to be our strategic depth..." It sounds as though he meant Afghanistan as Pakistan's client state, but he added "The way we understand it, if Afghanistan is peaceful, stable and *friendly* (emphasis added), we will have strategic depth because our western border secure..." By referring to Pakistan's western borders, he was referring to Afghanistan so that he can concentrate on Pakistan's eastern borders—with India. While he has used the concept many a time, he spelt it out in this rare foreign media briefing. He however, hastened to say, that his concept of strategic depth did not imply "controlling Afghanistan." Of course, he was aware that no one in history has been successful in controlling Afghanistan![6]

But it was clear that Pakistan desired to have a 'friendly' Afghanistan, positively doing what it desired, as a 'client state'. Obviously, when Kayani argues in favour of Western borders being secure he suggests that strategic depth enables Pakistan to concentrate on Indian borders. A friendly Afghanistan can help it to shift its moveable military assets to Afghanistan in case of a conflict with India. As it is, borders with Afghanistan are open ones. Durand Line drawn by the British as border between then India and Afghanistan is open and has not been accepted by Afghanistan even till now as it has divided the Pashtun tribe between Afghanistan and Pakistan. The British introduced this partition of Durand Line so as to provide a buffer zone between British India and the then imperial Russia.

Did Return of Democracy Push for Strategic Depth?

Did the return of democracy in 2008 in Pakistan induce the Army in any way to speak loudly on the concept of strategic depth? It is clear that despite having been a part of Indian cultural ethos to begin with, Pakistan has become a military dictatorship where even a semblance of democracy has not survived for more than a few years at a time. This has been begotten due to mainly Islamisation of society and polity and constant hate India campaign! After Zia, Benazir Bhutto ran a ramshackle democracy where all key decisions were taken by the Army.

Later, during Nawaz Sharif's democratic rule, again power was seized by the then Army Chief, General Pervez Musharraf in October 1999. Military dictatorship of Musharraf came to an end in January 2008. In Pakistan it is military alone that controls the nation's foreign policy, particularly India policy, nuclear policy and determines use of nuclear weapons!

The return of democracy in Pakistan in 2008 is only an outer shell without any democratic content or spirit in it. It is the Army that really laid down the strategic policy of Pakistan. Benazir Bhutto after demitting power had said that she had absolutely no knowledge of Pakistani status on the nuclear weapons. The government of Asif Zardari-Gilani elected in 2008 had no idea about 26/11 that was given the go ahead by the ISI with tacit consent of the Army.

Initially many were skeptical of Zardari's claim that it was a handiwork of 'non-state actors.' But subsequent developments in India-Pakistan political relations and continued dominance of Army in strategic affairs show that political establishment is often ignorant about the anti-India moves of the Military-ISI-Jihadi-Terror complex. Hillary Clinton spoke of ignorance on the part of Zardari-Gilani team, as it did not know "the connections…between elements within the military and ISI and various …terrorist groups."[7]

A Pakistani commentator, Shahzad Chaudhry argues that with the return of civilian rule in Pakistan, concept of strategic depth has been used by democratic forces in the country to hit the military.[8] During the last thirty years, the US has been the mainstay of Pakistan, but it has played 'In and Out' policy towards Pakistan. It was for Afghanistan that the US had to pull Pakistan in its orbit and also push it out as well. In 1979-1980, the US was keen to make Pakistan frontline state so as to pump-in arms, money and Mujaheedins into Afghanistan for forcing its then arch rival, Soviet Union, out of Afghanistan.

Having achieved that goal in 1989 and also seeing the demise of the Soviet Union, Americans abandoned Pakistan to develop as a university to train terrorists for the globalising world and left Afghanistan to their warlords! But Osama bin Laden forced

George W. Bush to invite Pakistan in 2001 to hunt for him in Afghanistan! In this period Pakistan received a bounty of over $40 billion as military and economic aid. It also got large unaccounted prize money for killing or capturing US-Wanted Pakistani terrorists that was an extra bonus of over millions of dollars.[9]

Obama's Elimination of Osama

Thus, Osama bin Laden played at least three significant roles in the triangular relations with the US, Pakistan and Afghanistan at three different phases. First, he was for the Americans and Pakistanis an anti-Soviet Islamic crusader who crusaded to get the Russians out from Afghanistan. Second, after Russian withdrawal and capture of power by the Taliban he was a welcome guest of Pakistan and a friend of Afghanistan. The Taliban which was trained in Pakistan-established, funded and protected *Madrasas,* for the first time created a hope in Pakistan of fulfilling their dream of creating space for their concept of 'strategic depth.'[10] Finally, since 9/11 he was hunted by the US during the Bush administration but protected by Afghanistan, but the hunt got over after Taliban was dethroned more particularly after Tora Bora escape of Osama to Pakistan in December 2001; thereafter he became a strategic asset of Pakistan with US as a likely financier, and Afghanistan as a strategic depth!

It is the US and Pakistan that really reaped the benefits of their changing relations with Osama. However, his presence became a liability for Afghanistan. An American spy, Lt Col. Anthony Shaffer, who has published his exploits in Afghanistan in a work called *Operation Dark Heart: Spycraft and special ops on the frontlines of Afghanistan* says that despite ground operators and his stating that "the intelligence indicates that most of leadership [of 9/11 terror] was... in Pakistan" their superiors forced them to focus on Hindu Kush mountains—their winter safe havens.[11]

Changes in Pakistan's Post-Osama Strategy

American daring and successful adventure of elimination of Osama brought about a change in Pakistan's Afghan strategy. American top policymakers like President, Secretary of State,

Secretary of Defence and Director of CIA, deliberately divulged information damaging credibility of the Military-Intelligence-Jihadi Complex of Pakistan. Pakistan, on its part, began to pretend sincerity and adherence to the terms of engagement as spelt out by USA. Pakistan's military establishment was weakened vis-à-vis the US since the killing of Osama bin Laden who was well protected till 2 May 2011 so as to claim a bigger price from the US. If the US had a secret understanding with Pakistan or it is possible that forces inimical to Kayani within the Pakistani Army might have leaked the presence of Bin Laden in Abbottabad, whatever may be the fact, but it weakened the Pakistani Army. The public perception was one of an Army that has weakened. This culmination led to three outcomes:

First, it emboldened the political democratic elite to assert to secure a greater say in strategic policy-making which was hitherto not permitted to it. It is evident that it began to perform its role as scripted by the US under the new situation; it had begun to strike at Pakistani Taliban. The political establishment of Pakistan has two components. One is the dominant Military, which inseparably includes ISI and another is a weak and subservient political democratic elite. In the beginning it has been made clear that in strategic policy formulation the democratic elite had a minimal role while military dominated, but now, under American calculated policy, post-Osama extermination onwards the military is being downgraded in matters of strategic policy formulation.

Second, it seemed to be clear that Pakistan will be forced to change its strategy in Afghanistan. Thus, President Obama said in his 22 June 2011 address on Afghanistan that US "will continue to press Pakistan to expand its participation in securing a more peaceful future for this war-torn region." In particular, Pakistan is expected to "address terrorist safe-havens", and root out "the cancer of violent extremism". The US officials publicly say that threat to US emanates from Pakistan and not from Afghanistan.

Third, Pakistan was warned that the US will continue to hit any terrorist hideout even in future, if that helps it to secure for itself greater safety and security. This is not an empty threat as American drones began to attack Pakistan's tribal areas more often from Afghan bases, demonstrating that it can still carry out its threat independent of the Pakistani cooperation including non-use of Pakistani territory.

Since American aid was essential to the survival of Pak Army, the US under Kerry-Lugar-Berman bill aimed to control promotions in Pakistan's military; Army was also made to give an undertaking that it would not derail democratic process if American funding was to continue. That left the Army with only to speak on Strategic Depth in Afghanistan, while ensuring the continuance of Zardari-Gilani democratic regime for its full term![12]

Futility of Strategic Depth

Pakistani scholars and journalists have questioned the description and validity of concept of Strategic Depth. In the event of an attack by India, the notion that Pakistan military would withdraw their military movable assets into Afghanistan is unsound for several reasons. One is that Afghanistan has been hostile to Pakistan for its promotion of Taliban; Pakistani politicians have openly described Taliban as 'Pakistan's strategic asset', that should convince Pakistani military that Afghanistan's forces might not cooperate with Pakistan if it decides to place its combat planes in Afghanistan. Even when Taliban was in power in Afghanistan, there was no such cooperation between the two.

The very idea of keeping aircraft in another country, instead of using them against the invading forces defies principles of warfare. Shahzad Chaudhry says, "In a war, a nation is meant to fight with what it has, not to hide away what it must be fighting with."[13] "What if Afghanistan permits Pakistan to hide their movable assets during war but refuses to return them after the end of the war? That was what Iran did to Iraq, where Saddam had moved his airplanes for safe custody!"

Relevance of Strategic Depth

What is the relevance of the theory or strategy of Strategic Depth to Pakistan's security today? Hillary Clinton was of the opinion that "Pakistan's concept of strategic depth is dead."[14] She advised Pakistan to focus all its strength on dealing with militants. US characterised Pakistan's selective fight against Taliban groups opposed to Pakistan as a 'double game.'

Pakistan is a state possessing nuclear weapons and its perceived source of national security threat emerges from India, which is also a Nuclear Weapons state. India has professed 'No First Use' (NFU) of nuclear weapons; it means India will not use them as the weapons of first strike in a conflict. India's nuclear weapons are not Pakistan-specific, as Pakistan's are India-specific. Pakistan has declared a nuclear doctrine in which it threatens to use nuclear weapons as weapons of First Strike.

Pakistan since 1998 has been boasting that its acquisition of nuclear weapons has equalised power between it and India. In the Kargil conflict India suffered heavy casualties in order to eject Pakistani soldiers from Kargil. Pervez Hoodbhoy has written, "Believing that a nuclear shield made Indian retaliation impossible, Pakistan coyly disclaimed any connection with the attackers..."[15] but after Pakistan acquired nuclear weapons, Pakistani leaders as well as the military officers have often boasted regarding the equalisation of power due to the acquisition of nuclear weapons. General Pervez Musharraf, for instance, had claimed that he "can do what he likes" as Pakistan now has "what other superpowers have."[16]

Same was the experience after India mobilised troops against Pakistan in response to its proxy attack on Indian Parliament by terrorist group *Jaish-e-Mohammad* on 13 December 2001 in which 14 men were killed. Despite ten months of Indian troops on eyeball to eyeball confrontation with Pakistani troops, India was not able to move beyond the borders. India was forced to withdraw troops from the border, eventually. Then Foreign Minister of Pakistan, Khursheed Kasuri had said, "We are not making any boasts but the Indians have come to the conclusion that the military solution is just not there."[17] While Kasuri is right, he and his likes need to understand that this conclusion is equally applicable to Pakistan as well, in relation to its sloganeering that the Kashmir dispute is the part of the historic incomplete process of division of India that began in 1947 on religious basis.

Conclusions

The above discussion clearly demonstrates that for the nuclear-armed Pakistan and India, the only war-option is of Nuclear War. In such an all out nuclear war scenario, the concept of 'Strategic Depth' is not going to help Pakistan in any way to protect and preserve its military assets by moving them to a distant geographic area. In a nuclear war, weapons can reach every nook and corner. Development of nuclear weapons has made concept of Strategic Depth irrelevant. It needs to be rejected as a geopolitical anachronism.

Why then has Pakistani military embraced the concept of Strategic Depth in the case of Afghanistan? The military leaders have used it in recent times vigorously, with a related dual purpose. First it has been a bugbear to Pakistan that was under the US presence in Afghanistan since the Taliban regime was dethroned by the invading forces of the US in October 2001. India has maintained a low profile in Afghanistan by undertaking several projects in socioeconomic area; Indian presence is widely admired and accepted by the Afghanistan's elite.

Second, post-US withdrawal from Afghanistan, Pakistan intends to play a decisive role; its all weather-friend, China, is also playing a major role in mining and economic development. This is acceptable to Pakistan. However, Pakistan has not accepted Indian presence as a helper of Afghanistan! Its hatred for India overrides everything else!

Notes

1. See Aditi Juvekar, *Partners in Conflict-Perceptions and Realties of Indo-US Relations* (Mumbai: Himalaya Publishing House, 1997), pp. 58-61.
2. Pakistani students visiting Mumbai reported to have said: "We were trained to hate India." See Hindustan Times (Mumbai) 24 November 2011.
3. See http://www.firstpost.com/printpage.php?idno=113492&sr_no=0
4. Strategic Depth-Wikipedia, the free encyclopedia http ;//en.eikipedia.org/wiki/strategic depth
5. General Pervez Musharraf writes in his memoirs to his best friend Bilal was killed in December 1971 war. When the cease-fire was announced and Pakistani troops had to surrender, he adds: Brave "soldiers cried with me. It remains saddest and most painful day of my life." See, *In Lines of Fire: A Memoir* (New York: Free Press, 2006), p. 545.
6. P. M. Kamath, "Pakistan's Strategy after Osama", Defence and Security Alert, Vol. 2, Issue 11 (August 2011), p. 32.

7. Pakistan needs to make hard choices now: Hillary" www.dawn.com/news/1114535
8. Strategic depth http://tribune.com.pk/story/863966/strategic-depth/ 3 April 2015
9. See Musharraf, In the Line of Fire, pp. 237-8.
10. See P M Kamath, "Pakistan's Strategy after Osama." *Defence and Security Alert*, Vol. 2, (August 2011), p. 33.
11. Pp. 191-2
12. See Strategic depth, Shahzad Chaudhry http://tribune.com.pk/story/863966/strategi-depth/April 3,2015
13. See his Strategic depth http://tribune.com.pk/story/863966/strategic-depth/April3, 2015
14. "Pakistan needs to make hard choices now: Hillary" www.dawn.com/news/1114535
15. "South Asia: Lighting the Nuclear Fire," http://www.wworld.org/crisis/crisis.asp?ID=247
16. Quoted in See P. M. Kamath, *India's Policy of No First Use of Nuclear Weapons: Relevance to Peace and Security in South Asia* (New Delhi: Anamika Publishers, 2009), p. 176.
17. See Owen Bennett-Jones, "Have Nuclear Weapons made South Asia Safe?" BBC News, 2003/05/09. http:/newsvote.bbc.co.uk/1/hi/world/south Asia/3015...

13

US Withdrawal from Afghanistan: Implications for India and the Way Ahead

KAVITA SHARMA

As the D-day for complete withdrawal of US forces from Afghanistan approaches, there is anxiety and a sense of pessimism regarding the future of Afghanistan and its potential impact on Regional and International dynamics. Like many countries, India too has a large stake in Afghanistan and needs to monitor various developments closely so as to understand its repercussions.

Background

Afghanistan is strategically located at the junction of Central Asia, South Asia and Middle East. It is a loosely knit conglomeration of a number of ethnic groups such as Pashtuns, Tajiks, Uzbeks and Hazaras. The ethnic composition and demography of Afghanistan have an important bearing on its power politics. Afghanistan's history is full of internal fighting, foreign interventions and unending instability. Instability and ethnic divide have led to its exploitation by both the superpowers and regional players.[1]

US involvement in Afghanistan is linked to cold war period. Soviet invasion, civil war, emergence of warlords and the rise of fundamentalism and Talibanism have been some of the important events which triggered US involvement in Afghanistan.

However, the main factor which brought in US forces in Afghanistan has been the 9/11 attack. US intervention resulted in the ouster of Taliban government and formation of Afghan Government under Mr Hamid Karzai in 2001. However, Afghanistan's internal situation continued to be chaotic. Taliban and insurgent factions had regrouped and posed formidable challenges for the new Afghan government. Prevalent security environment necessitated additional security forces and resulted into a surge of US Forces in Afghanistan. However, there has also been mounting pressure in US over casualties of US troops and demand for the withdrawal. Killing of Osama bin Laden came as a key event indicating defeat for the Al-Qaeda and in turn fulfilment of the primary objective of US mission. In a way, this cleared the road for the withdrawal of US forces, but, the contemporary environment in Afghanistan does not favour sudden removal of forces.[2]

US Withdrawal

Withdrawal of US forces from Afghanistan is inevitable. However, this has serious implications for the world and the region in particular. The withdrawal is likely to leave Afghanistan in a precarious situation because of numerous factors which need to be watched carefully.

Political System

Political system emerging post-withdrawal is one of the most important factors in the stability of Afghanistan. Karzai government has been in power since 2001 but it is generally perceived as the government imposed by the Western powers and has no clout to run a stable government. All elections held have been marred by rigging, violence and frauds. Insurgency has not been brought under control and the clout of Taliban has been on the rise. Though third general election has been concluded however, there is no clear cut positive outcome.[3]

Economy

Another important factor which would have significant bearing on Afghanistan's outcome is the likely drying up of financial assistance post-US withdrawal. Since 2001, numerous countries have been contributing to Afghanistan militarily, diplomatically, or financially. However, currently Afghan economy is facing severe revenue shortage. If Afghanistan does not receive extra funds needed, the government may not be able to pay salaries especially to security forces as they are generally being paid from foreign funds.[4]

Pakistan's Role

Pakistan is the most important player in Afghanistan. For Pakistan, a friendly government in Afghanistan is a must to nullify Indian advantage. Towards this motive, Pakistan has always pursued the policy of supporting insurgencies. Pakistan has been frontline state for US in forcing Soviet withdrawal by creating Taliban and in all probability will work towards bringing Taliban back to power. Pakistan has been playing a dual game of supporting the US agenda and as well as supporting Taliban. However, of late there appears to be change in its thinking towards Afghanistan policy by considering reconciliation process. Such change may be the outcome of domestic rise of terrorism in Pakistan. It will be very interesting to closely monitor Pakistan policy post-US withdrawal.[5]

The Taliban

Taliban since its inception in early 1990s had established its rule in most parts of the country by 1996. During the US attack in 2001, most of the Taliban cadre and leadership fled to Pakistan. They were provided shelter and allowed to continue pursuing their agenda. Subsequently they regrouped and increased their strength with the help of ISI, Army and terrorist groups present in Pakistan. They have recovered control of Pashtun-dominated areas of Afghanistan bordering Pakistan post-US diversion of forces to Iraq. Once again Taliban have become a formidable force and resorted to LED attacks, suicide bombings, armed attacks and infiltration of foreign terrorists. Further, Taliban have created serious ambiguity about the reconciliation process in which they have shown interest but refused to accept pre-conditions of laying down arms and accepting the Afghanistan constitution.[6]

Afghan National Security Forces

The second important factor is the Afghan National Security Forces (ANSF), especially created to take over full responsibility of the country's security. The readiness of ANSF to a large extent is considered as the guarantor for the Afghan Government to be able to function, post-US withdrawal. Afghan National Army (ANA) and Afghan National Police (ANP) are the two most important constituents of ANSF. ANA has been finding it difficult to recruit and retain skilled personnel and is plagued with graft and corruption. Patronage and nepotism remain perennial problems, while the attrition rate of personnel choosing to leave the forces continues to be high. The state of ANP is worse than ANA. ANP is closely linked to human rights abuses, drug abuses, and corruption. There is report regarding factionalism in the force because of ethnic divide. Under such circumstances ANSF readiness to take lead and assume full responsibility of security is highly doubtful.[7,8]

Regional Politics

Regional politics is another important factor which will play a significant role in the future of Afghanistan. Historically, constituents of Afghanistan have always made the country vulnerable to external influences because of neighbours exploiting ethnic divide for their own advantages. Iran is one of the neighbours which have historical and cultural ties with Afghanistan. Iran has interest in controlling land communication and pipelines to Central Asia which is feasible only when Pashtun- dominated areas remain stable.[9] China is another neighbour whose interest has specially risen after 9/11. China wants Afghanistan to be free of outside influences and would not like US to be present in their backyard. Further, China also has stakes in mineral rich Central Asian States and Afghanistan and therefore would like to have a government in Afghanistan which is friendly to her ally Pakistan.[10] Northern neighbours of Turkmenistan, Uzbekistan and Tajikistan would like to develop their own sphere of influence in the areas adjacent to their own borders post-US withdrawal.[11]

US Role

Likely role of US post-withdrawal is yet another important factor which as of now is not very clear. It will primarily depend on the number and type of troops left behind post-withdrawal. There is some indication that US may keep around 9000-10,000 troops for counter terrorism and training role. There are indications of US planning to maintain nine military bases and increasing diplomatic presence by opening US consulates at Herat, Mazar-e-Sharif and Jalalabad. This would require US to maintain far bigger presence. However, such military presence is dependent on the signing of the bilateral agreement with the new Afghanistan government. Any large presence of US forces will provide the new government much needed breather time for settling down and getting a firmer foothold. This may also check the Taliban from regaining grounds.[12]

Likely Scenarios Post-US Withdrawal

The factors discussed above are indicative of a number of possible scenarios shaping up in Afghanistan post-US withdrawal.[13,14,15,16]

Establishment of Stable Government Post-Karzai

Establishment of a stable government can be one outcome which can be achieved if the new Afghanistan government is able to bring in reconciliation and provide corruption free, effective and efficient governance. This would be an ideal situation which will bring peace and stability. There will be the conditions of improved security, legitimate and representative government working for sustained economic and social progress.

North-South Political Divide

There can be North-South divide situation mainly hinged on to mismanaged/ rigged elections and involvement of regional politics. Taliban and its supporters gain ground in the southern part of the country and Northern states.

Continuation of Afghan War

Another consequence can be the continuation of Afghan war. The ending of the US war in Afghanistan does not bring about the end of the Afghan war as ANSF may not have the capability to secure the entire country. Insurgency may rise and this could bring back civil war and instability.

Economic Crisis

Economic crisis can be another outcome. There is a likelihood of reduction in aids and support being received from international development agencies due to apprehensions of an unstable investment climate post-US withdrawal. There will be flight of capital, investment risks and a shortage of funds for reconstruction and development of logistics and transportation. This scenario is dangerous and may lead to increase in poppy cultivation, drug trafficking and finally rise in insurgency. This may also lead to drying up of funds for ANSF and the government's inability to pay them. Its consequence may be mass desertion in the force leading to lawlessness.

Operative Afghan National Security Forces

ANSF coming out strong and operative is also a possibility. Though the prospect of the ANSF being able to secure the whole country is bleak, yet there is a hope that better training and better equipment may enable ANSF to control insurgency with the support of normal public who may not like to see Taliban extremism returning to haunt them.

Taliban Wresting Power

Yet another possibility is of Taliban wresting power from the present incumbents. This has been in prominence because of the rising incidence of Taliban attacks in the last few years.

Thus, the likely scenario post-US withdrawal reflects a very complex picture full of uncertainties. All the discussed factors are indicative of the possibility of Afghanistan heading for chaos. Elected government may manage to survive for a while, but with highly diminished state authority leading to insurgents and local players gaining ground. The country may once again turn into a loose confederation of fiefdoms. Taliban is likely to emerge as the main insurgent group and its role will be central to the future of Afghanistan. It is quite certain that the Taliban will get in the centre of any set up which emerges in Afghanistan post-US withdrawal and there will be instability.

Implications for India in Afghanistan

The most likely outcome envisaged post-US withdrawal from Afghanistan predicts Taliban dominance. India has been partner in evicting Taliban from Afghanistan in 2001. India has earned a dominant position in Taliban affected Afghanistan, against the liking of Pakistan. India's interest is best looked after only if there is stability in Afghanistan. However, the emerging scenario post-US withdrawal is not at all indicative of a stable Afghanistan. Under these circumstances, implications for India are immense.[17,18,19,20,21,22]

Strong Relationship

Afghanistan and India traditionally have had strong and friendly relationships. India was the only South Asian country to recognise the Soviet-backed Afghanistan government in the 1980s. However, relations diminished during the Afghan civil war and the regime of the Taliban government. In the post-Taliban era of Afghanistan, India has once again built a very strong relationship with the country. Indians today are the most popular foreigners in Afghanistan. There is a natural understanding between the peoples of the two countries. This would be at stake with the return of Taliban.

Humanitarian and Reconstruction Aid Programme

India is the largest regional provider of humanitarian and reconstruction aid to Afghanistan. Indians are working in various construction projects, as part of India's rebuilding efforts in Afghanistan. Continuation of these efforts for betterment of Afghanistan is vital but will be at stake if Taliban returns to power.

Political Goodwill

Political goodwill has facilitated India having four consulates in Afghanistan. They are located in Herat, Mazar-e-Sharif, Kandahar and Jalalabad. These consulates facilitate expanding economic opportunities and improving contact with the larger population. Continuation of the consulates hinges on a stable Afghanistan.

Strategic Partnership

In the aftermath of the 2008 Indian embassy bombing in Kabul, the Afghan Foreign Ministry referred to India as a "brother country" and the relationship between the two as one which "no enemy can hamper". Relations between Afghanistan and India received a major boost in 2011 with the signing of a strategic partnership agreement, which is the first of its kind since the Soviet invasion of 1979. This will be a no go with the resurgence of Taliban power.

Energy Security Needs

India is an energy deficit country. Central Asian region is full of oil and gas reserves which are very crucial for Indian economic growth. Afghanistan is our natural gateway to Central Asia and beyond. Pakistanis and Chinese have been denying India the much needed linkage or access to Central Asia. However, India has built Zaranj-Delaram Road in Afghanistan and is helping Iran in developing the Chahbahar Port; both would provide India a direct access to Central Asia for trade and energy security for a long time to come. Another plan that has been floated is of the TAPI gas pipeline which is vital for meeting our energy security. All these initiatives are dependent on stability in Afghanistan.

Military Strategy

Good relations with any Afghan regime can allow us to maintain a military pressure on Pakistan from their west, which will prevent them removing deployed Army troops from their western border in case of any Indo-Pak hostilities. This military pressure has to be from the Afghan Army and any future re-created Afghan Air Force. Taliban's return would jeopardize this advantage.

Check on Terrorism

Terrorist groups inimical to India have gained strength in the past in Afghanistan. Afghanistan once again become a breeding ground for terrorism, particularly under Pakistan's dominance would naturally not be in our interest because of its geographical proximity to our northern state of J&K and the possibility of import of terrorism to India.

Initiatives for Democracy in Afghanistan

India has been assisting in the rebuilding of political institutions in Afghanistan. India has financed the construction of Afghanistan parliament building. India is the most respected country in Afghanistan as of now. If the Taliban regains power, these institutions will come under extreme Islamic rule.

Access to Afghan Market

Indian businessmen have been investing in a big way in Afghanistan and this would help in becoming part of the economic growth of Afghanistan in near future. Possibility of getting access to the Afghan market would be in danger if Afghanistan heads towards instability.

Way Ahead

It is very evident that India has a lot at stake post-US withdrawal. There is a need to realign her policies and exercise options which would enable her to safeguard her interests in the future too.[23,24,25,26,27,28,29]

Continued Support for Afghanistan Stability

Instability in Afghanistan benefits the Pakistani military the most. It provides leverage and control in their domestic and international affairs. The stability in Afghanistan benefits Indian foreign policy, domestic politics, and economic development. An unstable Afghanistan will become breeding ground and haven for terrorists which will help Pakistan in its mission Kashmir. As a result, India will require more expenditure on its internal security establishment. Conceding control over Afghanistan to Pakistan is totally undesirable, and therefore, India will have to **continue helping the Afghan government** rather more vigorously after US withdrawal in fighting insurgency so as to ensure stability.

Good Relations with Afghan People

We are known to have very good equations with Northern Alliance consisting of the Tajiks, Uzbeks and Hazaras. Yet we must not forget that the Pashtuns are the largest community comprising Afghanistan. Our vital stake in Afghanistan is the **goodwill of the Afghan people**. The economic and social contribution we are making in Afghanistan will yield rich dividends if it were to also involve the Pashtuns and not just the Tajiks, Uzbeks and Hazaras. There may be danger in pursuing this path in the beginning but that can be minimised if we open channels of communication with various Pashtun tribes. It is short sighted on our part to label all the Pashtuns as being Taliban. The Pashtuns are as fragmented as our polity and society on every issue including the future role of the Taliban. India has been working on small projects and on areas that directly benefit Afghan people. Several polls conducted by independent agencies show India on top of the popularity list in Afghanistan. These efforts must be continued and all opportunities to expand such efforts should be explored. India must continue building and running schools and hospitals.

Promote Indian Goodwill

India has a lot of goodwill in Afghanistan. India should continue to engage with Afghanistan in re-building its military and security forces by providing training, sharing its experiences in dealing with insurgency, but should not involve in any direct military engagement. India should help Afghanistan in redeveloping its power and energy sectors which will increase access of India to Central Asian Republic (CAR) countries. India should use her diverse groups within the civil society, for instance, political parties, NGOs, educational and research institutions, media groups etc. in fostering Indian goodwill in Afghanistan. The popularity of Indian cinema among the Afghans should be efficiently used in order to project India's 'Soft Power'.

Improved Afghanistan, India and Pakistan Relationship

Improved relations between Afghanistan, Pakistan and India, would in all probability be the best thing to happen to bring stability in the region. It would improve the trade connectivity which in turn would lead to economic development of the region. It will help in bringing stability to the entire region.

Economic Development of Afghanistan

Afghanistan is plagued with insurgency. Only economic development can help Afghanistan to discourage its youth from taking the path of insurgency. India should:

- Increase trade with Afghanistan and through it with the CARs.
- Increase business investment in Afghanistan.
- Assist Afghanistan to develop its natural resources.
- Increase reconstruction and capacity building programme.
- Enhance India's energy security.
- Assist Afghanistan to replace narcotics-based agriculture with regular agriculture.
- Work towards implementation of SAFTA.
- Promote India-China cooperation on Afghanistan.

It is only through sustained reconstruction and concerted socio-economic development that stability can be assured in

Afghanistan which is in the interest of India more than anyone else.

Convergence of Interest in Afghanistan with China

India and China can work together in Afghanistan for two reasons. First, both countries have economic stakes in Afghanistan. China has clearly shown its resolve to defend its economic interest and this can be common ground for India-China partnership in securing their common interest. Another area of cooperation can be in combating terrorist fallout from Afghanistan post-US withdrawal.

India and Iran Partnership

Afghanistan has been working on an alternative plan regarding Bilateral Security Agreement with US. Karzai government sees role for Iran and India in assisting peaceful transition in Afghanistan post-US withdrawal. India had always good relations with Iran. Signing of interim nuclear deal between Iran and US led to P-5+1 and has also come at the right time as it unshackles some of the constraints India felt in seeking Iran's support for ensuring stability in Afghanistan. India has been working with Iran to draw out alternative plan for access to the CARs. Iran has also been increasing influence in Afghanistan primarily through economic avenues. It has built roads, improved infrastructure and provided concessions enabling Afghans access to Chahbahar Port. This is a golden opportunity and must be seized.

Conclusion

Insurgency remains the root cause of instability in Afghanistan. Even US presence has not been able to eradicate insurgency. Insurgency cannot have solution in military operations alone. To eradicate insurgency one has to eradicate poverty and provide livelihood. India has been on the right track. India must continue to work for Afghanistan's stability by building strong democratic institutions, assisting Afghanistan military and security forces in capability-building and training so as to enhance their effectiveness in meeting their own security needs and helping in economic development of the country and its people. India should endeavour to work along with all the stakeholders to help contain problems arising out of US withdrawal, encourage positive development and bring peace, prosperity and stability in Afghanistan.

Notes

1. http://en.wikipedia.org/wiki/Afghanistan
2. Hasan Talal, (2009), Afghanistan Complex Situation And Its Implications On Pakistan, retrieved from, http://dspace.mah.se/bitstream/handle/2043/10761/ final%20thesis.pdf? sequence=1 &isAllowed=y
3. Wilson John, (2013), Future of Afghanistan Post-2014and Implications for India*, retrieved from http://orfonline.org/cms/export/orfonline/modules/issuebrief/ attachments/ibf_1377510555848.pdf
4. *Ibid.*
5. *Ibid.*
6. *Ibid.*
7. Frederic Grare, (2014), Afghanistan Post-2014: Scenarios and Consequences, retrieved from http://carnegieendowment.org/2014/02/04/afghanistan-post-2014-scenarios-and-consequences
8. Mariam Safi, Operation Khaibar–Taliban's Spring Offensive "Will the ANSF Prove Equal to the Challenge?, South Asia Defence and Strategic Review, May-Jun 2014, pp. 29-30.
9. *Ibid.*
10. Zhang Hong, (2014), China In Afghanistan, A Hesitant Neighbor Comes Knocking, retrieved from, http://www.worldcrunch.com/world-affairs/china-in-afghanistan-a-hesitant-neighbor-comes-knocking/afghanistan-china-strategy-war/c1s16150/#.VK7AfNKUeNA
11. Khalid Rahman, (2010). Situation in Afghanistan and its implications on the Central Asian region, retrieved from http://www.ips.org.pk/global-issues-and-politics/1278-situation-in-afghanistan-and-its-implications-on-the-central-asian-region
12. http://en.wikipedia.org/wiki/Withdrawal_of_US_troops_from_Afghanistan
13. Seema Mustafa, (2013), Post-Withdrawal Scenario in Afghanistan, retrieved from http:// tribune.com.pk/story/550670/post-withdrawal-scenario-in-afghanistan/
14. Stefan Olsson, Erika Holmquist,Samuel Bergenwall, Helene Lackenbauer, (2012), Afghanistan After 2014: Five Scenarios, retrieved fromhttp://www.academia.edu /3488447/Afghanistan_After_2014_Five_Scenarios
15. Muhammad Ibrahim, Post-US Withdrawal from Afghanistan and Its Impact on Internal Security, retrieved from, http://www.research publish. com/download.php?file=Post-US%20 Withdrawal%20From%20Afghanistan% 20and%20Its%20 Impact%20on%20Internal%20Security-158.pdf&act=book.

16. Clare Castillego, (2012), Regional implications of NATO withdrawal from Afghanistan: What role for the EU? retrieved from http://fride.org/download /PB_4_NATO_withdrawal_from_Afghanistan.pdf
17. http://en.wikipedia.org/wiki/Afghanistan%E2%80%93India_relations
18. Dr Dinoj Kumar Upadhyay, (2012), Security Transition in Afghanistan: Implications for India, retrieved from http://www.icwa.in/pdfs/VBsecurity.pdf
19. Shashi Tharoor, (2011), A question for India, if US leaves Afghanistan, retrieved from http://www.sundaytimes.lk/110717/Timestwo/t2_05.html
20. Naheed Anjum Chisti, (2013), The US Withdrawal from Afghanistan and its Impact on Indo-Pak Relations, retrieved from http://www.globalcentre.org/uploads /JGSI%2027-31%20dr%20naheed.pdf
21. Dr Shanthie Mariet D Souza, (2014), India In Post-2014 Afghanistan: Challenges And Opportunities – Analysis, retrieved from http://www.eurasiareview.com/10032014-india-post-2014-afghanistan-challenges-opportunities-analysis/
22. D Suba Chandran, (2014), Why is Afghanistan important to India?, retrieved from http://www.thefridaytimes.com/tft/why-is-afghanistan-important-to-india/
23. Debate, Afghanistan Post-2014: India's Option, Indian Foreign Affairs Journal Vol. 8, No. 3, Jul-Sep 2013, retrieved from http://www.associationdiplomats.org/publications /ifaj/DebateLeaders/8.3%20-Afghanistan%20Post%202014%20-%20India%27s%20Options.htm
24. Air Commodore (R) Khalid Iqbal, (2013), End of Afghanistan Game and Options for Pakistan, retrieved from http://www.criterion-quarterly.com/end-of-afghanistan-game-options-for-pakistan/
25. V Mahalingam, (2013), Post-US Withdrawal Scenario in Afghanistan-India's Concerns and Strategies, http://www.claws.in/986/post-us-withdrawal-scenario-in-afghanistan-indias-concerns-and-strategies-v-mahalingam.html#sthash.B7rIRV38.dpuf
26. Ankit Panda, (2014), Room for India-China Cooperation in Afghanistan?, retrieved from http://thediplomat.com/2014/04/room-for-india-china-cooperation-in-afghanistan/
27. Air Commodore (R) Khalid Iqbal, (2013), Afghanistan Sans Foreign Troops and Options for Pakistan, retrieved from, http://cpakgulf.org/wp-content/uploads/ 2013/06/ afghanistansan.pdf
28. Gareth Price, (2013), India's Policy towards Afghanistan, retrieved from http://www.chathamhouse.org/sites/files/chathamhouse/public/Research/Asia/0813pp_indiaafghanistan.pdf
29. Arvind Gupta, Ashok K. Behuria, Vishal Chandra, and Smruti S. Pattanaik, (2012), Post-2014 Afghanistan and India's Options, retrieved from http://www.idsa.in/ policybrief/Post2014Afghanistan AndIndias Options_180712.html

14

Pakistan's Afghan Policy in Post-2014 Scenario: Options for India

SUDHIR SINGH

Pakistan and Afghanistan relations have always been turbulent due to a gamut of factors. Pakhtunistan is top among them. After the 1979 Soviet intervention, Pakistan has adopted the policy of keeping Afghanistan volatile so as to achieve strategic depth against India. In the backdrop of 9/11 terror attack the NATO led attack commenced against Taliban in 2001. Since the last thirteen years despite being part of coalition against terror, Pakistan has been supporting terror elements preciously to score points against India. Despite civilian regime in Islamabad since March 2008 till date, military has been adamant to sustain old Afghan policy which is bound to inflict collateral damage on India if not managed properly and therefore we must reformulate our strategy to cope with the impending dangers.

Since millennia, Afghanistan has remained at the junction between Asia and Europe. The geography of the country has kept it in the chessboard of each and every global power game. The Greco-Bactrian (250-150 BCE), Kushan (30-375 AD) and Sassanid (224-651 AD) empires derived much of their wealth from the Silk Road, a series of interlinked trading networks criss-crossing the Eurasian land mass and centred around what is known as Afghanistan. Despite the decline of the importance of the Silk routes, Afghanistan's ability to act as a regional conduit never entirely faded from collective perception. Only a century ago, the modern father of geo strategy, Halford Mackinder, described the area as 'the heartland of Eurasia' and the 'geographical pivot of history.'[1] The country's location between four potentially wealthy but volatile and conflict ridden regions- Central Asia, the Middle East, South Asia and the Far East – endows it with extremely important geostrategic assets. Yet the Afghan instability, which has remained prevalent since the 1979 Soviet intervention, has prevented it from garnering the benefits out of this geographical situation. Although there are many players in Afghanistan, Pakistan has been one of the most important due to its variety of proximity and divergences with Afghanistan. Pakistan's Afghan policy has become extraordinarily important in the backdrop of NATO withdrawal by the end of 2014. This paper is intended to analyse these issues in detail.

By the end of 2014, NATO forces intend to withdraw from Afghanistan. NATO may leave behind some forces for imparting military training to the Afghan National Army (ANA) and this has been confirmed by the new President Ashraf Ghani. He has taken over in October 2014. In the meanwhile the number of armed forces has increased phenomenally. In the later part of 2013 the ANA had 1,87,000 soldiers and combined with Afghan police etc. their strength stood around 3,50,000. The new President intends to allow NATO forces to play a supportive role for the ANA after 2014. Since June 2013, the ANA however has taken over the security operations in all the thirty four provinces and NATO forces are supporting the ANA to contain the Taliban.

Pakistan never had peace with Afghanistan right from its inception till the 1979 Soviet intervention. Pakhtunistan remains a bone of contention between both countries. Although the Afghan rulers accepted Durand Line (1893), that cuts through the Pashtun homeland, they never really have given up their claims on 'Pashtunistan', the area right of the Indus.[2] The tribal areas along the Afghan border had retained a semi-independent status and were administered by political agents.[3] Before the First World War, Afghanistan had been an apple of discord between the British Empire and the Czarist Russia. After the bifurcation of United India in 1947 these areas are called Federal Administrated Tribal Areas (FATA) and remain turbulent even today. The leftover fighters after the withdrawal of the Soviet army in 1990 got holed up here and even today due to strategic and tough terrain of the area, have remained here. Since October 2001, the NATO forces have launched 'Operation Enduring Freedom' against the Taliban and Al-Qaeda and these leftover fighters were recruited throughout the Afghan Jihad era (1979-1990) and their next generation fought bitterly against the NATO forces and undermined NATO initiative for a peaceful and prosperous Afghanistan. Although Pakistan government kept promising the NATO forces that it is serious to erase these safe havens which are the breeding ground of international terror from this area but till recently it remains merely lip service. Sartaz Aziz, National Security Adviser of PM Nawaz Sharif, has stated about terror groups active in Afghanistan (November 2014) while giving an interview to BBC Urdu that "Some of them are dangerous for us and some are not. Why must we make enemies out of them all?", said he while speaking about the Haqqani Network.[4] He further said that, "The Afghan Taliban are Afghanistan's problem and Haqqani Network is a part of it."

In fact, Pakistan has extended sanctuary to the Haqqani group and used them as an asset to target Indian installations and keep Afghanistan destabilised. This group has been involved in the many attacks on Indian establishments in Afghanistan. Indian PM Narendra Modi had invited all SAARC leaders in May 2014 to his swearing in ceremony and after initial opposition from the Pakistan army Pakistani PM Nawaz Sharif's arrival was announced. But in the meanwhile Indian consulate at Herat near the Iran border was attacked. Later on international intelligence agencies identified Pakistani connection to this attack. After Mumbai carnage it was one of the worst attacks on an Indian establishment outside India. Fortunately only nominal casualty was suffered in this attack. Why was Herat attack planned when Pakistani PM Nawaz Sharif had already announced his New Delhi visit? A report by the US Department of Defence alleged Pakistan for "using proxy forces to hedge against the loss of influence in Afghanistan and to counter India's superior military"; this comment elicited a sharp response from Pakistan.[5]

Army Chief of Pakistan - Gen Raheel Sharif visited the US in November 2014, following an equally important visit to

Afghanistan in the first week of November 2014, it has been reported that in these visits Pakistan- an important military ally of the US, was deliberately snubbed. Pakistan has at long last launched a military operation in North Waziristan and has consistently asserted in recent months that the long-term goal is to eliminate all terrorist and militant sanctuaries on Pakistani soil. COAS, General Sharif accused India (during his November 2014 US visit) of not cooperating on Afghan front.

We could recall Kargil in this regard to understand this tango. It did happen because our PM, A.B. Vajpayee visited Lahore and inked the 'Lahore Declaration'. It was the first instrument after the 1971 Shimla agreement, which insisted about the bilateral mechanism to resolve bilateral issues including the core issue of Kashmir. Pakistani army was apprehensive that if Vajpayee visit goes well, it could lose its leverage from the corridor of power. In her recent book - *'The Wrong Enemy; America in Afghanistan 2001-2004'*, senior American journalist Carlotta Gall, who has spent ten years in Afghanistan has concluded that, "The embassy bombing (Indian Embassy, 2008 attack) was an operation by rogue ISI agents acting on their own. It was sanctioned and monitored by the seniormost officials in Pakistani intelligence." The evidence was so damning that the Bush administration dispatched the deputy chief of the CIA, Stephen Kappes, to Islamabad to remonstrate Pakistanis. The bomber struck before Kappes reached Islamabad. Gall writes, "Investigators found the bomber's cell phone in the wreckage of his exploded car. They tracked down his collaborators in Kabul, the man who had provided the logistics for the attack. The facilitator, an Afghan, had been in direct contact with Pakistan by telephone."[6] According to Gall, as the Afghan government investigated the attack, they became convinced that, "the ISI was working with Al Qaeda, the Taliban, the Haqqanis, and Pakistani groups such as Lashkar-e-Taiba for this attack". Gall concludes, "At the core of Pakistan's thinking was an obsessive desire to dominate Afghanistan in order to protect its own rear flank from India. In that way of thinking, the Taliban were guarantors of Pakistan's national strategic interests."[7] For the Pakistani army, Haqqani group is a favourite among all the other groups. During the last thirteen years India has been actively extending all round support for the reconstruction process of

Afghanistan. Pakistani army has been jealous of the growing Indian imprint and has engineered terror attacks on Indian establishments through Haqqani group and other state sympathetic groups like LET in Afghanistan. Haqqani group have been detrimental for the NATO force also and inflicted collateral damage on it. Speaking at a security forum in Colorado in the last week of July 2014, John Allen, the retired four-star general who led US and NATO forces in Afghanistan, voiced scepticism about Islamabad's past willingness to go after the Haqqanis, even as he acknowledged the opportunity presented by the ongoing offensive going on in North Waziristan.

"When I was commander there, the Haqqani killed or wounded over 500 of my troops, and the operations in Waziristan somehow missed them every time they conducted ops on the eastern side of the border".[8] In this conference Afghan Ambassador Eklil Hakimi, stated his information which suggested that Haqqani militants had safe passage inside Pakistan and were going elsewhere inside Pakistan.[9] United States urged Pakistan not to allow Haqqani fighters to escape but to target them during the ongoing military operation in North Waziristan; otherwise it is bound to lose US assistance. .

Since the last thirteen years, India has been among the top five contributors in the reconstruction of Afghanistan. From 2002 to 2010, New Delhi pledged $ 1.2 billion for the reconstruction and provision of humanitarian assistance to the country, of which $ 759 million has since been disbursed on highly visible projects.[10] It has built many infrastructure proects and provided transportation and key power assistance. India has also constructed Zaranj–Delaram road in western Afghanistan which connects Irani port of Chahbahar to Central Asia through Afghanistan. Through this route, Afghanistan has another outlet to the sea and in addition it has reduced its dependence on the same over Pakistan. Other schemes include the construction of electricity lines from Uzbekistan to eastern Afghanistan under the NEPS scheme, the new Afghan parliament and additional roads. In November 2011, an Indian consortium led by the state owned SAIL secured a mining contract for the Hajigak iron ore deposit, the largest such deposits in Asia, in the central Afghan province of Bamiyan. India is expected to invest $ 10 billion in Afghanistan over the next thirty years, and this has significant implications for the strengthening of relations between the two states.[11] Such cooperation was predicted from the overtures made by Karzai to the Indian government for providing it military aid under the 2011 Afghan-India strategic partnership agreement, a move that has further piqued Islamabad.[12] This has been accepted by the eminent Pakistani Afghan expert, Ahmed Rashid also. Pakistan is apprehensive that growing Indian presence in Afghanistan is intended to pursue anti-Pakistani activities, but somewhere it is again a miscalculation on Pakistan's part.

In November 2011 CBS poll, a majority of Americans said that Pakistan is either unfriendly (39 per cent) or an enemy (24 per cent). Only 2 per cent called it an ally.[13] For their part, Pakistanis don't see the relationship as healthy. The June 2011, Pew Research poll showed that most Pakistanis see the United States as an enemy and a potential threat to their country's security.[14] On the one hand, since joining hands in late 2001, Washington has been praising Islamabad for its commitment and sacrifice of more than 4,500 military personnel and as many as 45,000 Pakistani civilians in the "war against terror." In 2011, soon after the killing of Osama bin Laden inside Pakistan, President Barack Obama said, "We have been able to kill more terrorists on Pakistani soil than just about any place else. We could not have done that without Pakistani cooperation."[15] On the other hand, American officials have suspected and often accused the Pakistani military of supporting militant groups, particularly the Afghan Taliban. Although Washington and Islamabad have never been on the same page since 9/11, both sides have always made an effort to maintain their ties. This scenario has developed a status which could be termed as 'trust deficit' between both US and Pakistan. In its decade old experience, the US has realised that Pakistan is part of the problem and not part of the solution in Afghanistan. The parochial prism of the Pakistani army about Afghanistan is still dominant in the power corridor despite seven years of post-military democratic governance. The military has jealously guarded its stance on Afghanistan. It is the holy cow for the sustainability of the dominance of the army over the ruling civilian oligarchy. Former Pakistani PM, Yusuf Raza Gillani had once stated during his official tenure as PM (2008-2012) that "Pakistani army is not within the Pakistani state but Pakistani state is within the

Pakistani army." This tendency remains a bone of contention between civilian - military trust deficit. Former Secretary General of the United Nations, Boutros Boutros Ghali has carried out a comprehensive study on the interlinking democracy and the military. The central argument of his findings is that in those societies where military is powerful, democracy could not sustain for a long time merely because both can't survive together. Pakistan is perhaps a classic country suited for his thesis.

Pakistani military therefore will not allow Afghanistan to stabilise. In the scenario of the backdrop of NATO forces the Afghan people and the international community is anxious about the post-withdrawal security situation. Nawaz Sharif is in power and his past has given anxiety to Afghan people. Interestingly, many Afghans are also uncomfortable with the return of Nawaz Sharif as Pakistan's Premier. One of Nawaz Sharif's 1993 election campaign slogans (targeting the Pakistan People's Party at that time) was 'You gave up Dhaka, we took Kabul'. Till today, these words are recalled with equal dismay and honour by Afghans.[16] Nawaz Sharif was basically planted as a stooge by military dictator, General Zia-Ul-Haq to contain the might of the then PM, Mohhamad Khan Junejo. Later on military extended covert support to him to contain Pakistan People's Party and its leader, Benazir Bhutto particularly during the civilian interlude during 1988-1999. Due to sustained protest and demand for his resignation by the opposition comprising PTI led by Imran Khan and PTI led by Maulana Qadri, he has become weak and practically in the prevailing scenario Afghan policy will be formulated and implemented by the army.

Pakistan feels insecure with the deepening Indian interests in Afghanistan. Herat attack was a fresh testimony of that mindset. These kinds of attack will be occurring in future as well. It was basically a provocative attack engineered by the military to derail any initial bonhomie between PM Modi and Nawaz Sharif.

The Pakistan government has launched a military operation called 'Zerb-A- Herb' in North Waziristan in FATA in June 2014 to remove these terror groups in the aftermath of terror attack on Karachi airport in June 2014. The NATO forces have already announced that they will withdraw by the end of 2014. In this backdrop an operation to remove terror elements in one of the most suitable place for the Jihad factory is not going to yield any purpose. As discussed above the most dangerous terror outfits like Haqqani, LeT etc. have been protected by the Pakistani army as an asset. These groups have been instrumental to the army to sustain bloodshed in India and Afghanistan. These groups have been provided 'Safe Passage' even during the so-called military operations.

As I have already stated Afghanistan never accepted Durand Line as legitimate border line between both countries. Even the Taliban regime, which was promoted by Pakistan (1996-2001), refused to accept it and its take on the line was that, "a Muslim does not require to obtain visa to visit another Muslim country". Right from independence, Pakistan has perceived Afghanistan as courtyard which is providing it 'strategic depth' vis-à-vis India, while India supports Afghanistan in order to sandwich Pakistan from the western side. It is also an open secret that this prevailing proxy war in Afghanistan has been the biggest stumbling block to more intense economic relations between South and Central Asia. Networks of gas pipelines are also not established despite hectic efforts between South and Central Asia due to prevailing anarchy in Pakistan and Afghanistan. The connectivity by road and rail between South and Central Asia would have been yielding enormous economic dividends for both India and Pakistan. This is well argued by Hussian Haqaani, former Pakistani Ambassador to the United States, "The Policy tripod I wrote about has become less sustainable. Among the factors that have changed is the stress within Pakistan. The issue of India as an eternal enemy has come under a lot of strain. Before the Bin Laden raid, Pakistan was a subject discussed only among American foreign policy experts. Now Pakistan has become part of the American pop culture. Pakistan's elite should embrace a new liberal paradigm. There is no eternal enemy of Pakistan, there is no existential threat to Pakistan, it should maintain an effective military, it should maintain a minimum nuclear deterrent, and after that it should focus on educating its people. Put their 48 per cent children who do not go to school into schools, open up the economy, organise agriculture, create jobs and take advantage of being at the centre of trade ties from India to Central Asia, from Iran to India, from the Middle East to India and China. For the last 66 years, the elite have thought that Pakistan is strategically important because it sits at the crossroads of conflict. I say that Pakistan should now look at itself as sitting at the crossroads of opportunity."[17]

It seems that the sagacious advice of Ambassador Haqaani has not been duly taken by the Pakistani security establishment. Pakistan must learn a lesson that a weak Afghanistan will be detrimental for its own stability and prosperity.

The sustainability of NATO operation since last thirteen years in Afghanistan has further exposed Pakistan. In the meanwhile due to this operation terror factory has shifted to Pakistan and created a huge loss to people and economy, to contain this threat, Pakistan promoted political Islam in Afghanistan and thus tried to remain an important player. It is also an open secret that the 2014 Pakistan is not the 1979 Pakistan. It has become not only weak by losing 55,000 people and 6,500 soldiers in their home grown insurgency but also by all counts it is a crumbling state. The United States has poured $ 30 billion[18] in Pakistan since the onset of Operation Enduring Freedom till July 2014, but Pakistan is not cooperating adequately. Few of America's bilateral ties have been as fraught as those with Pakistan.[19] Despite all round support by the United States, the country has provided safe haven to the Taliban at Quetta and Haqqanis in FATA. The elimination of Osama bin Laden in May 2011 at Abbotabad vindicates the fact.

According to a book *Duty; Memories of a Secretary at War*, written by former US Defence secretary Robert Gates, "I gave him a list of specific actions we wanted Pakistan to take. The US also instructed Musharraf to disrupt certain major infiltration routes across the border; enhance intelligence cooperation and streamline Pakistani decision-making on targeting. Musharraf kept a straight face and pretended to take all this seriously."[20]

Pakistan has used all negative means to keep Afghanistan turbulent despite international community's consistent request to contribute positively. Today Pakistan is one of the most hated countries in Afghanistan.[21] This hostility is no longer confined to the Northern Alliance or elements in the Afghan government, but now runs so deep that most Afghans have stopped differentiating between Pakistan's military and the general population.[22]

Since last many decades Pakistan has used terror as an instrument of its foreign policy and has intended to sustain it. Destabilisation in Afghanistan is a must for the pursuance of this project. Given the situation, it seems that Pakistan will not cooperate to stabilise Afghanistan because its all powerful Army feels that it could convert Afghanistan again as its courtyard and thus achieve the 'Doctrine of Strategic Depth' against India. In 1988 November, Benazir Bhutto was elected PM of Pakistan after a general election in the aftermath of the General Zia-Ul-Haq's plane crash in August 1988. But the army first took three assurances from her then only she was allowed to enter into the corridor of power. These three assurances were that Kashmir, Afghanistan and nuclear policy will not be changed and military will be allowed to pursue it. Since March 2008, civilian regimes are ruling over Pakistan but still they are not autonomous to take their own decision on the Afghan front. Army has always considered Afghanistan as an instrument to sustain its monopoly over power. Of course, Kashmir is also connected with the project because their dominance over Afghanistan is intended to create anarchy in Kashmir. Despite seven years of present democratic rule there are certain limitations of elected regimes in Pakistan and they cannot bypass the army's dictate while formulating any policies about Afghanistan and Kashmir.[23] Therefore a trust deficit is prevailing between the army and the civilian dispensation on these critical issues. Civil-military trust deficit in Pakistan on Afghan affairs has also reduced the space of positive role for Pakistan. It intends to sustain the Hobbesian state of nature in Afghanistan. For this particular project of the military a stable and peaceful Afghanistan could be detrimental therefore they are compelled to keep Afghanistan volatile.

It may be safely said that despite all round destruction by home grown Jihad factory, Pakistan perhaps will not change its old Afghan policy. To cope with the situation the Modi government has to reformulate its policies to ensure attainment of national interests.

Policy Options for India

Afghan society has already witnessed rampant violence since the last three and half decades. There is hardly any Afghan family today which is not either led by a widow or a disabled. It is high time to establish peace and stability. Afghan people are ready. Only Pakistan needs to be prevented both by persuasion and arm twisting against destabilising Afghanistan. International community needs to be present in Afghanistan with a gamut of reconstruction efforts. It could stretch to decades. Since the last three and half decades the efforts have been shaky due to the power game of the stakeholding nations. For a stabilisation process to set in, another decade post-withdrawal of the NATO forces is required. Since 2001, the NATO forces had engaged in "Operation Enduring Freedom" and somehow security situation has improved comparatively. With all round reconstruction efforts, Afghanistan may stabilise within the next decade. If this happens then it will be a great help to bolster peace and prosperity in not only South, Central and South West Asia but the entire globe.

For the last three and half decades Afghanistan has remained a den of international terror. It could have been a heaven of peace and stability through consistent and collective international efforts. Due to geographical proximity the support of Pakistan would be crucial for the stabilisation of this war torn and devastated country. Bypassing Pakistan may be possible if India reformulates its strategy to cope up with the post-2014 NATO withdrawal situation. India has to understand in clear terms that in case Taliban takes over or gains dominance in Afghanistan, Pakistan will be in a dominating situation which has been denied to it by the thirteen year long NATO operation. In this scenario it is possible that a new wave of terror will prevail particularly in Kashmir because the leftover Afghan *jihadis* may be diverted towards Kashmir. Pakistan is struggling with the civil-military cold war. In the backdrop of the NATO withdrawal the military will wish to dominate power structure of Pakistan covertly or overtly. For that project, Kashmir needs to boil. Despite relative peace in Kashmir since last one decade the seed of unrest is prevailing and it can be ignited again by way of provocations. Needless to say that such a situation will have an imprint on the rest of the country as well. Therefore, peace and prosperity in Afghanistan is a must for sustainable development in India.

Since the end of the cold war, India has done well by all counts and has been considered as a force to reckon with. NDA-1 regime denoted atomic weapons and demonstrated its power to the entire globe. This event proved positive for Indian strategic calculations because traditionally India is considered as a shy emerging global power. Today India's status is rising. It has a GDP of $ 1.8 trillion,[24] a projected GDP growth rate of seven per cent in the fiscal year of 2014-15,[25] a 46.8 billion dollar defence budget, a nuclear stockpile of more than 80 warheads and ballistic missiles,[26] a newly built aircraft carrier,[27] and expectations that by 2020 it will overtake Japan, France and Britain to become the world's fourth largest military spender.[28]

As Kautilya had stated that a country must demonstrate its capability to secure its border, India must secure its border from the incoming terror onslaughts. For that, besides strengthening its external and internal security system it also requires to solicit the support of the like-minded countries. China has all weather relationship status with Pakistan but the Chinese western province of Xinjiang is also infested with terror which also has linkages with the Afghan Jihad. India needs to garner Chinese support as well because besides the security threats from terror networks based in AF-PAK, China also has commercial interests in this region. Russia is one of the worst sufferers of the reign of terror and therefore we must solicit Russian support as well. Russia was part and parcel of the Northern Alliance support mission against the Taliban along with Iran and India during the Taliban regime in Afghanistan. In the backdrop of the IS advances in Syria and Iraq, threat is knocking on the door of Iran. The Central Asian Republics are also extremely vulnerable because of weak governance and presence of IMU and drug trafficking. The Taliban have been connected with the IMU and in the June 2014 attack on Karachi's Jinnah airport, Pakistani authorities have identified both Uighurs and the IMU terrorists among the attackers.

The western powers led by the United States are equally concerned for peace and prosperity in Afghanistan. They have learnt a lesson that until Afghanistan stabilises they cannot also remain in peace. By early 2012, Pakistan's repeated and deliberate efforts to undercut US policies had clearly prompted US officials to reconsider the value of the overall security partnership with Islamabad. This became clear when Secretary of Defence Leon Panetta, during a June 2012 trip to Afghanistan and India, issued Washington's starkest criticism yet uttered against Pakistan and pointedly stated that Washington was "reaching the limits of (its) patience" with Islamabad's refusal to crack down on terrorist safe havens operating in its territory.[29]

Panetta further noted India's positive contributions to Afghanistan's economic and commercial development and, arguably and more significantly, expressed support for Delhi's training programme of Afghanistan's nascent armed forces and encouraged it to continue with this security assistance mission. Panetta's implicit nod to Indian military engagement in Afghanistan represented a significant shift in US policy away from Pakistan and an acknowledgment that Delhi had more to offer in terms of promoting Afghanistan's internal stability. The United States has already delinked its Pakistan policy from Indian policy and this was vindicated by 2010 visit of President Obama, when he visited New Delhi but avoided Islamabad. The tendency is sustainable due to wider convergences of interests between India and the United States on the larger canvas of the Asia-Pacific. Foreign secretary, John Kerry visited New Delhi in July 2014 and expressed his desire to sustain the process. Prime Minister, Narendra Modi has strengthened this process through his Washington visit in September 2014 and President Obama has indicated enough to sustain the process. It is a new beginning after a small thaw in bilateral relations of both countries in last few years of UPA-2. (2009-2014)

We need to solicit the support of all concerned to stabilise Afghanistan and prevent Iraq type situation there.

Eminent Indian security analyst, Raj Mohan has rightly stated in November 2013, "Any nuclear deal between Washington and Tehran will immediately bring down oil prices, relieve the current macroeconomic pressures on India and improve Delhi's energy security calculus over the longer term. US – Iran rapprochement will help to strengthen Afghanistan against the Taliban and Pakistan and expand India's room for regional manoeuvre after 2014".[30] The interim deal between Washington and Tehran has already been concluded and it is time when Indian diplomacy must act and bring Iran and United States on the same page to ensure peace and stability in Afghanistan. Iran has also contributed huge resources in the reconstruction of Afghanistan. During 2002-2010, Tehran pledged $ 673 million, most of which has been spent on infrastructural development in western Afghanistan.[31] Iran is an important player and part and parcel of the efforts to contain Taliban during its rule over Afghanistan (1996-2001), along with India, Russia and Central Asian Republics. Although Pakistan has been increasingly jealous of the growing Indian and Iranian involvement in Afghanistan, it is nowhere in a position to contribute to match these contributions by India and Iran.

Global balance of power has played and is still playing its devastating role in this war torn country since centuries. But the regional rivalry has also spoiled the situation. In November 2014, the new Afghan President, Ashraf Ghani, visited Islamabad and had a long delegation level meeting with Pakistani PM, Nawaz Sharif, but despite that there is little hope that Pakistan will become part of the solution of the Afghan problem. Pakistan is an important neighbour of Afghanistan but despite part and parcel of global war against terror it has not collaborated properly and instead has worked with the tacit collaboration of Haqqani networks and others to keep Afghanistan volatile. As part of this approach, Pakistan has been more eager to see that regional cooperation processes and projects are shaped in ways that make Kabul economically and strategically dependent on Islamabad than to enable Afghanistan to emerge as a regional player in its own right.[32] While seeking to secure strong leverage in Afghanistan in order to control the nation's politics after the withdrawal of the NATO, Pakistan has also sought to deprive its regional rival, India, of any significant foothold in the country, and to check what it perceives as Iran's regional ambitions. Pakistani democracy remains fragile and subject to the military's manipulations. The Sharif government is too weak to move forward with serious talks with India. There will be definitely an attempt by the Taliban and their backers to grab power as they did in the chaos following the Soviet withdrawal".[33] Elements within the Pakistani military have been sympathetic to the Taliban resurgence in Afghanistan and turbulence in Kashmir, both as a means of self-preservation and to enhancement of Pakistan's leverage in a complex and unpredictable region. Sharif seems to have recognised that Pakistan's stability and security are critically linked with Afghanistan and India, but as vindicated from prevailing situation PM Nawaz Sharif is unable to convince the army that a stable Afghanistan is in the larger interests of

Pakistan too. Therefore it is crystal clear that Pakistani army and their stooges will try their level best to capture power in Kabul. Pakistani military, however, has become weak due to the sustained volatile domestic situation but as an institution it is unlikely to accept Sharif's wish over both the critical issues. Pakistani Military also protested Sharif's participation in the swearing in ceremony of Indian PM, Narendra Modi.

Pakistan's Afghan policy is decided by the military. Given the prevailing security architecture of South and South West Asia, it seems unlikely that military will allow any stabilisation in Afghanistan. Needless to say those situations in Afghanistan will determine security architecture of India, South, and Central Asia and will also make an imprint on global peace. India must take all possible steps to ensure peace and stability with tacit understanding with like-minded countries in Afghanistan. It will be a marathon litmus test for the Modi led NDA-2 Government.

Notes

1. H.J. Mackinder, (1904) 'The Geographical Pivot of History,' *Geographical Journal*, Vol. 23, No. 4, April-1904.
2. The last British governor of the NWFP sees it differently, referring to documents from 1893 to 1956 concerning the Durand. Caroe, Olf Kirkpatrick (1976) *The Pathans 550 B.C-A.D 1957*, Karachi, Oxford, p. 466.
3. The rulers of the Princely states of Swat, Dir, Chitral, and Amb joined Pakistan shortly after independence but not the Khan of Kalat, who wanted to remain independent, Baloch, Inayatullah (1987). *The Problem of Greater Baluchistan, A Study of Baluch Nationalism.*
4. Militants not dangerous to Pakistan should not be targeted: Sartaj Dawn, Karachi, 18 November 2014.
5. Pentagon's view, (7 November 2014) Dawn Editorial, Karachi.
6. Lalit K. Jha, (24 March, 2014) ISI executed Kabul Indian Embassy attack, US couldn't stop it, *The Indian Express,* New Delhi.
7. *Ibid.*
8. Do not let Haqqani fighters resettle, (26 July 2014) US tells Pakistan, *Reuters.*
9. *Ibid.*
10. Afghan Ministry of Finance (2010), *Development Cooperation Report*, Kabul, p. 95.
11. Etlaf Najafizada, (6 December 2011) 'Indian Group Wins Rights to Mine in Afghanistan's Hajigak, *Bloomberg Businessweek*.

12. Hamid Shalizi, (19 May 2013) Afghanistan's Karzai seeks Indian Military Aid Amid Tensions with Pakistan , *Reuters*.
13. "Poll: Americans' views on foreign policy," (11 November 2011) *CBS News*.
14. "US Image in Pakistan Falls No Further Following bin Laden Killing,"
15. "Obama: (8 May 2011) US, Pakistan Can Find Ways to Improve Cooperation."
16. Hina Baloch, (28 January 2014) Afghans and Pakistanis; friends turned foes?, *Dawn*, Karachi.
17. The Idea Exchange, (20 October 2013) *Indian Express,* New Delhi.
18. C. Fair, (27 July 2014) *Times of India*, New Delhi.
19. Sumit Ganguly, (April 2014) "The Pathological Alliance", *Current History,* p. 165.
20. Mushraaf refused to act Against Al-Qaeda, (12 January 2014) Taliban; US ex-defense secretary, PTI, *The Indian Express*, New Delhi, p. 12.
21. Dr Pervez Hoodbhoy, (18 March 2012) "What Pakistan should do in Afghanistan?," *Express Tribune,* Lahore.
22. "Helmand despatch: (1 August 2010) "Pakistan is the true enemy," *Daily Telegraph*, London.
23. Singh, Sudhir, (2013) Limits of Electoral Mandate in Pakistan, *Politico,* Vol. 1, p. 67.
24. World Bank, India, http;//data.worldbank.org/country/india
25. India's GDP growth Forecast to 6 percent for FY 14; (13 August 2013) Credit Suisse, "The *Financial Express,* New Delhi.
26. India as a Great Power; (30 March 2013) Know Your Strength, *The Economist*. .
27. Indian-Built Aircraft Carrier INS Vikrant Launched, (12 August 2013) *BBC*.
28. The Idea Exchange, (20 October 2013) *Indian Express,* New Delhi.
29. Jim Garamone, (7 June 2012) "US Reaching Limit of Patience with Pakistan on Safe Havens," *American Forces Press Service*.
30. C. Raja Mohan, (20 November 2013) The Great Game Folio, *The Indian Express,* New Delhi.
31. *Op. cit.*, No. 6.
32. Mary Anne Weaver, (2002) Pakistan; *In the Shadow of Jihad and Afghanistan,* Farrar, New York.
33. Military pushing Imran Khan-Nawaz govt. too weak for talks, (22 August 2014) *Times of India,* New Delhi.

15

Post-2014: Likely Relapse of Afghanistan to Terrorism? India's Options

P.G. KAMATH

Historical Perspective

Afghanistan has been called the Heart of Asia. It is the geographical centre of Asia and the junction where Eurasia, Middle East, Central Asia, South Asia and Sinkiang meet. Civilisations have criss-crossed this turbulent country for several thousands of years and no outsiders could ever rule it in the correct sense of the word. The Greeks, Persians, Mauryans, Kushans, Mongols, Turks, British, Sikhs, Soviets and Pakistanis (Taliban) have come and gone and now the Americans are about to go. Afghanistan is indeed called the 'Roundabout in History' and has been aptly described along with Vietnam as 'the fabled graveyard of empires'.[1]

The British in the First Afghan War had made the mistake of installing an unpopular Shuja Shah Durrani as the Emir of Afghanistan. The British, satisfied that the country would not come under the Russian influence, withdrew the entire Army of 16,500 from Kabul to Jalalabad in Jan. 1842. Their rout was monumental and complete. The entire army was decimated save for one British surgeon, who reached the safety of the British Garrison at Jalalabad.[2] Shuja Shah Durrani was also assassinated. The Soviets when they invaded Afghanistan had also installed Babarak Karmal, a local puppet who was exiled to Moscow, in favour of Najibullah - another puppet of their choice as the President of Afghanistan. Ultimately, when the Soviets left they also left behind chaos and an intense civil war. Mujahedeen entered Kabul in 1992 and Najibullah took refuge in UN compound for four years. Ultimately his body was found hanging from a traffic light in Kabul on 27 Sep 1996; the Taliban had tortured and killed him.

The Soviet withdrawal was the handiwork of the US, Pakistan and the Mujahedeen. The Americans were known to have given $40 billion in addition to other weapons and equipment and 2000 stinger shoulder-fired Surface-to-Air Missiles.[3] Lt Gen Akhtar Abdur Rehman the ISI Chief was directly conceiving and controlling the operations.[4] It was hailed as an Islamic victory–a victory for Jihad and defeat of a superpower by Islamic freedom fighters. There is a grave danger of misinterpreting the US withdrawal as victory for Jihad, such thinking will again make the *jihadi*sts claim victory over another superpower and boost their morale. The release of five Taliban prisoners from Guantanamo Bay in exchange for Sgt Bowe Bergdahl is another indicator of the Super Power having yielded to terrorists, indeed a first sign of soft state in the making. Already Mullah Mohammed Omar, the Taliban Chief has hailed the release as a great victory.[5] The likely relapse into civil war and subsequently the country becoming a sanctuary for the Al Qaida would indeed strengthen the clout of the Jihadists who would then claim to have achieved a total victory for the cause of Jihad.

Afghans are brave and fiercely independent people and would not accept any foreign hand in determining their future. There is a saying that an Afghan is at peace only when he is at war. If anyone is to replace an emir in Afghanistan, it will have to be the people of Afghanistan themselves. The British and the Soviets have learnt it the hard way.

The Americans have been more prudent in handling the country's affairs. They had planned to leave behind a President elected by the will of the people. The runoff between the two presidential candidates was most unfortunate as it has got stuck into rough weather. Though the Independent Election

Commission has declared Ashraf Ghani as the winner, the rival Abdullah Abdullah has threatened to form a parallel government alleging industrial scale fraud. With over 1.3 million more votes cast in the runoff than in the first phase of election and with some of the ballot papers without the signature of the voters, Abdullah Abdullah's claims do not look unjustified. US Secretary of State John Kerry brokered a deal to audit all the 8.1 million votes and meanwhile both the candidates were asked to enter into a power sharing agreement which was accepted by them. The power sharing again would need a constitutional amendment. The path to a stable government seems indeed tortuous. With some hiccups the auditing is continuing, however political uncertainty prevails in Afghanistan.

As and when the government is formed, should one of the candidates express discontent the entire process will be misconstrued as American manipulation to foist a President of their choice on the Afghan people and whoever the President can go the same way as Shah Shuja or Najibullah and the resultant Civil War would be ideal for restoration of Taliban and return of Al Qaeda. Hence, it is most important that the legitimacy of the government formation is accepted by the Afghan people and the two contesting candidates.

It is the longest war the Americans have ever fought. After investing over six trillion dollars[6] as cost of Iraq and Afghanistan wars it would be irresponsible, if not outright foolish, to leave the country in a civil war and thereby create conditions for safe return of Al Qaeda; the raison d' etre of their initial intervention. President Barack Obama in his West Point address in the last week of May 2014 said that he had got an assurance from both the prospective presidential candidates, who are tipped for a rerun, that they would sign the Bilateral Security Agreement with USA and he would keep 9800 American troops by the end of 2014 and will ultimately withdraw all of them in 2016[7] before the end of his presidency, a promise he made during his election.

Scenarios

Post-American withdrawal, what would be the situation in Afghanistan? Will it relapse into a civil war, or would Afghanistan surprise the world by a stable democracy? Will the US, NATO and the world watch Afghanistan relapse into civil war and become a sanctuary to the Al Qaeda to pursue their agenda of turning the world into an Islamic Caliphate? Obviously not, it is the collective responsibility of the world at large that Afghanistan becomes a stable state to pursue her policies as per the will of her people. We will examine different scenarios which could emerge and what Afghanistan, the world at large and India need to do in pursuance of global interests.

Scenario 1: Civil War in Afghanistan

Its proof is in history that as and when occupying foreign regimes have left Afghanistan the country has hurtled towards Civil War. It happened during the First Afghan War. It happened after the Russians left and could happen again after the Americans leave.

Not surprisingly there are differences in the end states sought by Soviets and Americans in Afghanistan: The Soviets wanted stoppage of all hostilities on Afghan borders and non-interference in its internal affairs by outside countries and to ensure its non-aligned status before pulling out of Afghanistan[8]. Not surprisingly, the Americans forced their entry into Afghanistan to ensure that the country should be cleansed of 'Al Qaida' and they never again use Afghanistan to launch attacks against America.[9] One could blame the Soviets for entering Afghanistan, supposedly on an invitation from government? The American entered as a retaliation to the 9/11 incident after tracing the conceiver of the plan, Osama bin Laden, to Tora Bora Caves in Afghanistan.

Secondly, once the Russians withdrew in Feb 1989, the Mujahedeen took over the rural part of the country and entered Kabul in 1992. As per Peshawar Accord 'Islamic State of Afghanistan' was established. Pakistan was not happy with the end state. She started training Islamic fighters under the 'Taliban philosophy'. They were unleashed into Afghanistan, and took over the lawless countryside and entered Kabul in 1996. Unlike the Taliban, the Al Qaida residing in Afghanistan had harboured international ambition. Their ambition culminated in 9/11 incident and its aftermath proved very costly for the Osama bin Laden and Al Qaida and posed an existential threat to him and his organisation.

The Taliban would demand their price in kind for giving Al Qaida a safe sanctuary. Two days prior to 9/11, Al Qaida carried out the assassination of Ahmad Shah Massoud as the necessary pay back to the Taliban for giving them a safe haven in Afghanistan. They had withstood the intense pressure of the Americans to hand over Osama who had masterminded the embassy bombings in Tanzania and Kenya and subsequently 9/11.

The Soviets, who were war weary and ripe for disintegration then, failed to appreciate the situation in Afghanistan after their withdrawal. Even if they had, they were not inclined to do much, as the withdrawal was the only face-saving option, which they readily clutched at before it disappeared in the molten state of world's 'real politik'. Post-US withdrawal, with Al Qaida waiting to enter the fray and with little chance of Northern Alliance sans a person like Ahmad Shah Massoud's calibre holding out, would Afghanistan relapse into complete take over by Taliban? The Americans are leaving behind a 'Training and Assistance Force' of 9800 till end 2016, which would definitely delay if not deny an early takeover by Taliban.

In the earlier instance the arrival of Osama bin Laden from Sudan to Afghanistan with his son on a special plane in May 1996, symbolised the Prophets *hijra* from Mecca to Medina[10]. Symbolism is important as Osama a devout Muslim had got an opportunity to re-enact Prophet's *hijra* with a view to appealing to the believers to come and join him to liberate Islam across the world from its perceived subjugation and suppression by waging the Holy War of Jihad. The appeal was well received and 'Al Qaida' grew strong and spread in Middle East, Africa, Maghreb and South East Asia. It was strongest during the period of 9/11.

Presently the Al Qaida has lost its founder 'Osama bin Laden' following Operation Geronimo, and now Al Zawahiri is the current leader. He and his headquarters have moved to Pakistan. Should he return to Afghanistan from Pakistan, the symbolic *Hijra* would be re-enacted for the third time.

Currently the Afghan Taliban are under training and shelter in Baluchistan under the aegis of the ISI, and Pakistan would certainly want to re-enact what they had done post-Soviet withdrawal. If the Afghan Taliban takes over the country under Mullah Omar, the situation would be ideal for Pakistan and also would ensure the safe return of Al Qaida. A literal 'back to square one' situation after thirteen years of war and trillions of dollars down the drain besides loss of over 3441 lives[11] and other casualties adding to over 20,000.[12] It would be a classic case of rout of an Eliphinstonian scale. No responsible government in the US would ever like such a situation to emerge with an additional disadvantage of giving a 'walk over' to the Democrats in 2017 US elections.

Regime only in Kabul and a Few Cities and Rural Countryside under Taliban

In this scenario it is possible the formal government writ runs only in Kabul and a few cities and the rural countryside relapses into chaos and strife. The Afghan Taliban encouraged and supported by Pakistan would slowly take over the rural countryside and would enforce Sharia. Sharia is one law that the Muslims cannot protest, in doing so they could be charged with blasphemy. It is a Catch-22 situation and most fall in line for the diktats of the draconian law. Rural Afghanistan falling back to medieval age with Kabul and other cities slowly slipping out of control in the long run is the possibility that cannot be ruled out. It will do well for the ANSF to keep their domination in the countryside as well. The local chieftains and tribal heads owing their allegiance to Taliban and Al Qaida have enough influence over all the tribes that they control so as to make them walkover to their side. Al Qaida will continue to flourish under such a situation under a benign Taliban regime helping the latter to take over the cities as well and to pursue its own global agenda.

A Repeat of Post-Russian Withdrawal Scenario

The North South Divide that was experienced post-Soviet withdrawal, under which the Northern Alliance of Tajiks and Uzbeks held on their own, with the help of Russia, Iran and India against the onslaught of Taliban, is a likely scenario that could repeat itself post-US withdrawal. In this the Afghan Taliban comprising mainly of Pushtos could take over the Southern and Eastern parts of Afghanistan starting initially with the rural areas and further expanding to other cities and population centres. Thereafter the mountainous areas of Afghanistan again would become a safe haven for terrorists of all hues to perpetuate and prosper and pose a threat to the whole world.

The capacity of Northern Alliance in the absence of a Military Leader of the stature of Ahmad Shah Massoud holding out for long against a combined Al Qaida and Taliban threat is doubtful. However, the Northern Alliance cannot be written off with still powerful members like Amrullah Saleh who worked under Massoud in the line-up for Tajiks and good old warlord Abdul Rashid Dostum among the Uzbeks. The shortcoming would be compensated by additional financial and military support they are going to get as most of the big powers including US, Russia, India, EU and other regional powers would lend their support to them. The Taliban would get some support from Islamic World of Sunnis led by Pakistan and probably Saudi Arabia and Qatar. Afghanistan again can become a battlefield of proxy war? However, in this instance both the Russians and Americans would be on the same side. A total situation of irony in real geo-politics, under which they continue as adversaries in Ukraine but become allies in Afghanistan?

Liberated Terrorist Zone in Trans Afghanistan and Pakistan Border

The entire FATA has virtually become a zone, which Pakistan has not been able to bring under control. This area in conjunction with most parts of North West Frontier Province and Southern Areas of Afghanistan could become a de-facto 'Taliban Land'. The liberated zone would stretch 100 to 200 Kms on both sides of Durand Line. The zone on the Afghanistan side could also encompass the areas up to Wakhan corridor. The area already plays host to multifarious terrorist organisations such as Al Qaida, TTP, Haqqani network, LeT, Afghan Taliban, Swat Taliban, Hizb-e-Islami etc. These bad lands under the control of local chieftains could become a no-man's land between the two countries. If both the countries lose control over this area it would be an ideal place for global terrorism to prosper and perpetuate itself.

All these terrorist organisations have their own agenda. The TTP focuses on Pakistan, the LeT on Kashmir, Haqqani network and Afghan Taliban on Afghanistan and the Al Qaida on 'far enemy' i.e. USA.[13] Hence it would not be possible to get all of them to work on one agenda. Al Qaida feels that they should neutralise the distant enemy that is US and other regimes would then fall on their own. If they can convince the other terrorist organisations and bring them under one umbrella it would give a big boost to their agenda. Their strategy would be not to disturb the host countries and follow the policy of 'live and let live'. This would enable them to pursue their plans against the US, Israel, EU and India with a secure operational base in the liberated zone. They can finance themselves with narco-dollars through poppy cultivation, have training areas, intermingle with locals, manufacture and buy arms and ammunition and give a clarion call for the world's Jihadis to join them.

Preventive Measures to be taken by Afghan Government

To obviate this possibility the Afghan government should take certain preventive measures. The various commands which the Americans have created should be replicated and the force should be spread out to all districts in Afghanistan depending on the level of remoteness, possibility of Taliban re-emerging and attitude of the local population. Afghanistan has been for years been characterised by tribal loyalties, factional fights, and societal feuds woven in to a loose conglomerate with low level of central control. Major decisions were driven by *Loya Jirgha* or the High Peace Council. Afghanistan's 2004 constitution caters to the representation in the government of various ethnicities such as the provision of each president to have two vice- presidents of different ethnicities etc.. However, it leaves most of traditional tribal chiefs out of the governance. This is likely to be the centrifugal force working against the cohesion of the country. Malaysia is a good example, when different states of Malaysia were formed into a single country the erstwhile kings were made heads of provincial governments and became the titular heads of their respective states. Thus, democracy was formed without breaking the traditional institutions. Some such arrangements should be done by incorporating traditional structure into the democratic framework. Even in India our Panchayat System of governance is an age old practice that has been incorporated in the governance framework thus ensuring almost universal direct participation in governance at the grass-root levels.

In practice the Chieftains and Warlords have been brought in to governance by Presidential nomination to Meshrano Jirga (house of elders). They have been the chief beneficiaries of government contracts and corruption has been rampant. To keep the country together it is necessary for the government in power to get support of the clergies, tribal chieftains and warlords. Institutionalised arrangements within the framework of the constitution should have been made to keep the traditional societal structures intact. India became a republic by the union of over six hundred independent states and all the heads of states were given privy purses so that all the kings big or small had a stake in Independent India.

The first task of the government is to seal the country's borders with Pakistan and establish an effective counter infiltration grid. Like India it would be fruitful if they are able to fence the borders like the Indo-Pak border. The fencing in no way rescinds our stand on POK as an integral part of India. Similarly, Afghanistan can fence the border without compromising her stand on the Durand Line. Deployment of a multi-tier counter infiltration grid should be the first task the ANSF should undertake as this would be the precursor to a stable Afghanistan. Though the Af-Pak border in no case can be hermetically sealed if it can stop the inflow in large numbers, the smaller numbers can be tackled by other tiers of the grid and the troops deployed in the hinterland.

Second-most important requirement is to ensure the security and governance in Kabul and other provincial cities. Similarly a strategy should be worked out for enabling the ANSF to hold on to the population centres and cities of Afghanistan in situations under intense pressure from terrorists. These cities should act as bases for launching future operations to reclaim the rural areas.

The third important task of ANSF is to dominate the rural areas. The ANSF need to occupy a geographical grid across the whole of Afghanistan including the rural areas. It is the strategy of Taliban to first spread into rural areas, empathise with people and propagate the familiar story of 'threat to Islam' to earn public support. US could indeed help in surveillance over the remote areas of Central and North Eastern mountains. The presence of security force among civil population, however remote, with effective communication means can ensure the presence of Taliban is nipped in the bud. The surveillance should be a combination of effective electronic surveillance from satellites, drones and human presence. The use of drones by US should be restricted to surveillance and for destruction only on confirmed information. Indiscriminate use of drones for destruction and the collateral killings of innocent civil population would certainly alienate the mass base who could gradually start supporting 'the call of Islam' by Taliban. The US has lost the support of Pakistani people in spite of having pumped billions of dollars, basically due to killings of innocents in the drone attacks.

The Afghan National Police should take care of the internal security and the ANA deployed in garrisons spread through out the country so as to take charge during emergencies when the task in hand goes beyond the control of the police. Once the terrorists are spotted the ANSF should have adequate helicopters to concentrate forces and accurate firepower to neutralise them and thereby militarily should acquire the capability to control the entire geographical extent of the country. Each province should have a base where adequate reserves of troops are located with helicopters and other means of communication and transportation so as to move the troops to the point of crisis. It should also act as a logistic base with means of support to the troops in its area of responsibility. Knowing the nature of terrain the task is stupendous and needs highly motivated and trained troops with state of art surveillance capability, communication and weaponry. Adequate boots on the ground are important otherwise the security forces would only control the bases and the countryside would be under the sway of Taliban. Armies who rely more on technology are prone to fall in to 'high tech trap' and get alienated from ground realities. ANSF being locals should use technology to the optimum without diluting their grass root image and ground proficiency. The absorption of technology by troops would take considerable time and training and this has to be done during the period when 'Training and Assistance Troops' of US remain on Afghan soil from end 2014 to end 2016.

Afghanistan needs to shake off its dependence on Pakistan. This is difficult due to their intertwined history and geography. However, the dependence needs to be minimised. Afghanistan is a land locked country and is dependent on Pakistan for port facilities. She should slowly start using Chahbahar port of Iran. Indian Border Road Organisation has already constructed a road linking Zaranj to Delaram to connect to the road link to Chahbahar. It would also enable Afghanistan to re-negotiate Afghanistan-Pakistan Trade and Transit Treaty in her favour while retaining the alternative of route through Iran. Both these options enhance the negotiating power of Afghanistan.

Afghanistan should reassert her disputed borders with Pakistan and not accept the Durand Line. The concept of 'Pashtun Nationalism' needs to be kept alive. This way Afghanistan will have some cards up its sleeves while negotiating with Pakistan and be enabled to put the latter under pressure.

India's Options

In the past Afghanistan was a starting point for myriads of invasions against Indian subcontinent from invaders like Mohd Ghori, the infamous Mohd Ghazni, Taimur, The Huns, Babur and Sher Shah Suri. Hence to say that we have nursed good relations with Afghanistan from time immemorial is not correct. However, geo-politically it is important because if these invasions took place in the past, there is no reason why it should not take place in future? The movement of all terrorist organisations including Al Qaida from Afghanistan to Pakistan is a type of invasion. History has a habit of repeating itself, albeit the versions could be different. It is Pakistan that is bearing the brunt of political volatility and foreign interventions in Afghanistan. A host of problems have been the bane of an unstable Afghanistan these mainly include more than a million refugees[14] in refugee camps with the attendant problems of violence and crimes, smuggling of arms and narcotics, a myriad of terrorist organisations infiltrating to and fro across Durand Line, having to cope with a liberated zone of world terrorism astride the frontier, intense law and order problem in FATA and Pakistan's state policy of nursing terrorism. Rather in this particular situation Pakistan has become a buffer between India and an unstable and volatile Afghanistan.

It is in the interest of India and the region to have a strong and stable Afghanistan which is more assertive in safeguarding her frontiers especially against Pakistan. Pakistan's dream of making Afghanistan her strategic depth is ridiculous to say the least. For Pakistan, a country which is tottering and with many vouching for its demise sooner rather than later, harbouring a dream of keeping Afghanistan as her client state is beyond the realm of comprehension. In fact, with the FATA and southern part of Afghanistan coming under the writ of terrorists, whatever strategic depth she wanted to achieve has had the opposite effect of making Pakistan much shallower.[15] Afghanistan's claim for Pashtun speaking areas of Pakistan, and not recognising the Durand Line with her formations quartered in cantonments in southern parts of the country would pose a threat to Pakistan. Not to forget that in the Third Afghan War in 1919, it was the forces of Amanullah which had attacked Bagh in NWFP and the British could only extract a facile tactical victory and conceded her authority to manage the Afghan foreign affairs. Afghan forces postured on its Southern Frontier with an unresolved border would pin down Pakistani 11 Corps based at Peshawar to the West, if unable to pull them out for war against India. Such an arrangement is strategically advantageous to India. With Baluchistan also under the spectre of insurgency even the Pakistan 12 Corps could be tied down in Baluchistan. This indeed would be an ideal situation for India in the event of a war with Pakistan, more so in a two front war situation of combined threat from both China and Pakistan simultaneously. It is in the interest of India to create geo-political conditions both internally and externally to force Pakistan to deploy her forces on her Western Frontiers and internally in the event of hostilities against India.

In 2011, India had signed a 'Strategic Partnership Agreement' with Afghanistan encompassing issues of economy, infrastructure, Science and Technology, foreign relations, governance and security. Unfortunately their request for supply of arms and ammunition has been marked by delays due to bureaucratic red tape, a hallmark of our governance. It was politely put across indirectly by President Hamid Karzai in his interview on 'Times Now' on 28 May 2014 that India should give arms, weapons and equipment and train Afghan National Army both for conventional and counter insurgency operations.

To keep an unstable Pakistan between India and a stable Afghanistan is in the interest of India. A Pakistan that is internally simmering and with unresolved borders both on the Eastern and Western fronts would not have time and energy to unleash terrorists against India and Afghanistan. Hence it is in India's interest to work towards a strong and stable Afghanistan. Economically India is assisting Afghanistan in building infrastructure and public amenities like a hospital and has spent $2 billion and another $500 million have been committed.[16] Post-US withdrawal, should a requirement arise to send troops to Afghanistan under the aegis of the UN, India should not feel shy and be ready to induct a division or two, so as to work towards establishing normalcy over a particular sector of Afghanistan. All the terrorist organisations such as Al Qaida, TTP, Haqqani network, LeT under the umbrella of ISI would be targeting Indian forces. Some casualties should be expected in the initial phases till the troops settle down and establish their intelligence network. However, in the long run there is no doubt that the Indian Armed Forces would get better with each encounter. An attack by terrorist should be taken as an opportunity to destroy him. If he does not attack or make contact it is always more difficult to trace and destroy him.

There is a school of thought which opines that once the Afghanistan problem is resolved all the terrorist organisations would be free to be unleashed against rest of India in general and J&K in particular. Hence an unstable Afghanistan with a constant strife between the ANSF and Taliban with the latter having established a safe haven in Afghanistan would ensure the terrorists would be tied down and will not be diverted to India. An unstable Afghanistan again would not be able to control ETIM activities in Sinkiang. Hence disturbances in Sinkiang would aid India as troops of Lanzhou Military Region that is deployed against Ladakh, Himachal and Uttarakhand will have their logistics tails on fire. Notwithstanding the above a strong, stable and friendly Afghanistan can assist India in pursuit of our goal of keeping Pakistan nervous and China concerned. Pakistan's dream of having Afghanistan as a 'strategic depth' should be made into a 'strategic threat'. Hence, instead of banking on Afghanistan's instability to ensure our security it is better to ensure mutual security in the event of two fronted war against India. Our security would be ensured by a volatile and unstable Pakistan: Mired in her self-created cesspool she would not be able to devote time to plan hostilities against India. With Pakistan neutralised, India would be able to contend with the threat from the North.

China has been helping our insurgents in the North East since the fifties and India has not been able to pay back in kind. With a friendly Afghanistan, Tajikistan and Mongolia, India should not hesitate to support ETIM in Sinkiang. By keeping alive both the Sinkiang and the Tibetan Freedom Movements, India would be able to leverage her national interest vis-à-vis China. We should not hesitate to counter China's 'string of pearls strategy' against India, with a 'girdle of diamonds' by forging strategic relationship with South Korea, Japan, US, Philippines, Taiwan, Vietnam, Australia, Afghanistan, Tajikistan, other CAR countries with Mongolia and Tibetan Government in Exile.

Conclusion

Even the most stringent critic of US cannot help but appreciate her initiative in bringing peace and stability to a war torn Afghanistan. A country in absolute chaos and violence has been salvaged and today is having a government of its own. The world cannot afford to see Afghanistan again in the vortex of misrule and violence. With Al Qaeda waiting on the wings to make it their operational base again, the Afghan people, their government, regional players, UN, US, EU, India and China need to play their part. So far China, which claims a superpower status is free riding on the international security provided by US. There has been very miniscule effort by China in contributing to world peace. In this case Afghanistan is in her backyard and still she prefers US and NATO countries to do the dirty work but makes forays in East China Sea, South China Sea and Ladakh to assert her claims on her weak borders. It is high time China exerts her influence on Pakistan to curb terrorism that is flourishing within her borders and stop the latter from interfering into the internal affairs of Afghanistan. Should Afghanistan relapse into terrorism then the next initiative should come from the region. The world should continue to financially contribute as per the July 2012 Tokyo Conference on Afghanistan attended by over 70 donor countries for economic reconstruction and military aid pledged in May 2012 Chicago Conference. India on her part should not hesitate to provide troops under the UN flag. As discussed it is in India's interest to have a strong and stable Afghanistan and it is high time we pursued our national interest and wielded our comprehensive national power in the interest of the region and our nation.

Notes

1. Seth G Jones, *Britain's Afghan Agony*, available at http://nationalinterest.org/bookreview/imperial-britains-afghan-agony-6530
2. William Dalrymple, *Return of a King*, Bloomsbury Publishing, London, 2013, p. 387.
3. Wikipedia, *History of Afghanistan*, available at http://en.wikipedia.org/wiki/History_of_Afghanistan
4. Mohammad Yousa and Mark Atkin, *The Bear Trap*, available at http://therearenosunglasses.files.wordpress.com/2012/10/the-bear-trap.pdf, Preface.
5. Tim Stelloh, *Taliban Leader Mullah Omar calls Bowe Bergdahl's Swap "Victory"*, NBC News, 2 Jun 2014, available at http://www.nbcnews.com/storyline/bowe-bergdahl-released/taliban-leader-mullah-omar-calls-bowe-bergdahl-swap-victory-n119816
6. Sabir Saha, *US Wars in Iraq and Afghanistan cost $6 trillion*, Global Research, available at http://www.globalresearch.ca/us-wars-in-afghanistan-iraq-to-cost-6-trillion/5350789
7. Mareesa Nicosia, *West Point Graduation: Obama offers new foreign policy*, Lohud Journal News, 29 May 2004, available at http://www.lohud.com/story/news/local/rockland/2014/05/28/obama-west-point-graduation/9660543/
8. V.V. Swaminathan, *Problems of Peace and Security in Asia*, Sterling Publishers Private Ltd, New Delhi, 1986.
9. Anwar Iqbal, *US close to achieving objective of Afghan War, says Obama*, Dawn, 13 Jan 2013, available at http://www.dawn.com/news/778451/us-close-to-meeting-objective-of-afghan-war-says-obama
10. Peter L Bergen, *The Longest War*, Simon and Schuster UK Ltd, London, 2011, p. 21.
11. Staff Writer, *American war deaths through History*, updated as on 24 May 2014, available at http://www.militaryfactory.com/american_war_deaths.asp
12. Wikipedia, *United States Military Casualties of War*, available at http://en.wikipedia.org/wiki/United_States_military_casualties_of_war
13. Bergen, n 11, p 24.

14. Alan Taylor, *Afghan Refugees in Pakistan*, In Focus, available at http://www.theatlantic.com/infocus/2014/02/afghan-refugees- in-pakistan/100673/
15. Amit Singh Dabas, *Endgame in Afghanistan: Debating Kashmir Connection* CLAWS , Journal, Winter 2013, p. 148.
16. Gurmeet Kanwal, *Post-2014 Transition in Afghanistan: Options for India*, CLAWS , Journal, Winter 2013, p. 140

16

Stability under Threat: Post-US Withdrawal from Afghanistan

NAVASIKHA DUARA

There is a lot of speculation regarding the future of Afghanistan after the final withdrawal of US led ISAF from the Afghan territory by the end of 2016. It has been feared that post-withdrawal will see Afghanistan collapse into Civil War or return of the Taliban Militants to the centre stage of Afghan politics. Will the post-US Afghanistan be similar to post-Soviet Afghanistan of 1989? These apprehensions can neither be fully accepted nor fully rejected. While the Soviet pullout was sudden and abrupt, US President Barrack Obama has provided a time line for the withdrawal of troops.[1] The process of political transition is already underway in Afghanistan, though the post-election crisis posed a challenge to the US President to leave behind an effective legitimate Afghan government. The final signing of the American initiated power-sharing deal between the two presidential candidates as a political settlement helped in ending the five month-long post-election crisis. Yet the future of Afghanistan is far from safe and certain. The new Afghan government under President Ashraf Ghani has the difficult task of establishing stability in post-US Afghanistan, of securing the Afghan border and preventing the misuse of the Afghan territory. A weak and corrupt Afghan government can revert the country into a safe haven for Islamic Fundamentalist terror groups. This will defeat the initial objective of US-led ISAF's invasion of the Afghan state back in 2001.

It is to be noted here that Afghanistan's strategic location has always made the Afghan state a natural theatre of Great Power rivalry.[2] Regional power dynamics always had a role in Afghanistan. Thus the approaches and perspectives of the neighbouring states regarding the stability and security of post-US Afghanistan are important in shaping her future. The paper deals with the crucial issue of establishing stability and security in post-US Afghanistan, particularly the challenge of Taliban resurgence to the stability of Afghanistan. The paper endeavours to address the conflicting interests of states bordering and in close proximity to Afghanistan particularly the implications of Indo-Pak relations on the future of Afghanistan after US-led ISAF's final pullout. The first part of the paper deals with the Taliban insurgency–its rise with Pakistan's support and continued nurture by the Pak-army and ISI. This part also deals with the steps to counter Taliban Insurgency. The second part of the paper deals with the dynamics of Indo-Pak relations (rivalry) on the future of Afghanistan.

The Taliban Militancy: the Biggest Challenge to Afghanistan's Future Stability

The internal stability and security of post-US Afghanistan is crucially linked to the Taliban Militancy. Will the Afghan state see the return of the Taliban to power in Kabul? Will there be divided authority? Will the post-US Afghanistan be like the post-US Iraq or Syria or Libya?

Rise of the Taliban

The Taliban is predominantly a Pashtun Islamic fundamentalist group under the leadership of Mullah Mohammad Omar, described as commander of the faithful by his supporters.[3] The withdrawal of Soviet troops and ouster of Moscow backed communist government of President Nazibullah resulted in infighting between the contending Mujahedeen groups. The years of conflict that followed from 1992 to 1996 after the removal of Nazibullah ended when the Taliban seized the capital Kabul from President Burhamaddin Rabani, an ethnic Tajik, whom the Taliban viewed as anti-Pashtun and corrupt. In 1999, the UNSC imposed sanctions on the Taliban regime for harbouring terrorist group Al-Qaeda. In the wake of the 9/11 terror attacks on USA, the Taliban accused of sheltering the attackers collapsed in the face of US-led coalition forces military operation.[4] Mullah Mohammad Omar and other senior members of the Taliban leadership reportedly fled to the city of Quetta in Baluchistan province of Pakistan. The city of Quetta is bordering Afghanistan, enabling the Taliban to recruit, train and conduct high level meetings and conferences necessary for insurgency. The Taliban leadership - the Quetta Shura Taliban enjoys sanctuary in Pakistan and has the support of Pak military and Pak intelligence service - the Inter Services Intelligence or ISI. Thus, after removal from power in Kabul, Pakistan is accused of allowing and enabling the Taliban to regroup and reorganise. For years, relationship between Afghanistan and Pakistan has been poisoned by Afghan anger at the presence of the Quetta Shura, the presence of virtually all of the Taliban senior leadership in Pak territory. The Pak Army and the ISI regard the continued support to Taliban as a method to ward off Indian influence in Afghanistan.

Pakistan's Continued Patronage to Afghan Taliban—the Biggest External Obstacle to Stability in Post-US Afghanistan

The resurgence of the Taliban is closely linked to its mentor Pak Army and Pak ISI's continued support. The Soviet initiated negotiation, for a negotiated end to the civil war reportedly failed due to an extensive support network in Pakistan which had dissuaded the insurgents from a compromise and gave them little reason to make peace. The Pak Army and ISI want the Afghan Taliban to gain power in post-US Afghanistan, they like to see a government in Kabul which, if not directly controlled by Islamabad should at least be well disposed towards Pakistan and should be free of India's influence. With this objective Pakistan has been maintaining a distinction between 'bad' Taliban (their Taliban, the Pak Taliban-Tehreek-e-Taliban Pakistan or TPP those that target the Pakistan state itself) and 'good' Taliban (our Taliban, the Afghan Taliban, the *jihadi*sts who are fighting against the Afghan state and US-led coalition forces in Afghanistan). The Haqqani network, an affiliate of the Afghan Taliban maintains a safe haven in North Wazirstan, Pakistan, across Afghanistan's south eastern border. Pak security establishment regards the Haqqani network as useful ally and proxy force to represent their interest in Afghanistan. Haqqani forces have repeatedly targeted Indian infrastructure and construction projects in Afghanistan. In recent time there is report of growing cooperation between the Afghan Taliban, the Haqqani network and TPP causing the Pak establishment to share an uneasy relationship with the Afghan Taliban.

The Taliban leadership after their removal from power in Kabul was given a safe haven in Pakistan, but in launching an insurgency in Afghanistan the Quetta Shura helped in the creation of Pak Taliban. The agenda of Pak Taliban is the establishment of the Islamic Emirate of Waziristan in FATA area of Pakistan, on the pattern of Mullah Omar's Islamic Emirate of Afghanistan. At present the safe haven provided to the Afghan Taliban leadership in Pakistan is keeping the 'Quetta Shura' subservient to Islamabad. However, in future, the relation of the Afghan Taliban and their sponsor, the Pak Army and the ISI may not be the same. The Taliban may not remain Islamabad's proxies if they recapture the Afghan government. This will defeat the very objective of Pak's support to them as a 'strategic asset' against India.

The long standing demand of the Pashtun nationalists for a new state of Pashtunistan uniting the Pasthun areas on sides of the Afghanistan-Pakistan border is a cause of concern for Pakistan. The Durand Line drawn by the British in 1897 to split the tribal Pashtuns between Afghanistan and British India has always been disputed by the Afghans as a 'geographical myth'. Will the TPP be the ideal vehicle for the advent of a new Islamic Pashtunistan? With the growing nexus between the Afghan Taliban and the Pak Taliban, Pakistan may not want the Taliban to win exclusive power in Afghanistan fearing a threat to the territorial integrity of Pakistan.

Good Governance: the Best Way to Counter Taliban Resurgence

An effective and transparent Afghan government can ensure stability and security after the pullout of US troops and counter-Taliban resurgence. The early popularity of the Taliban was largely due to their success in removing corruption, curbing lawlessness that followed immediately post-Soviet withdrawal and ouster of Nazibullah's government. The Taliban got popular support by promising to impose stability and rule of law after four years of conflict between rival Mujahidin groups. The corruption of the previous Hamid Karzai Government was used by the Taliban, who otherwise failed to offer an alternative that could provide a better future to the Afghan people.[5] The new Ghani Government can win the battle of legitimacy with the Taliban by providing a stronger and more efficient government at all levels, national, provincial and district.[6]

A major challenge to the new Afghan President will be his willingness and capacity to counter the opium trade which allegedly is financing the Taliban insurgency.[7] Reportedly many officials of the previous Karzai Government were benefiting from Afghan narcotics trade.[8] The new Afghan President thus faces the challenge of removing 'narco-corruption' of the Afghan Government. The ability to deliver positive results despite challenges of opium economy, strong Taliban offensive, diminishing international financial aid and reduced presence of international troops, will alone fetch the credibility for the new Afghan government.

Negotiating with the Taliban: an Exit Strategy to Ensure Stability in Post-US Afghanistan

A political solution to end the war on terror has resulted in pursuing the policy of negotiation with the Taliban. However, a negotiated end to the war as the exit strategy of the US and her allies may not result in the desired reconciliation and stability.[9]

Challenges to Negotiated Peace

The opening of the political office of the Afghan Taliban in Doha on 18th June 2013 to facilitate peace talks with Afghan authority and the USA appeared to be more symbol than substance. This is due to the fact that the two sides remained far apart on their final objectives.

The US goal of Peace Talks is to make the Taliban recognise the Afghan constitution including the rights for minorities and women and participate in the democratic process. The Taliban agree to the key American demand of not using Afghanistan as a base to threaten other countries. Yet the Taliban consistently refuses to stay away from the west sponsored political transition.[10]

In his traditional Eid message in August 2013 Mullah Mohammad Omar, the Taliban supreme leader, said that his group favours an 'Afghan inclusive government' based on Islamic principles. The Taliban boycotted the Afghan Presidential election of 2014 to elect a new Afghan President and termed it a 'fake process.' Hence it is unclear whether the Taliban is really interested in working towards a comprehensive peace settlement as desired by the US and her allies, or are they mainly ensuring that US-led ISAF forces close their operation as scheduled and thereby remove a major obstacle in their return to power?

The pessimism over negotiated peace settlement was evident when the recent prisoner–exchange (one US soldier held captive by the Taliban was given back to US in exchange for five senior Taliban officials detained in Guantanamo Bay, Cuba) was followed by fierce fighting between the Afghan Taliban and the Government forces in the district of Sangin in Helmand province. The Taliban offense of seizing territory and attacking police outposts and Afghan government facility even before US-led ISAF have completed their withdrawal does not give much hope to the peace process.[11]

Benefits to Taliban from Peace Talks

Politically the opening of Peace Talks is intended to end the isolation of the Afghan Taliban. The Taliban has exploited the opening of the Doha office and Peace Talks to gain recognition as a legitimate movement and political entity.[12]

Dynamics of Indo-Pak Relations on Stability of Post-Afghanistan

With no negotiated peace settlement with the Taliban in sight the prospect of a stable, peaceful Afghan state post-US withdrawal appears to be uncertain. The relationship of regional rivals India and Pakistan is invariably linked to the future stability of Afghanistan. The mutual suspicion of these two neighbouring states has long made a mess in Afghanistan. Both the states have the capacity to become a source of stability or instability for Afghanistan. An improved relation between these two neighbours will enhance the prospect of regional stability and prosperity.[13] The two regional rivals must contribute meaningfully to stabilise a weak Afghanistan. It is in the best interest of both these states for in the long run an unstable, lawless, divided Afghanistan is not good for either of the states.

India's Involvement in Afghanistan

India has tried to pursue a pro active policy in post-Taliban Afghanistan. The removal of Taliban from power in Kabul happened at a time when India was doing well as a rising power[14]. As a rising power India is adopting a pro active policy to make her presence felt. India's interest in the Afghan state is many. It ranges from countering Pakistani influence, containment of Islamist extremism, prevention of the misuse of the Afghan territory by terrorists and its emergence as a safe haven for terrorism, the use of Afghanistan as a gateway to the energy rich and strategically important Central Asian region and most importantly ascertaining her credibility as a regional and emerging global power. A resurgent Taliban in Afghanistan is indeed of concern to India, for it would encourage anti-India militants like Lashkar-e-Taiba. This was noted by Henry Kissinger too who said that, "In many respects, India will be the most affected country if Jihadi Islamists gain impetus in Afghanistan."[15]

Ironically India's success in Afghanistan has driven Pakistani security establishment into panic mode with a perception that India is aiming to take over Afghanistan. In a confidential report submitted to the US President Barack Obama in 2009, US commander in Afghanistan, General Stanley McCarystal, had warned that an increasing Indian political and economic influence largely benefitting the Afghan people is likely to exacerbate regional tension and encourage Pakistan's counter measures in Afghanistan or India.[16]

Islamabad views New Delhi's disproportionate involvement in Afghan affairs as a strategic ploy to encircle Pakistan strategically as India and Afghanistan flank the two sides of Pakistan border. Former Pakistan's Foreign Minister Shah Mohmad Qureshi had once expressed Islamabad's concern over India's growing involvement in Pakistan's neighbouring state. The Pak Foreign Minister said that New Delhi needs to justify its interest in Pakistan's war-torn western neighbour which shares no border with India. In an interview with the *Los Angeles Times* Mr Qureshi reportedly said, "India's level of engagement has to be commensurate with the fact that they do not share a border with Afghanistan, whereas we do—. At times this concerns us."[17]

Pakistan's Stake in Afghanistan

Pakistan's policy towards Afghanistan is primarily motivated to counter an impending Indian attack. The guiding factor in the engagement of Pak Army and the Pak ISI in Afghanistan since long has largely been prompted by the motive of safeguarding itself from its historical enemy, India. Pakistan views Afghanistan as a means of attaining 'Strategic Depth' to combat any possible Indian attack.

The vision of 'Strategic Depth", arising out of Pakistan's imagined fear of 'encirclement by India' was said to be first articulated in the 1980's and this had guided Pakistan's policy with regard to Afghanistan in the 1990's. The international abandonment of Afghanistan post-Soviet withdrawal and the ensuing civil war gave Islamabad an opportunity to pursue its policy of treating Afghanistan as its source of 'Strategic Depth'. This stand made Pakistan provide the Taliban insurgency with logistical, military and political support to enable it to capture Kabul in 1996. Afghanistan is treated by the Pak security establishment as a possible strategic territory for retreat in case of a hypothetical Indian invasion. This concept of 'Strategic Depth' was re-worded by Pakistani Army chief of staff, General Kayani in early 2010 so as to make Afghanistan kind of proprietary hinterland for Pakistan, independent of the threat factor from India or other outside influence as had been the case from 1992-2001.

Alexander Thier, Director for Afghanistan and Pakistan at the Washington-based US Institute of Peace (USIP) commented about Indo–Pak regional dynamics and its implications for the Afghan state in the following words - "Pakistan has existential concerns about India's involvement in Afghanistan, as they see it as a form of encirclement aimed at the weakening or dismemberment of Pakistan. Pakistan relies on Afghanistan for 'Strategic Depth' – pro-Islamabad government in Kabul will support Pakistan in the event of another war with India including providing a retreat area for conventional forces."[18]

India's Growing Economic Role in Afghanistan: Concern for Pakistan

Except during the Taliban rule, India has historically supported the Afghan government. Pakistan views India's growing involvement in post-Taliban Afghanistan's infrastructure and economic projects with suspicion. Pakistan assumes that India is employing 'soft power' tactics to serve India's strategic goals of developing pro-Indian Kabul Government. Pakistan believes that India is purposely developing its economic ties with Afghanistan so as to displace Pakistani influence.

The construction of the 218 km Zaranj–Delaram Highway, Route 606 in southwest Afghanistan near the Iranian border is making it possible to transport goods from Iran to Kabul across Afghanistan. With the building of the highway India has developed a land route to Afghanistan bypassing Pakistan. This new road certainly threatens Pakistan's commercial position in Afghanistan. The highway will eventually link Afghanistan to the Iranian port of Chabahar. It will reduce the landlocked Afghanistan's dependence on Pakistan to access the Arabian Sea.[19] This will also give India easier access to Afghanistan and the energy rich Central Asian Region.

What is Next

New Delhi and Islamabad have been levelling accusations about each other's involvement in the Afghan state for years. Pakistan and India try to counter each other's influence in the Afghan state. Each side has a different interest to achieve by involving in Afghanistan.

Pakistan perceives good relation between Kabul and New Delhi as India's attempt to gain 'Strategic Encirclement' which the former perceives as detrimental to its security. While New Delhi's main objection is the continuing patronage of the Pak Army and Pak ISI to militancy. India's fight against terrorism is closely intertwined with the rise of extremism in Afghanistan and in Pakistan. India accuses Pakistan of exporting terrorism in J&K and other parts of India by sending militants to India who have been recruited from Afghanistan and trained in Pakistan. India's national interest demands aiding Afghanistan in the process of building a stable, democratic and prosperous Afghanistan. A radical Taliban regime in Kabul with close ties with Pakistan will make India's fight against terrorism a difficult task. This will also put an end to India's aid, investment and trade in the country and cut off India's access to the resource rich Central Asian Region.

Normalisation of Indo–Pak Relations to Establish Stability in Afghanistan

For regional stability and for the best interest of both India and Pakistan, the two rival nuclear powers must contribute meaningfully to establish stability in post-US Afghanistan. A radical Taliban regime in Kabul is a threat to India's security. Pakistan may also not be benefited by a Taliban regime in Afghanistan. The return of the Taliban may embolden the Pak Taliban in their campaign against the Pak state. Hence stability along the Durand Line is in Pakistan's national interest. To that extent stability in post-US Afghanistan is in the interest of both the states.

Pakistan must arrive at a civil-military consensus on Afghanistan. This will pave the way for normalisation of relations with India eventually leading to stability in Afghanistan. On her part India must allay Pakistan's fear of an impending attack from India, while Pakistan must prove itself as a reliable partner in the war against terror by going against terror of all hue and colour and dismantling all terrorist sanctuaries on her soil.[20]

Involvement of both the arch rivals, in joint projects like TAPI-Trans–Afghan Pipeline to ship Turkmenistan gas across Afghanistan and Pakistan to India may serve as confidence building measure for New Delhi and Islamabad. The project will fulfil energy demands of both India and Pakistan. Economic integration of these two states is to be encouraged for stability in the region. Projects like TAPI may make both the regional rivals realise the importance of giving up historical enmity and come to a consensus on Afghanistan affairs. Growing economic cooperation between the two states on Afghanistan can deter the onset of actions and counteractions, not to forget expanding US-China trade relation compels both the states to adjust their differences.

In the long run no stability in post-ISAF Afghanistan is possible unless all the sides comprising India, Pakistan and Afghanistan resolve their suspicions about one another. The new Afghan government seems to have realised that no settlement with the Taliban will be possible without the blessing of the Pakistan Army and ISI. Therefore, the endeavour to assure the Pakistan security establishment which harbours deep suspicions about India's influence and intention in Afghanistan is tending to appear like a policy of distancing from India, at least on the surface.

After the Peshawar school massacre the Pak army is insisting that a distinction between 'good' and 'bad' Taliban no longer exists. The massacre of school children seems to be compelling the Pakistani security establishment to realise that the terror apparatus set up to hurt India and for strategic gains has backfired on them. There has been a visible shift in the approach of both Afghanistan and Pakistan on the issue of Terror. Fugitive TTP chief Mullah Fazllullah is believed to be hiding in the north eastern Afghan provinces of Kunar and Nuristan. Earlier inaction on the part of the Afghan government to dislodge militants from their side of the Durand Line was due to the trust deficit with Pakistan. While Pakistan's concern was reluctance of Afghanistan to cooperate against TTP, Kabul believed that Pakistan security establishment is supporting Afghan insurgents.

There is however now hope for a new beginning. The Afghan authority is going against TTP hideouts in Afghanistan and assuring that Afghanistan soil will not be allowed to be used for terrorist activities. Pakistani Government has announced the banning of the Haqqanni network and Lashkar's political wing Jammaat-ud-Dawa, the terror outfits which acted as proxies for ISI. These steps are indeed positive steps though there is room for suspicion considering Pakistan's previous record. Only time will prove how serious Pakistan is in acting against terrorists of all shades. Pakistan must immediately get the Afghan Taliban leadership to enter into peace talks, otherwise the new Afghan president accused of getting too little in return for a policy that is not going well with the Afghan people may be forced to rethink of agreeing to cooperate with Pakistan in their strike against TTP.

Notes

1. Most importantly while Mikhail Gorbachev regarded Afghanistan as the 'bleeding ground', US President Barrack Obama termed the Afghan war as a 'good war'.
2. Political and Military campaigns demanded the creation of Afghanistan as a Buffer State between British India and Imperial Russia during the Anglo-Russian conflicts in the 19th century. The soviet invasion of Afghanistan in 1979 was primarily to deter the US interference in the

neighbouring region. Whereas the US support to the Mujahedeen's fight against the Pro-Moscow communist government was to check further soviet expansion in Southwest Asia.

3. The ideology of the Taliban is a combination of strict anti-modern Pashtun Tribal ideology mixed with radicalised Deobandi interpretation of Islam. The Taliban rule in Afghanistan from 1996 to 2001 enforced their own austere interpretation of Sharia or Islamic law.
4. On 28th September, 2001 UNSC Resolution 1373 affirmed the UNSC's condemnation of the terror attacks and confirmed for such acts as constituting a threat to international peace and security.
5. In a public opinion survey conducted in 2014, 62.4 per cent of the respondents regarded corruption as the main reason for pessimism about the direction of the country. The proportion of Afghans citing corruption as the major problem in their daily life significantly increases from 55.7 per cent 2013. (Source: Asia Foundation survey on Afghanistan, 2014http://www.asiafoundation.org/resources/pdfs/Afghanistanin2014final.pdf
6. Senator Ted Kaufman in The World Political Post, November 2009http://www.huffingtonpost.com/sen-ted-kaufman/best-defense-in-afghanist_b_369314.html?ir=India
7. Despite $7 billon spent on counter narcotic effort since the beginning of operation Enduring Freedom and 13 $ billon on agriculture programme designed to provide alternative to farmers, opium poppy harvest which also help finance Taliban Insurgency was at an all time height in 2013. Recent UNODC statistics has shown that between 2008 and 2012 opium cultivation increased in Taliban controlled areas. Governor-led poppy eradication campaigns were less active in all the regions of Afghanistan in 2014 than in 2013. The security situation continued to be unfavourable for Governor-led poppy eradication campaign in all provinces where eradication campaign was launched. (Source: Report published by UN Office on Drugs and Crime (UNODC) http://www.unodc.org /documents/crop-monitoring/Afghanistan/Afghan-opium-survey-2014.pdf
8. Reports link Karzai's brother to Afghanistan Heroin Trade http://www.nytimes.com/ 2008/10 /05/world/asia/05afghan.html?pagewanted=all&_r=0James Risen October 4, 2008, The New York Times (Asia Pacific)
9. The Soviet also tried to negotiate with the Mujahideen to facilitate orderly withdrawal of its troops and ensure the survival of Moscow baked Najibullah government. But it was without success. This time too, to bring the Taliban to negotiating table a number of significant concessions has been offered. The Prisoner swap deal in May 31, 2014 has been seen by the US as confidence building measure to get the Taliban involved in power sharing with the Afghan Government.

10. In his August 6, 2013 e-mailed id message to news organisation, Mullah Omar said that "our fundamental principle according to our unchanging policy is that we do not intend to harm anyone nor we allow anyone to harm others from our soil", echoing the original language used by the Taliban in June 18, 2013 when they announced the opening of a political office in Doha, capital city of the Gulf state of Qatar. Source Mullah Omar is still willing to talk, August 6, 2013; The Hindu http://www.thehindu.com/news/international/south-asia/mullah-omar-is-still-willing-to-talk/article4995606.ece
11. Taliban kill dozens to take former Afghan stronghold, The Washington Post, June 20, 2014, http://www.washingtonpost.com/world/taliban-kills-dozens-attempts-to-retake-former-afghan-stronghold/2014/06 /28 /ddbd9132-1b60-41d2-af3e-4a76643abced_story.html
12. The opening of the Doha office was used by the Taliban to gain international credibility. At the opening ceremony, the Taliban representatives played their official anthem, raised the white flag atop the Doha office along with a sign reading. The Political Office of the Islamic Emirate of Afghanistan, the name used during Taliban rule in Afghanistan. The office was supposed to have opened as the Afghan – Taliban Political Office in Doha. The then Afghanistan President Karzai accused the Taliban of presenting the Doha office as the embassy of a government-in-exile. The Afghan authority's protest was followed by removal of the Taliban sign and flag atop the Doha office which resulted in temporary closure of the office less than a month of its opening.
13. US Secretary of state John Kerry and Sartaz Aziz, Pakistan's National Security adviser stressed that a peaceful, stable, independent and united Afghanistan is in the interest of the region. In a joint statement Kerry and Aziz recognised the potential for enhanced stability and prosperity from improved bilateral relations between India and Pakistan benefitting the lives of citizens on both sides of the border. http://www.firstpost.com/world/improved-indo-pak-relations-enhances-regional-stability-1362611.html
14. According to Hans Morgenthau the interests of a state are shaped by it's power. An increase in state's relative power capabilities will result in a concomitant increase in it's interest in the realm of Foreign Policy.
15. Harsh, V Pant India's changing Role, The Afghanistan Conflict, in Middle East Quarterly, Vol. xviii, No. 2, Spring 2011. http://www.meforum.org/2895/india-afghanistan
16. Securing India's interests in Afghanistan, October 23, 2009, The Hindu, http://www.thehindu.com/todays-paper/tp-opinion/securing-indias-interests-in-afghanistan/article167056.ece
17. Pakistan has nothing to gain from Quetta Shura: Qureshi October 4, 2009, Daily Timeshttp://archives.dailytimes.com.pk/main/04-Oct-2009/pakistan-has-nothing-to-gain-from-quetta-shura-qureshi

18. Christopher .L.Budihas, What drives Pakistan's interest in Afghanistan, The Institute of Land Warfare, (Association of the US Army) 2011http://www.ausa.org/ publications /ilw/ Documents / LWP_82_web.pdf
19. Chabahar would be the shortest transit way connecting Afghanistan to a sea harbour and through Afghanistan. http://www.afghanembassy jp.com/en/news/1654
20. Sartaz Aziz Pakistan National Security Adviser said that military operations in FATA in June, 2014 is against all militants. http:// www.ndtv.com/article/world/no-distinction-between-good-bad-taliban-pakistani-official-548305

17

Indian Perception of the American Withdrawal from Afghanistan in December 2014: Developmental Issues and Related Policy Options

AMRUTA DESHMUKH

Afghanistan is a key element for India in the framing of her Foreign Policy and also a strategic partner. This is mainly due to its geopolitical status of being a neighbour's neighbour. Furthermore, in the light of the terrorist threat to the security of India, especially from Pakistan-based camps, the role of Afghanistan assumes greater significance.

The US withdrawal from Afghanistan in December 2014 could have serious repercussion on Indo-Afghan relations. These would be more so, in the military, and security arena. Even so, Afghanistan and India share close ties in the field of development and infrastructure. The changing dimension of the Indo-Afghan relations after US withdrawal would surely impact the military and security ties and subsequently the same would be reflected in the developmental issues. While the US presence in Afghanistan serves as a security check for India, the withdrawal of the same would demand from India adoption of more viable policy options.

India has always extended its assistance and has undertaken infrastructure projects for the development of Afghanistan. The vacuum that would be created in Afghanistan as a result of the US withdrawal in 2014 would prove worrisome to India. Therefore, the Indo-Afghan strategic partnership needs to be viewed in the context of US troop withdrawal from Afghanistan. India's policy aims at promoting its security interests by helping Afghanistan so that it becomes stable and democratic. At present the future of Afghanistan remains uncertain.

Afghanistan is one of the poorest and most ravaged countries in the world. The US is waging a war against militants in Afghanistan by every possible means. Colonel Stammer is the commanding officer for primarily the 700 or so soldiers of the 2nd Battalion (Airborne), 503rd Infantry Regiment, based in the dusty town of Qalat in Southeast Afghanistan. The US is at war with the Taliban fighters. Taliban leaders, many of whom work hand in hand the opium growers with do not have to spend much to outwit the Afghan army.

Colonel Stammer estimated that in Zabul province in his 'battle space' there are probably fewer than 300 active Talibans. As a military power they are insignificant. Over the past four years the US has spent a total of \$1.3 bn. for the reconstruction of projects in Afghanistan. The developmental efforts have been tarnished by the disturbing incident of graft, inefficiency and scandals.

Afghanistan, like Iraq, has been a strife-torn country and is sliding back into conflict. The US-led coalition in Afghanistan failed in ousting the Taliban and committed a mistake in adopting a 'peace-time approach'. There has been no progress in democratic governance in Afghanistan after the end of the Soviet occupation. Former British Prime Minister Tony Blair urged NATO allies in 2006 to do more in Afghanistan, saying that the alliance's credibility and global security were at risk. He had stressed the need for strengthening NATO.[1]

India signed a trilateral agreement to help Afghanistan on governance, development and security, although both the US and Pakistan have separate agreements with Afghanistan. A joint statement issued by India and US on June 13, 2012, said: "India and the US intend to explore opportunities to work together to promote Afghanistan's development, including in areas such as agriculture, mining, energy, capacity building and infrastructure."[2] India's foreign Minister S M Krishna stated

Afghanistan's peace and stability could form a part of the dialogue.[3]

India had already committed to Afghanistan's security in October 2011 agreement. It is thus clear that as US prepares to leave Afghanistan in 2014, it is eager to encourage regional partners to share its erstwhile load. In November 2011, Turkey hosted a conference of Afghanistan's neighbours. India attended the conference after being forced out by Pakistan in 2010. India hosted a conference in June 2012 to encourage investment in Afghanistan. The US Defence Secretary Leon Panalta has encouraged India to play a more active role in Afghanistan as the US combat troops leave in 2014. India is one of the biggest donors in Afghanistan, with a spending of about $2 billion on projects, and it has also got an iron ore concession in an $11-billion investment.[4]

As the US prepares to wind up its military operations in Afghanistan, other stakeholders such as India are, unsurprisingly, anxious. Western powers believe that, measures like strengthening the Afghan armed forces and building multiple revenue streams for Afghanistan will help stabilise the situation.[5] They seem confident that the measures would help keep Islamic fundamentalists, Taliban and the ISI at bay.[6] Hence, there is a hurry to construct the long-planned Turkmenistan, Afghanistan, Pakistan and India (TAPI) gas pipeline. The 1,735 km gas pipeline, with a total gas capacity of 90 million cu. m per day, will follow the ancient trading route to India, passing through Herat and Kandahar in Afghanistan, Quetta and Multan in Pakistan, before landing in Fazilka, Punjab. On completion in 2017, India is supposed to receive 38 MMSCMD of gas from the transnational pipeline.[7]

Getting gas via TAPI "is not just a good business idea, it could herald peace in South Asia". TAPI promoters, to lure investors and new consortium partners, mostly from the western countries and Indian based Public Sector Undertaking GAIL (India) Ltd. are predicted to face " a tough scrutiny of the project, particularly on the issue of the pipeline's security in war-torn Afghanistan and in the Baluchistan region where Pakistan's own domestic gas pipeline are bombed regularly by separatists."[8]

However, western powers claim that they have new technologies which will take care of such concerns. It is argued that TAPI can be almost fully protected by keeping it underground and by wiring it up with computer and satellite-controlled devices to counter any terrorist attack. "The pipeline, when completed, would probably become the shining symbol of the growing India-Pakistan economic cooperation on the one hand, and of deepening India-Afghanistan bonds on the other."[9]

TAPI is projected more as "an economic cooperation initiative than a geopolitical one". TAPI can change the future of the entire region and may prove to be the catalyst for a new South Asia. India needs to show enthusiasm for the 2,775 km Iran-Pakistan-India (IPI) gas pipeline too which is now in progress. The US is opposed to IPI for its own reasons, but it is for India to decide what is good for its 1.21 billion energy consumers. India cannot afford to break its ties with Iran, which has been its partner for ages.

India hosted the first investment meet and pitched for greater private investment in Afghanistan which is poised to become a regional trade and transit hub which links the energy-rich Central Asian region with dynamic markets of India, China, Russia, Turkey and other east and south-east Asian economies[10]. According to Afghan foreign Minister Zalmal Rassoul, Afghanistan had "accorded high priority to private sector and the public and private investments in Afghanistan had touched $10 billion in 2012.[11]

India is stepping up its engagements with central Asian countries, the key neighbours of Afghanistan. India and Tajikistan also supported the Northern Alliance in their fight against the Taliban regime. India is using the Ayni airbase in Tajikistan which gives "an impetus to the growing strategic ties" between the two countries.[12]

At the Tokyo conference on Afghanistan, India's former External Affairs Minister S M Krishna expressed the view that India visualised the Shanghai Cooperation organisation as a forum to resolve the Afghan crisis, once the NATO forces withdrew. India also considers the Eurasian region important for its energy purposes. China also has a keen interest in the region, especially in Turkmenistan and has also ambitious railway plans for the region. India is keenly working on the gas pipeline from Turkmenistan that passes through Afghanistan and Pakistan and wants to develop its ties with countries of Eurasian region for energy purposes.[13]

The obvious concern for India is that the greater the uncertainty Afghanistan feels about the US support, the more willing it is to seek an accommodation with Pakistan. The years of Taliban rule in Afghanistan coincide with the years of insurgency in Kashmir. The US troops pullout would benefit India as long as a long-term international aid commitment is ensured to war-torn Afghanistan. The degree of US commitment also remains a key and is unpredictably variable. India's own commitment remains fixed.

Afghan President Hamid Karzai, during his 2012 visit to India, had discussions with Prime Minister Manmohan Singh and President Pranab Mukherjee on various issues that would strengthen bilateral relations. The two countries entered into a strategic partnership in 2011, that has the potential to stabilise Afghanistan and would transform the regional security environment. India's policy towards Afghanistan is based on the twin pillars of democracy and development that would bring stability to the war torn country.

India has over several decades, invested enormous amount of effort and money to nurture its relationship with Afghanistan, which explains the cordiality that characterises India-Afghan relations.

The strategic location of Afghanistan will always be important for India, particularly in the context of the difficult India-Pakistan relations. However, the importance of Afghanistan for India is much bigger than normally perceived in this narrow context. Once Afghanistan becomes stable, trade through Pakistan, Afghanistan and Central Asia has the potential to alter the nature and character of India's continental trade. So far the majority of Indian trade is conducted by sea. Looking beyond Central Asia, it is clear that India trades a great deal with other CIS countries, Iran and of course with the European continents. In 2012-13, India's total trade with these countries amounted to about US $173 billion. Just before the global economic slowdown, India's trade with this region was growing very fast particularly with Afghanistan, Pakistan and Iran. Simple calculation on the basis of past trends shows that India's trade with Europe, CIS countries, plus Iran, Afghanistan and Pakistan would be in the range of about $400-500 billion annually within the next few years. Even if 20 per cent of this trade is conducted through road, $80-100 billion of Indian trade would be passing through Afghanistan and Central Asia. With improvement in India-Pakistan relation, an important portion of Indian trade (particularly from the landlocked northern states including Jammu and Kashmir) will be moving through Pakistan and Afghanistan and central Asia, most of the infrastructure projects in the region will become economically viable.

The Afghanistan-Pakistan Transit Trade Agreement (APTTA) had been reached after years of negotiation and active US encouragement. Despite its limited nature and serious initial problems in implementation, the agreement can be seen as a major development in regional economic cooperation. It has also generated interest beyond Afghanistan and Pakistan. Both Pakistan and Afghanistan have decided, in principle, to include Tajikistan in the APTTA. To make this initial small project into serious regional economic force, it is imperative to include Turkmenistan, Uzbekistan (and perhaps Iran) into the broader agreement. However, the project will be of very limited interest to Central Asian countries if traffic of India is not allowed in both the directions. Once Central Asia and India are included in the expanded APTTA, the region will be ready to take advantage from the Eurasian Economic Union space within a few years.

Despite tension at the political level, there are some positive developments between India and Pakistan on the trade matter. Both have agreed on the three agreements viz. redressal of trade grievances, mutual recognition and custom cooperation. Pakistan will allow bilateral trade through Wagah for all goods (presently restricted to 137 items). India has agreed to reduce the number of items under the restricted list by 30 per cent. There are some signs that Pakistan may provide most-favoured nation (MFN) status to India soon. While India had given Pakistan MFN status in 1996, Pakistan had been refusing to do so. Once that happens, India will bring South Asian Free Trade Area (SAFTA) sensitive list to just 100.[14] Pakistan will do so in the next five years. By 2020 the peak tariff rate will not be more than five per cent. Both have also agreed to cooperate in investment, banking, electricity and gas trade, railway and better air connectivity. In addition, they have signed new liberalised Visa agreement.

In the last few years, all four countries involved in Turkmenistan-Afghanistan-Pakistan-India pipeline (TAPI) project have signed most agreements required for its commencement. These include: an Inter-Governmental Agreement (IGA), a Gas Pipeline Framework Agreement (GPFA) and Gas Sales and Purchase Agreement. A broad agreement on transit fees has also been agreed upon. Recently, Indian Minister for Petroleum and Natural Gas M. Veerappa Moily asserted that the framework for TAPI is moving forward on a fast track basis by the four shareholder nations. A transactional advisor for the project has also been appointed. He announced confidently that "gas is expected to reach the border of the India by August 2017." The Indian public sector giant, Oil and Natural Gas Commission (ONGC) also plans to bring Russian Hydrocarbons to India via Central Asia, Afghanistan and Pakistan.

Within the broad context of increasing regional economic cooperation, India continues to support both the Regional Economic Cooperation Conference on Afghanistan (RECCA) as well as the "Heart of Asia" process. In the Istanbul process, India leads the Trade Commerce and Investment Opportunities Confidence Building Measures (TCI-CBM). Uncertainty concerning post-2014 Afghanistan has also added a new dimension to India's relations to Central Asian republics. The failure of the Afghanistan project poses common security challenges but any positive outcome will open tremendous economic opportunities to both India and Central Asia. These two factors have increased the strategic significance of the region considerably and perhaps are the reason for announcing a 12-point "Connect Central Asia" policy. As the Shanghai Cooperation Organisation (SCO) may play a bigger role in Afghanistan in any post-2014 situation, India is also hoping to get its full membership soon. Overall, economic integration both within and between South and Central Asia is limited at the moment. High economic growth in both the regions, however, will be pushing policy-makers to work for integration strategies. Regional economic integration is also important for sustainability of Afghanistan as ultimately it has to play its traditional role of facilitating trade and commerce through its territories. Between 2006 and 2009, the issue of regional economic cooperation through Afghanistan was becoming serious. Since then, however, the focus on exit and later on "negotiated settlement" in discussions pushed the issue into the background. Even if a single major project like the TAPI takes off, it could become a "game changer" in regional geopolitics and the whole discourse on Afghanistan may change.

Afghanistan views India as a good friend. India has not interfered in Afghanistan's domestic affairs like other countries. India has always extended its assistance and has undertaken development measures like infrastructure projects in Afghanistan.

The US decision to withdraw from Afghanistan in 2014 would prove worrisome to India.[15] The Indo-Afghan strategic partnership therefore needs to be viewed in the context of US troops withdrawal from Afghanistan. Apparently, India's policy towards Afghanistan aims at promoting its security interest by helping Afghanistan, so that it becomes strong and democratic.

India has long opposed the return of the Taliban regime because of its addiction to terrorism. However, geography and India's aversion to risk make it difficult for India to play more than a marginal role in Afghanistan. In recent times, the Taliban and the ISI of Pakistan have worked hard to sabotage peace talks with the international community, including $10-billion a year and the US promise to build a strong Afghan security force.

The US and allied military planners have drawn up the broad outlines of a special force that would remain in Afghanistan following the handover of Afghan security to the Afghanistan government after 2014. In a parallel effort, NATO forces will guide Afghan forces after the withdrawal of US and allied forces, but most likely will have a minimal battlefield role. The final decision on the size of the forces and its precise configuration has not been made by US and its allies.[16] As of now, the future of Afghanistan remains uncertain.

The challenge in the newly commenced saffron era for Indian Politics, as regards to Afghanistan would be to strike a balance between the national security and military issues and the bilateral economic cooperation and development.

Nonetheless terrorism may continue to pose a threat to the security of India. A new chapter in the Indo-Afghanistan relations in post-December 2014 could also be viewed from a positive angle.

If India keeps in mind the above observation in the foreign policy towards Afghanistan, may be, conflicts would lessen. Further more and more importantly the US withdrawal will also add newer dimensions to Indo-Pakistan relation, which may not be necessarily that of conflict but in fact of closer cooperation and economic ties. The world community cannot afford to ignore the Human Rights violations by Taliban. Nonetheless, US withdrawal of troops in December 2014 would liberate and further license the Taliban which will be a whistle blower for the National Security of the neighbouring States in terms of National Security.

Notes

1. "America's Forgotten War", *Society*, Vol. 1, No. 27, September 2006.
2. Quoted in Yashwant Raj (2012), "India, US Team up on Afghan Security", *Hindustan Times* (New Delhi), June 15, p. 1.
3. *Ibid.*
4. *Hindustan Times*, June 18, 2012, p. 15, New Delhi.
5. Narendra Taneja (2012), "Peace in the Pipeline", *Tehelka*, June 16, p. 18.
6. *Ibid.*
7. *Ibid.*
8. *Ibid.*
9. *Ibid.*
10. *Hindustan Times* (New Delhi), June 29, 2012, p. 17.
11. *Ibid.*
12. Jayanth Jacob (2012), "Afghanistan Endgame Leads to Tajik Gambit", *Hindustan Times* (New Delhi), July 3, p. 17.
13. *Ibid.*, see also Jyotsna Bakshi (Ed.) (2007), *India's Engagement with Central Asia with Focus on India-Uzbekistan relations*, Lal Bahadur Shastri Centre for Indian Culture: Centre for Political Studies, Tashkent.
14. The sensitive list defines products which will not be eligible for lower import tariffs in the South Asia Free Trade Area (SAFTA).
15. Bidanda Chengappa (2012), "Soft or Hard Power", *The Sunday Indian*, November 25, p. 60.
16. *Hindustan Times*, November 28, 2012, p. 19, New Delhi.

Appendix

V. S. SHETH

I thank Professor Kamath for giving me this opportunity to participate in this Seminar and ask me to preside over the session on, "India, USA and Pakistan in Afghanistan and Changing Perspectives".

I believe facts of History and Geography have relevance for finding solutions to the contemporary situation. During Soviet occupation of Afghanistan, BBC produced serial titled 'Gateway of India' and in the nineties serial Chanakya was aired by Doordarshan. These two serials stressed importance of land routes to Indian subcontinent and the unity of the Indian heartland in the face of threats emanating from Northwest, if the local political units are unable to face them. The British came by sea but then they realised that the frontiers of India lay through Afghanistan and secured them by capturing Kabul in nineteenth century.

Recently, a book by Robert D. Kaplan has put forward a thesis that facts of geography are taking revenge on those of history and politics. The geographic unity and economic primacy of area stretching from Gangetic-belt to Kabul has been disturbed in recent times by politics and technology. The area has lost its political, cultural, and commercial primacy in post-independence period. The resultant socio-cultural vacuum has been filled by terrorists and fundamentalists. Kaplan argues that if one has to establish peace between India, Pakistan and Afghanistan then the exchange of people, trade and commerce from Indian subcontinent to the west and central Asia via trade routes has to resume.

Indian interests in Afghanistan are in establishing land connectivity with Iran and Central Asian countries, promote infrastructure, economic and educational growth, and strengthen democratic rule. This can be done at bilateral and multilateral levels. Policy makers have to search for new policy models and paradigms which will increase and strengthen trade and cultural constituencies at societal level in Afghanistan, deepen democratic rule and tradition and localise terrorist and fundamental influences.

I know this is a tough call but then political rulers of Indian subcontinent will have to take the challenge and attain results without fail.

P.G. KAMATH

1. Afghanistan should be used as a Strategic threat to Pakistan

Strengthen Afghan National Army, Arms, weapons and equipment and training should be given to them for both Conventional Warfare and for Counter-Insurgency warfare. Ensure that they pose a threat to Pakistan's western borders and tie down troops so that Pakistan is not able to concentrate them against India during the next war. Create geo-political conditions in Pakistan both internally and externally to tie it down in internecine warfare so that it drowns in the cess pool of her bad governance and ethnic conflicts. There is no other way to deal with Pakistan.

2. Direct Land Access to Afghanistan

Ask Pakistan to grant direct land access to Afghanistan for non-lethal goods for the benefit of Afghan People. In case it is not given declare that India has no option but to explore the possibility of finding a route through Northern Territory or POK both of which are integral part of India.

3. Troops under UN Flag

The country side is already under the Taliban and the Karzai's regime was only in cities. Once the Americans leave altogether, then it is more than certain that the Taliban will cross over from Pakistan in large numbers and hold their sway.

Afghanistan going the Iraq way is a distinct possibility. India needs to plan now. We should not hesitate to send troops under UN Flag and with Afghan Consent.

MOHAMMAD ATTA ROSHANGAR

Regarding India's policy options concerning Afghanistan after US withdrawal from this country, as an Afghan citizen and one of the participants of the seminar who believes in India's constructive and vital role in the region as well as my country, I would suggest that India should follow these policies simultaneously:

1. India should continue training, equipping and supporting the Afghan National Security Forces (ANSF); as I came to know, India trains Afghan officers in India. For making it more cost-effective, I suggest that if possible Indian government should send trainers to Afghanistan instead of bringing Afghan officers to India; the reason is very simple, for instance, if India sends 10 trainers to Kabul, they will be able to train up 1000 officers or soldiers directly, but, if Afghan's officers come to India, it's more costly and they may not be able to train officers and other soldiers back home as Indians can directly.

2. As we know there is a huge trust deficit and suspicions between India and Pakistan in their policies and relationships regarding Afghanistan; Pakistanis believe India tries to destabilise Pakistan through Afghanistan specifically under the cover of its consulates in the provinces neighbouring Pakistan's border. In return India believes that Pakistan's government and its Army intelligence service seek to install a puppet government in Kabul which is intended to be loyal to Pakistan and hostile to India, and Pakistan's generals and policy-makers see Afghanistan as "strategic depth". If this mistrust continues, Afghanistan would be a battlefield for both the countries, which will destabilise the entire region. Indians have to negotiate with their Pakistani partners and convince them that Indian presence in Afghanistan is not against national security of Pakistan. By doing so, the mistrust between them will decrease and cooperation could be accelerated.

3. Many participants in the seminar including Indian diplomats were of the view that India being the fifth largest donor to Afghanistan is one of the most popular countries in the eyes of Afghans, this perception is only partially true. The main reason behind this admiration is non-interference by India in Afghanistan's internal affairs, India unlike Pakistan and Iran which have been involved and interfered in the national politics of Afghanistan, has not interfered directly or its intrusion is not visible to the eyes of ordinary Afghans. So, India in comparison to other countries is popular; it will be favourable for the long-term benefit of India to continue the policy of "non- interference".Yet, it does not necessarily mean that India should not support Afghanistan's government; helping a democratic, inclusive and legitimate government in Kabul is in the best interest of India as well as the people of Afghanistan.

NAVASIKHA DUARA

The stability of Afghanistan post-US withdrawal is indeed uncertain. The question is whether Afghanistan will see the return to the dark days of Taliban Rule or continue as a democratic, united, stable Afghanistan.

If Taliban's emergence is the most serious challenge to Afghanistan after 2014, its return can undo what the international community has achieved in Afghanistan during the last fourteen years. The Taliban insurgency is invariably linked to the regional dynamics of Indo-Pak relation. Pakistan's policy of regarding Afghanistan, as the 'strategic depth' to be used against an impending Indian attack has led to ISI-Pak Army's continued support to the Afghan Taliban. Pakistan's search of 'Strategic Depth' is thus an 'existential' issue arising out of an imagined attack from India. Therefore, Pakistan's policy towards Afghanistan is India-centric, aimed to minimise India's role in Afghanistan. It is no secret that India's deep involvement in post-Taliban Afghanistan is viewed by Pakistan as aimed to 'pressure' it from both sides. As a result, very often if not always, it results in Islamabad taking counter measures either in Afghanistan or in India. That explains Pakistan's support to Pak-based militant groups. India's fight against terrorism is invariably intertwined with terrorism in Afghanistan. That is why India wants to see a democratic and stable Afghanistan; a radical regime is a threat to Indian security.

The present uneasy relationship of the Pakistan's security establishment with Afghan Taliban can be explored for improving the relations between the two regional rivals. The reported nexus, between Afghan Taliban and Pak Taliban, is a cause of worry for Pakistan, for this may defeat the purpose of sponsoring the Taliban. Rather the success of Afghan Taliban might encourage the TTP to revive the demand for creation of Pastunistan under the Islamic Jihadi banner, thus posing a threat to the territorial integrity of Afghanistan. Therefore, pushing for the Afghan Taliban's return to power in Kabul might not be helpful to Islamabad. If that is the case, both India and Pakistan have a common interest in having a stable Afghanistan free from radical forces.

An improvement of Indo-Pak relations via economic integration can be explored to achieve stability in Afghanistan. Afghanistan can be used for economic development of both the Nation States. Joint projects either bilateral or multilateral projects like Trans–Afghan project involving both the states should be encouraged. Economic benefits of such projects may prevent Pakistan from seeing Afghanistan as a mere battle field to wage proxy wars against India. However, a lot depends on Pak army and civilian government reaching a consensus on policy towards Afghanistan; mainly, Pakistan is proving her credential as a reliable partner in the war against terror in Afghanistan. India on her part can take the process of dialogue to improve relations and build confidence between the two rivals.

R.G. GIDADHUBLI

India should explore the possibilities of setting up joint ventures to promote Small and Medium Enterprises in Afghanistan to facilitate agro-processing particularly wide range of fruits, and export to India. In this regard regional cooperation with the Central Asian States such as Uzbekistan, Tajikistan etc. might be of great help.

A project to study the status and socio-economic conditions of ethnic community of Sikhs in Afghanistan by our Centre may be worthwhile.

Seminar Report

Anand V and Vineeth Krishnan

The national seminar on "American Withdrawal from Afghanistan in December 2014: Post-Withdrawal Puzzle of Policy Options for India, Pakistan and Afghanistan" held by the VPM's Centre for International Studies at Mumbai during 29-31 July 2014 comes at a time when the US has planned a phased exit strategy after December 2014, generating regional concerns. It also came at a time when the fear of Taliban resurgence is complemented by the events in West Asia in the aftermath of the Arab Spring, including the rise of the ISIS (Islamic State of Iraq and Syria). As a result, it becomes important to assess the implications of the US withdrawal from Afghanistan for the regional security as well as for India's national security.

The discussions which ensued were based on the three transitions which have been underway in Afghanistan concerned with matters of security, politics and economics. At the core of the discussions on the security transition was the question of readiness of the Afghan National Security Forces (ANSF) to deal with the security challenges emanating from the re-emerging Taliban. Scepticism was expressed regarding the adequacy of training given to the ANSF by the ISAF (International Security Assistance Force) to deal with conventional conflicts. The political transition in Afghanistan towards achieving a stable political system is mired in the domestic hurdles. Notwithstanding the debate between effective and democratic models of governance, the trajectory that the then ongoing Presidential election traced was seen to be of critical value to Afghanistan's future. The economic transition has been mostly seen from that of the opium and foreign aid-based economic model to one which is sustainable and capable of reinforcing the development of Afghanistan and the regional security in its neighbourhood. The constructive role of external players has been seen as integral to the comprehensive transition of Afghanistan into a peaceful and stable state. A social angle was also added to this transformation, wherein Afghanistan's demographic youth bulge could be diverted from violence to constructive nation-building through effective human resources management in collaboration with neighbouring states, especially India.

The objectives and strategies of the various regional and extra-regional players with vital stakes in Afghanistan's security scenario were discussed in depth. For Pakistan, being one of the most significant stakeholders, Afghanistan has been seen to be a vital part of its quest for strategic depth vis-à-vis India. In this context, it was debated as to whether Pakistan's interest lies in a stable or an unstable Afghanistan. An effective Pakistani control over the government in Kabul has been found to be Pakistan's preferred objective in Afghanistan. However, it was indicated that the backing given to Taliban for this purpose by Pakistan might subsequently lead to surge in Pashtun nationalism which will have negative consequences for Pakistan's territorial integrity and national security itself.

Other stakeholders like Iran and Central Asia have long standing and strong civilisations old links as well as security stakes with Afghanistan related to the cross-border drug trade menace and the Taliban threat respectively. These countries have been found to hold considerable sway over its non-Pashtun ethnic groups and regions. Russia, even though having a high potential for supporting the nation building efforts of Afghanistan, has been highlighted to be constrained by its negative historical baggage rooted in the Soviet intervention of 1979. China, on the other hand has already developed considerable economic clout in Afghanistan through its infrastructure development activities by free-riding on the US-led efforts to maintain security within the country.

Afghanistan plays a key role in India's national security considerations. Since historical times, invaders have entered India from Afghanistan, which highlights its geostrategic significance. India's role in bringing peace and stability to Afghanistan and transforming it into a positive force in the region has been deliberated in much detail. India has involved directly in the post-intervention reconstruction of Afghanistan through capacity building in various sectors. India has also been working through other countries and stakeholders in this respect. There were debates as to whether a stable or an unstable Pakistan will ensure advancement of India's strategic objectives in Afghanistan. There have been arguments supporting India militarily countering Pakistan and attempting to fracture it domestically along ethno-political lines, against those supporting economically luring potentially favourable constituencies within the nation. India's role in establishing connectivity to Afghanistan through Iran, as well as projecting its influence through neighbouring Central Asian states was also highlighted. India's role in arming Afghanistan through Russian support has also been indicated as a model for the way forward in utilising third countries for enhancing Indian interests in Afghanistan. There were even suggestions about bringing in regional organisations like the SAARC (South Asian Association for Regional Co-operation) and SCO (Shanghai Co-operation Organisation) in ways which will augment Indian efforts to stabilize Afghanistan.

The seminar therefore covered a wide ground in understanding and analysing the complex issues involved with the withdrawal of American forces from Afghanistan. However, the seminar has also left open the scope for further debate and discussion, based on certain salient considerations. Firstly, the general mood reflected during the seminar was that the Taliban would re-emerge and gain administrative control over large parts of Afghanistan in the aftermath of the US withdrawal. However, considering that the Taliban has no air force, their progress from the southern province of Kandahar to the capital Kabul and northwards to Mazar-e-Sharif is bound to be slow. Even in their initial surge to power, it took Mullah Omar four years to reach Mazar-e-Sharif after initially gaining control over Kandahar. This temporal factor can have considerable influence on the regional and international responses.

Secondly, much apprehension was recorded about the ability of the ANSF to defend the state from a resurgent Taliban. However, a comparative study about the capabilities of the Quetta Shura Taliban and the ANSF could throw more light on the likely security situation post-2014. When the Taliban did secure power, they were helped by the civil war that had divided the various tribal militias. The present condition on the ground, in spite of the political divide over alleged rigging of the Presidential election, is much better off.

Thirdly, although there has been a dominant emphasis on the ethnic divide in Afghanistan and its ramifications on national stability, the fact remains that there has also currently been political attempts to balance power between the different ethnicities. In particular, the practice of naming first and second Vice Presidential candidates representing the ethnic mix has been undertaken by the Presidential Candidates Ashraf Ghani and Abdullah Abdullah, giving the ethnic issue a complex dimension.

Finally, apart from economic, ethno-political and demographic factors, the role of leadership is a major aspect which could bring in an additional dimension to understanding the emerging scenario in Afghanistan. For instance, a major element lacking in the current Afghan system is the presence of a leader who commands respect across ethnicities, a personality of stature akin to Ahmed Shah Massoud.

Index

A

9/11

Attack on US, 12, 15, 174

Massacre, 114

Shock, 45

Terror Attack, 187

Abbotabad, 152

Abdul Rashid Dostum, 209

Abdullah Abdullah, 60, 63, 104-107, 205

President Aspirant, 23, 24

ISI's Worst Neighbour, 105

Abu Bakr al Baghdadi, 29

Addiction, 139

Afghan

And Iraq War, 146

And Pakistan, Strategic Location, 54

Communities, 24

Elections, 105

Ethnic Groups, 51, 136

Foreign Ministry, 171

Jihad, 189, 198

Market, 180

Mission, 147

Narcotics Trade, 223

National Army (ANA), 14, 39, 94, 115, 117, 132, 142, 175, 188, 212, 214

National Police (ANP), 14, 20, 49, 132, 150, 164, 175, 212

National Security Forces (ANSF), 139, 131, 175F, 178, 208, 211, 245

Population, 117

Refugees, 71, 73

Regime, 180

Security, 130

Security Forces, 39

Society, 116, 131, 132, 135

Society Rebuild of-, 53

Stability, 181

Taliban, 27, 48, 55, 56, 58, 94, 119, 189, 192, 208, 209, 210, 221-224

Taliban or Tribal Chiefs, 58

Terror Group, 21

Haqqani Network, 21

Taliban, 21

Tribes, 113, 114

War, 18, 58, 96, 118, 146, 172

War of 1989, 16, 119

Afghanistan

And Eurasia, 77

And India, 179
Strong and Friendly Relationship, 179
And Kashmir, 196
And Pakistan, 12, 74, 148, 155
And Regional Peace Building, 69-84
As US Proxy, 57
As Vital Security Interests, (for India and Pakistan), 39
Buffer Zone, 70
Civil War, 155
Collapse into Civil War, 219
Crisis Ridden Society, 112
Crisis, 45, 93-107, 156, 157
Dependence on Pakistan, 71, 73
Development, 21
Mining, Energy—, 21
Economic Importance, 16
Economy, 18, 140
Elections, 101
Energy, Bridge, 70
Ethnic Conflicts, 16
Extraction Sector, 26
Feudal Structured Country, 112
Future of Democracy in-, 135-144
Future of-, 25
Future Stability, 220
Gas Cooperation, 91
Goods, 46
Grave Yard of Empires, 145
Grave yard of Great Empires, 45
Hell of Extremism, 114
India Relations, 41
Insurgency, 100
Internal Situation, 20
Isolation, 71
Land of Warriors, 117
Landlocked—, 69
Military, 91
Mujahideens, 44
National Forces (ANF), 24, 26, 94, 142
National Security Forces (ANSF), 20, 21,
Natural Resources, 77
No Sign of Lasting Peace, 13
Pakistan Trade Tariff Agreement (APTTA), 46, 238
President Elections, 103
Problems, 200
Security, 94, 114, 118, 125
Security Forces, 78, 107, 126, 127, 157, 240
Security Threat to-, 14
Strategic Partnership Agreement, 192
Subject of Great Game, 113
Taliban Movement, 75
Train International Terrorist, 12
Untapped Raw Material Resources, 118
Afghanistan's Najibullah Government, 141
Afghan-Pakistan Taliban, 52
Af-Pak
Border, 119, 211, 222
Trade and Transit Treaty, 213
Afzal Gani, President Aspirant, 23, 24
Ahmad Rashid, Scholar, 52
Ahmad Shah Massoud, 207, 209
Akhtar Abudr Rahman, Lt. Gen. ISI Chief, 21, 204
Akshardham, 36

Al Qaeda, 12, 13, 18, 41, 48, 52, 55, 73, 75, 78, 106, 114, 129, 146, 152, 162, 190, 204, 205, 206-209, 210, 213, 214, 215, 216, 220

And Taliban, 114

Islamic Extremists, 146

Operative Trained in Pakistan, 52

Sponsored Attack on US, 55

Taliban Nexus, 105

Al Qaeda's Global Jihadism, 130

Alexander The Great, 15, 113, 145

American

(NATO) Military Presence, 53

Aid, 168

Economy, 59

Funds, 40

Hegemony, 64

Hunting, 15

Intervention in Afghanistan, 14

Military Forces, 28

Military Intervention, 12

Misadventure, 146

Mission, 114

Mission in Iraq and Afghanistan, 111

Political Game Plan of Global Hegemony, 49

Presidential Elections, 45

Protectionism, 65

Security, 49

Super Power, 15

Troops, 205

Troops in Afghanistan, 16, 127

Withdrawal from Afghanistan, 2014, 12, 21, 39, 67, 233-241

American's Divide and Rule Policy, 44

Americans, 203, 204

Training and Assistance Force, 207

Amrullah Saleh, 209

Amu Darya and Pyanj Basins, 75

Anglo-

American Diplomacy, 44

US Consensus in Iraq War, 43

US Interests in Iraq War, 43

Anti-

American Afghan Group, 54

India Mission of Pakistan, 120

Indian Regime in Afghanistan, 46

Pakistan Activities, 28

Soviet Islamic Crusader, 166

Taliban Northern Alliance, 104

Arab Sunni Charities, 24

Arms Race, 40

Asaf Zardari, Pak President, 162

Ashfaq Kayani, General, 28

Ashraf Ghani, Afghanistan Pres., 60, 200, 219

Attack on Saddam Hussain Iraq, 64

Ayub Khan, 162

B

Babarak Karmal, Local Puppet, 151, 204

Bagdad and Kabul, 23

Bagran Airfield, 16

Balance of Power, 40, 141

Baluchistan, 149

Bamiyan

Buddha, 147

Province, 191

Bangladesh, 148, 149
Alienated in 1971, 47
Independent State, 161
War in 1971, 19, 61, 163
Barua, Arpita, 13
Beijing
Afghan Policies, 79
Run Terrorist Camps, 119
Bhutan, 57
Bhutto, Benazir, former Pak PM, 165, 196
Bifurcation of United India, 1947, 188
Big Powers, 209
US, Russia, India, European Union, 209
Bigger Powers of Asia, 62
Japan, India and Pakistan, 62
Bilateral
Security Agreement, 205
Security Arrangements (BSA), 106
Bill of Rights, 112
Bin Laden in Abbotabad, 167
Birth of Pakistan, 1947, 161
Bloodshed in Kunming Province, 119
Bomb Blasts, 13
In Mumbai (26/11), 51
Bonn Agreement, 2001, 115, 137
British
Art of Diplomacy, 44
Empire, 145
India, 19
India and Russia, 70
Buddhism, 147
Burhannuddin Rabbani, Assassination, 98
Bush, George W, US President, 12, 55, 166
Administration, 14, 96, 166, 190
Presidency, 56

C

Cabinet Committee on Security (CCS), 102
Carter, Jimmy, President, 48
CBS Polls, 192
Central
And North Eastern Mountains, 212
Asia, 72, 112, 119, 150, 155, 157, 173, 176, 194
Asian Natural Resources, 43
Asian Oil Gas, 61
Asian Region, 88, 179, 225, 227
Asian Republic Countries, 216
Asian Republics (CAR), 29, 78, 89, 80, 81, 153, 154, 155, 182, 239
Central Asian States (CAS), 74, 75, 88, 98, 247
Tajikstan, 88
Turkmenistan, 88
Uzbekistan, 88
Centre for Conflict and Peace Studies in Kabul, 143
Chahbahar
Irani Port, 26, 29, 77, 102, 183, 190, 191
To Delaram, 91
Chechen Muslims, 155
Check on Terrorism, 180
Chhatrapati Shivaji, Maratha Leader, 50
Chieftains and Warlords, 211
China, 13, 42, 48, 49, 61, 63, 74, 80, 81, 120, 154, 170, 176, 198, 216

And Pakistan, 214
Axis, 57
Pakistan, Nepal, Bangladesh, 57
In Muslim Uyghur, 30
Mission—in Afghanistan, 120
Pak Axis, 57
Strategic Planning, 62
War, 18
China's
Metallurgical Group, 62
Strategy in Afghanistan, 79
Chinese
Comprehensive National Plan (CCNP), 61
Diplomacy, 61
Economy, 74
Rise of-, 58
Investment and Energy Network, 71
Muslim Terrorists, 79
Pakistani Nexus, 61
Security Interest, 30
Sinkiang, 69
CIA, 167, 190
CIS Countries, 237
Civil
Society in Afghanistan, 129
War, 141, 173, 205
War in Afghanistan, 206
Clinton, Hillary, 19, 55, 162, 165, 168
Administration, 56
Cold War World Order, 43
Combating Terrorism in Punjab, 33
Communist Manifesto, 112
Conduits and Carriers, 33
Confederation of Fiefdoms, 178
Construction Projects, 179
Consulates in-, 77
Herat, 77
Jalalabad, 77
Kandahar, 77
Mazar-e-Sharif, 77
Contract Farming, 25
Conventional War Mechanism, 36
Counter
China's String of Pearls, 216
Insurgency Operations, 204
Terrorism, 31
Counter-Insurgency, 130
Crush Pakistan, Economy, 56
Cultural War Against US, 12
Czarist Russia, 188

D

Dari Language, 85
Dawn, Pakistan Newspaper, 150
Delaram with Zaranj, Iran Border, Connecting of-, 25
Delhi's Training Program of Afghanistan—, 199
Democracy
In Afghanistan, 17
In Pakistan, Return of-, 165
Democratic Government, 47
Democratization
Brief History, 136
Of Afghanistan, 116
Process, 135
Development
And Infrastructure, 233
Issues, 233-241
Disputed Border, 19
Dobbins, James, US Special Representative, 103

Doctrine of Strategic Depth, 196
Domestic Issues, 40
  Poverty—Religious Cultural Conflicts, 40
Drone War, 24
Drones, 212
Drug
  Dealers, 43
  Trafficking, 14, 74, 76, 79, 80, 89, 90, 155, 178, 198
  Trafficking in Eurasia Region, 90
Dukhtar-e-Millat, 33
Durand
  And Radcliffe Lines, 100
  Line, 19, 73, 148, 164, 188, 194, 211, 213, 222, 228
  Border Between India and Afghanistan, 164
  Line in Afghanistan, 27

E

East
  China Sea, 216
  Pakistan, 19, 161
  Turkistan, 156
Economic
  And Political System, 40
  Crisis, 177
  Development, 21, 87, 170, 182
  Of Afghanistan, 182
  Growth, 180
Economy, 40, 128, 174, 175, 195
Educational And Research Institutions, 182
Election
  Campaign, 146
  Commission, 116, 117
Electronic Surveillance from Satellites, 212
Embassy Bombing in
  Kabul, 179
  Tanzania and Kenya, 207
Energy
  Supply Routes, 79
  Trade, 71
Ethical Groups, 173
Ethnic
  And Cultural Tensions, 70
  Conflicts, 112, 115
  Groups,
  Hazaras, 173
  Pashtuns, 173
  Tajiks, 173
  Uzbeks, 173
  Minorities, 93
  Polarization, 14
Eurasia, 188, 203
Eurasian
  Land Mass, 187
  Region, 237
Europe's Economy, 43
European
  Colonialism, 15
  Colonialism, Era of-, 112
  Powers, 50, 59, 60
  Dutch, 50
  France, 50
  France, 59
  Germany, 59
  UK, 59
  US, 59
  Union, 49, 216
Extra Regional Powers, 39
  China, USA and Russia, 39
Extremism and Terrorism, 74

Extremist
Islam, 30
Movement, 55
Of Afghanistan, 119

F

FATA (Federally Administered Areas), 56, 152, 188, 193, 195, 213, 214, 222
Fazilka Settlement on Pak-India Border, 91
Ferdowsi University, 76
Financial Operations, 34
First
Afghan War, 203
Gulf War, 64
Foreign Invasions, 15, 112
Forums, 28
Ankara, 28
Chicago, 28
France and Germany, 43
Fratricidal Conflicts, 115
Freedom Movement, 50
Fundamentalism, 32

G

GAIL, 235
Gandhara Art, 147
Gandhi, Late Mrs. Indira, 105
Gandhi, Late Rajiv, 105
Gas Pipeline Framework Agreement, (GPFA), 239
Geneva Accords, 14
Ghali, BB, former UN Secy. Gen., 193
Gidadhubli, RG, 14
Gilani, Pak PM, 48, 62, 63
Global
And Regional Security, 16, 115
Jihad/Terrorism, 31-38
Jihadism, 129
Power Game, 187
War on Terrorism, 125
Globalization, 47
Good Governance, 222
Gorbachev, 12
Great
Game, 70
Power Rivalry, 220
Greeks—Pakistanis, 203
Guantanamo Bay Cuba, 204, 224
Guerrilla Fighters of Third World, 111
Gulf
Oil, 44
States, 24
Gwadar Port, 63

H

Hajigalmo, Arc, 191
Hajigath Region, 25, 26
Hamid Karzai, 23, 25, 60, 85, 102, 103, 104, 106, 107, 120, 151, 174
Afghanistan President, 88, 94, 97, 101, 139, 214, 237
Government, 58, 60, 148, 223
Haqqani
Clan, 27
Group, 46, 48, 53, 189, 190
In FATA, 195
Militants, 191
Network, (HN), 21, 93, 151, 156, 189, 194, 200, 210, 215, 221, 222, 229
Hazaras, 76, 98, 104
Herat, 76, 179, 235
Attack, 189, 193

Jalalabad and Kandhar Population, 138
Heroin
Poppy, 24
Processing Centres, 25
High Peace Council, 98
Himachal Pradesh, 215
Hindu
India, 46
Ḳush, 79
Hitler Defeat, 64
Hizb-e-Islami, 151, 156, 209
Holy War of Jihad, 207
Home Building Projects, 86
Human Rights, 40
Organisation, 34
Hydroelectric Power, 74

I

Illegal
Drug Trafficking, 25
Weapon Trafficking, 80
Imperial
Powers, 151
Russia, 164
Import of Terrorism in India, 180
Improvised Explosive Devices (IEDs), m142
Imran Khan's Tehreeq-e-Insaff Party, 27
IMU Terrorists, 198
Independent Election Committee, (IEC), 103
India and
Afghanistan, 19, 194
Central Asian States, 70
China, 16, 111, 121, 183, 194, 216
Policy Option for-, 111-121
China Great Game Between-, 118
Iran Contribution, 200
Kashmir, 119
Pakistan, 18, 39, 40, 41, 45, 51, 78, 147, 162, 182
Part of Enduring Peace (In Afghanistan), 40
Russia, 14
Common Interest in Afghanistan, 14
US, 21
India,
Afghan Historical Ties, 54
China Partnership, 183
Developmental Work in Afghanistan, 41
Implications in Afghanistan, 178
Jewel in Crown, 40
Pakistan, China, Triad of Conflict, 42
Political and Economical Cooperation with Afghanistan, 71
Six Great Power, 51
India's
Afghan Policy, 105, 120
Conventional Superiority, 41
Development Assistance, 53
Economic Investment in Afghanistan, 77
Economic Investment in Natural Resources, 29
Economic Role in Afghanistan, 226
Foreign Policy, 233
GAIL, 91
Interest and Policies in Afghanistan, 80

Investment (in Afghanistan), 53
Involvement in Afghanistan, 225
Options, 213
Presence in Afghanistan, 17
Soft Power Diplomacy, 51
Strategic Location, 42
Strategic Partnership Agreement, 214
War with China, 1962, 61
Indian
Armed Forces, 215
Army, 162
Border Road Organization (IBRO), 213
Borders, 19, 46
Consulate Jalalabad, Bombing of-, 15
Consulates, 26
Herat, 26
Jalalabad, 26
Kandahar, 26
Development Program (Afghanistan), 53
In Afghanistan, 50
Infrastructure, 222
Iranian Cooperation, 72
Military, 28, 29
Military Assistance, 28
Military Engagements in Afghanistan, 199
Military Training Centre, 26
Nuclear Retaliation, 41
Ocean, 42
Trade, 237
India-Pakistan Political Relations, 165
Indo-Afg
Relations, 240
Afg Strategic Partnership, 240
Afghanistan Strategic Partnership, 234
Indo-China-Russia Cooperation in Afghanistan, 81
Indo-Pak
Border, 211
Cooperation in Afghanistan, 80
Relations, 220, 224, 233, 237, 238, 241, 247
Relations-Stability in Afghanistan, 228
Rivalry, 80
Indo-Pakistan Hostilities, 180
Infiltration
Of Foreign Terrorists, 175
Routes, 79
Information Technology Professionals, 33
Infrastructural Projects, 191
Insurgency, 174, 182, 183, 195
In Kashmir, 237
In North East India, 33
Insurgent
Camps—In Myanmar and Bangladesh, 34
Groups, 178
Organizations, 34
NDFB, 34
NSCN(IM), 34
ULFA, 34
Inter-Governmental Agreement (IGA), 239
International
Border, 73
Ethnic Conflicts, 15
Human Rights, 116
Relations, 40

Security Assistance Force (ISAF), 24
Security Assistance Program, 90
Terrorism, (IT), 12
Terrorist Group, 12
Terrorists, 112
Invaders, 213
Babar, 213
Greeks, Huns, Persians, 112
Infamous Mohd Ghazni, 213
Mohd Ghori, 213
Sher Shah Suri, 213
Taimur, 213
The Huns, 213
Iran, 27, 155
Border, 189
Iran's
Aid to Taliban, 76
Borderland, 27
Nuclear Program, 73
Policies in Pakistan, 76
Iranian
Backed Militant Groups, 76
Hamas, 76
Hizbollah, 76
Iran-Pakistan-India (IPI), 235
Iraq, 37, 47
And Afghan War, 205
And Afghanistan, 59
And Libya, 93
Incursions, 1990, 44
Into Shia and Sunni and Kurdish Sections, 14
War, 18, 43, 146
Iron Ore, 25
ISAF (International Security Assistance Force in Afghanistan), 142, 151
Operation, 78
ISI, 46, 51, 55, 58, 222, 229, 235
Agents, 190
And Pakistan Military, 73
And Pakistan, 73
Backed Taliban, Al Qaeda and Lashkar-e-Toiba, 105
Created Taliban Regime, 150
Led ISAF, 219
Of Pakistan, 19, 52, 119, 120, 150, 152, 153, 154, 165, 167, 175, 204, 207, 215
Pakistan's Intelligence Agency, 47, 48
ISI's Game, 48
ISI-Interstate Intelligence of Pakistan, 33
ISIS (Islamic State of Syria and Iraq), 21, 24, 37, 42, 47, 66
Taliban Fighters, 29
Islam World of Sunnis, 209
Islamabad Foreign Policy Radar, 28
Islamic
Bank, 61
Caliphates, 206
Card, 48
Countries, 42, 63
Emirate of Waziristan, 222
Extremism, 114
Extremist Group, 25, 114
Extremists, 55
Extremists from Xinjiang, 156
Faith, New Nationalism, 47
Freedom Fighters, 21, 204

Fundamentalism, 89, 97
Groups, 153
Identity, 137
Jihad, 12, 90
Jihadi Banner, 247
Jihadism, 152
Jihadists, 154
Movement for Uzbekistan, 90
Radicalism in Afghanistan, 156
Radicalism, 118
Reform Movement, 136
Rule in Afghanistan, 47
Rulers, 46
State, 36, 61
State of Afghanistan, 206
Terrorism, 63
Terrorism and Extremism, 156
World, 23, 136
Islamist Military, 46
Issues of Economic Infrastructure, —, 214
ITBT, 65
Paramilitary Force, 53

J

Jalalabad, 179
Jamaat-ud-Dawa, 229
Jammu and Kashmir, 215, 227
Japan, 48
Jasih-e-Mohammad, 169
Jidadi/Terrorist Groups, 33
Jihad, 21, 27, 32, 35, 47, 204
Against Chinese Regime, 30
Factory, 194
Militancy, Terrorism, 38
Jihad/Terrorism, 31-38
Jihadi, 74, 153
Attacks, 46, 147
Concept of War, 31, 36
Groups, 37, 154
Islamists, 225
Organization, 34, 35
Terrorism, 105
War, 37
Jihadi/Terrorism Concept, 31
Jihadi/Terrorist, 38
Group, 35, 36
Movement, 33
Jihadi/Terrorists, Types and Concept, 32
Jihadis, 29, 105
Jihadists, 152, 204
Jimmy Carter Regime, 44
Jinnah, Mohammad Ali, 54
Joint EU-Russian Agency, 90
Jundullah Instability, 73
Junejo, Mohammad Khan, PM, 193

K

Kabul, 16, 23, 29, 53, 62, 72, 74-76, 103, 105, 138, 148, 190, 191, 200, 201, 203, 206, 208, 220, 221, 226-229
House Building Factor, 86, 87
University, 88
Kalashnikov, 29
Kamath, PG, PM, 19, 20
Kamra Air Force Base, 27
Kamran Shafa, 150
Kandhar, 179, 235
Herat, Jalalabad and Mazar-e-Sharif, 148
Kappas, Stephen, Dy Chief CIA, 190
Karachi
And Gwadar Ports, 46

Harbour, 27
Kargil, 190
Conflict, 169
Crisis, 41
Karzai, 77, 192 See under Hamid Karzai also
Abdulla and Ghani, 25
Government, 53, 65, 86, 88
Karzai's
Pakistan Alliance, 93
Political Alliance, 14
Regime, 93
Kashmir, 20, 33, 37, 42, 46, 48, 52, 54, 154, 196, 197, 210
Affairs, 29
And Afghanistan, 163
And Xinjiang, 118
Issue, 190
Valley, 100
Kashmiri Militants, 16, 119
Kautilya, 50
Kayani, Former Army Chief General Pakistan, 19, 41, 46, 93, 150, 226
General, 164
Kazakhstan, 65, 78
Kennedy, Edward, 66
Kerry, John, 199, 205
US Secy. of State, 23
Kerry-Lugar Berman Bill (US), 168
Key Players, Pakistan, Sri Lanka, Myanmar, 42
Khar Hina Rabani, 162
Khurshid Kasuri, Pak Foreign Minister, 169
Khyber Pass, 50
Khyber-Pakhtunkhwa, 148
Kill American Concept, 56
King
Amanullah Khan, Reformist, 136
Zahir Shah, Afghan King, 113
Kissinger, Henry, 225
Krishna, SM, Minister, 236
Kunar and Nuristan, 229
Province, 15, 100
Kurdish, 93
Kushan, 187
Kyrgyz Republic, 90
Kyrgyzstan, 78

L

Labour Room of Terrorism, 114
Ladakh, 215
Lahore Declaration, 190
Lanzhou Military Region, 215
Lashkar-e-Toiba (LeT), 15, 73, 75, 100, 120, 156, 190, 194, 209, 210, 215, 225
In Afghanistan, 191
LED Attack, 175
Liberated Terrorist Zone, 209
Life Expectancy, 17, 138
Line of Control (LOC), 15, 100
Low Intensity Conflict, 41, 51
Loya Jirga, or High Peace Council, 106, 210

M

MAD (Mutual Agreed Destruction), 40
Madarsas, 166
Mafias, 43
Magna Carta, 112
Mahabharata, 37
Major Powers of Europe, 43

Manmohan Singh, former Indian PM, 102
Maoists, 33
Marijuana Trade, 46
Maternal Mortality Rate, 17, 138
Mazar-e-Sharif, 179
Mehran Naval Base, 27
Mehrishi, BN, 14
Meshrano Jirga, 211
Microryan, 87
Middle
  East Oil, 48
  Eastern Oil, 44
Militancy, 105
Militarism, 40
Military
  And Security Forces, 183
  Intelligence Jihadi Complex, 167
  Operation, 183, 190
  Operation 'Zerb-a-Herb', 193
  Operation Against Taliban, 147
  Operation in Iraq and Afghanistan, 23
  Strategy, 37, 180
  Valuation in Aghanistan, 40
Military-ISI-Jihadi Terrorist Complex, 165
Minahjul Qura Movement, 27
Mini-Hydro Power Plants, 86
Minority
  Islamic Group, 155
  Religious Group, 153
Mirza ASlam Beg, GeneraL, 163
Mittal, Ashita, 104
Mobile Terrorist Group, 27
Modern Education System, 13
  Replace Madarsa Culture, 13
Modi, Indian Prime Minister, 105, 106, 120, 121, 189, 193, 199, 200
Modi's Leadership, 105
Mohammed Atta Roshangar, 245
Mohite, Dilip, 13
Moily, M Veerappan, 239
Mortality Rate, 138
Most Favored Nation (MFN), 238
Movements of Baluch and Sindh and NWFP, 47
Mujahideen, 51, 113, 204, 206
  Group, 220
Mukherjee, Pranab, President, 237
Mullah Fazlullah, 93
Mullah Mohammed Omer (Mullah Omar), 23, 29, 58, 99, 152, 208, 220-223
  Pakhtun Afghan Taliban, 24
  Taliban Chief, 204
Multiethnic Afghan Society, 155
Multi-National Security, 13
Multi-Tier Counter Infiltration Grid, 211
Mumbai Carnage, 189
Musharraf, 195 see under Pervez Musharraf also
Muslim
  Community in Pakistan, 153
  Interest, 57
  League (N), 28
Mujahedeen, 65
  Ahmadi, 153
  Sects, 153
Vohra, 153

N

Najibullah, 105, 151, 204
  President, 220

Regime in Afghanistan, 151

Najibullah's Government, 222

Narcotics, 34, 74, 80, 82

Narco-Trafficking, 75

Natural Gas In—, 49

Central Asia, 49

Middle East, 49

Persian Gulf, 49

Nawaz Sharif, Pak Prime Minister, 27, 200, 150, 165, 189, 193

Regime, 27

Naxalites, 33

NDA-1 Regime, 197

NEPS Schemes, 191

New Powers, 43

Brazil, 43

China, 43

India, 43

Nixon and Ford Administration, 44

NIZAMNAMA First Afghanistan Constitution, 136

No First Use (NFU), 169

Non-Pakhtun Ethnic Groups, 155

Tajiks, Uzbeks, Hazaras and Shais, 155

Non-Pashtun Afghan Tribes, 114

North Atlantic Treaty Organization (NATO), 44, 45, 46, 60, 74, 75, 93, 127, 128, 151, 157, 187, 205

Allies, 234

Forces, 47, 55, 59, 188, 189, 191, 193, 197, 236, 236, 240

In Europe, 30

Operations, 195, 197

Troops, 89

Troops Withdrawal from Afghanistan, 16, 125-133, 188

War Plans, 48

North

South Divide, 208

Waziristan, 190, 191

Northern Alliance, 25, 28, 77, 90, 155, 181, 195, 198, 207-209, 236

Hazaras, 181

Leaders, 98

Tajiks, 181

Uzbeks, 181

Northern Route, 153

Nuclear

Armed Pakistan and India, 169

Capability, 42

Exchange, 41

Holocaust, 40

War, 42, 170

Weapons, 73, 154

Nuristan and Kunar, 119

NWFP, 148, 214, 215

O

Obama, Barak, US Pres. 15, 18, 44, 45, 59, 96, 97, 100, 101, 126, 127, 146, 162, 192, 205, 219

Administration, 97, 106

Obama's Election, 56

Oil

And Natural Gas Commission (ONGC), 239

Resources of West and Central Asia, 43

Operation

Dark Heart, 166

Enduring Freedom, 146, 156, 187-201

Opium

From Marjah, 104

Production, 89

Trade, 104
Organized Crimes, 80, 82
Osama Bin Laden, 113, 114, 115, 125, 147, 152, 165, 167, 192, 194, 206, 207
Al Qaeda Chief, 12, 44, 52, 56-58,
Elimination of-, 166
Killing of-, 152, 174
9/11 Mastermind, 57
Responsible for 9/11, 147
Saudi Billionaire, 12

P

Pak
Security Threat to India, 50
Taliban, 222, 247
Pakhtun
Community, 23
Sunni Fighters, 27
Sunni Jihadists, 155
Sunni Taliban, 155
Tribes, 26
Pakhtunistan, 187
Pakhtuns, 19, 25
In Pakistan and Afghanistan, 19
Pakistan, 13, 15-22, 29, 31, 33, 39, 40-42, 44-49, 39-66, 70, 72,·73, 75, 77-82, 89, 113, 114, 119, 120, 121, 132, 146, 149, 152, 153, 154, 162, 165, 167, 175, 181, 189, 194, 195, 205-208, 211
Afghanistan is Lifeline and Obsession, 41
And Afghanistan, 19, 27, 148, 150, 156
And Afghanistan Problems, 151, 152
And Afghanistan Relations, 187
And China, 65
And China, Stakeholders, 60
And India, 13
Direct Stakes in Afghanistan, 13
And Iran, 71, 147
And US, 157
Army, 28, 48, 56, 150 168
Army and ISI, 48, 220, 228
Army's Military Operations in North Waziristan, 27
Backed Mujahedeen, 53
Based Camps, 233
Created on Foundation of Islam, 47
Dependency on Arms (from US), 48
Double Game in Afghanistan, 152, 153, 168
Doubled Edged Policy, 41
Dubious Role in Afghanistan, 151
Frontline State, 52
Imperial Mission, 151
Intelligence Service ISI, 221
Interference in Afghanistan, 154
ISI, 151, 153
ISI Influence, 65
ISI to Militancy, 227
Jihadists, 154
Linkages, 48
Military, 27, 195
Nuclear Capability, 41
Nuclear Weapons, 154
Occupied Pakistan (POK), 63, 211
Peoples' Party (PPP), 193
Policy Towards Afghanistan, 148
Population, 149

Role in Afghanistan, 155
Route, 153
Security, 221
Establishment, 226
Forces, 19, 153
Short Sighted Policy of Strategic Depth, 154
Soft Power, 42
Strategic Depth in Afghanistan, 161-170
Taliban, 27, 55, 61, 167
US Cleavage, 57
Pakistan's
Afghan Policy, 20, 187-201
Diplomatic Card, 45
Division in 1971, 161
Eastern Border, 164
Foreign Policy, 41
Game Plan Against India, 52
Game Plan, 100
Logistic Support to US, 147
National Security, 129
NWFP and FATA Areas, 41
Recruiting Ground for Jihadis, 41
Perspectives in Afghanistan, 145-160
Policy in Afghanistan, 226
Proxy War Against India in Kashmir, 16
Role, 175
State Policy, 213
Strategic Policy, 149
Western Borders, 164
Pakistan—China, 72
Pakistan-Chinese Axis, 62
Pakistani
Army, 27, 75, 129, 163, 191, 192, 193
Inter-State Gas System, 91
Nuclear Weapons, 27
Proxy War in Afghanistan, 105
Sunni, 30
Taliban, 73
Tribal Areas, 167
Pakistan-US Relationship, 48
Pamirs Mountains, 69
Parvez Musharraf, 48, 56, 165, 169
General and Military Dictator, 163
Military Dictator, 165
Pashtun
Language, 73
Nationalism, 21, 213
Pashtun
Population, 73
Tribes in Pakistan and Afghanistan, 148
Pashtunistan, 188, 222
Pashtuns, 79, 104, 181
And Tajiks, 60
Peace
And Stability, 40, 125, 133
Security and Security of Afghanistan, 147
Talks, 224
Persian
Gulf Regime, 44
Gulf, 72, 73
New Year, 85
Peshawar
Accord, 206
Shura, 75
Attack on Military High School, 19
Pew Research Poll, 192

PNS Zulfikar, Pakistan Navy Frigate, 27
Policy Options for India, 145-160, 196
Political System, 174
Poppy
  Cultivation, 178
  Farming, 25
Post-9/11 Afghanistan, 135
Post-ISAF Afghan, 228
Post-NATO Era, 121
Post-Taliban
  .Afghanistan Infrastructure, 227
  Era, 116
Post-US
  Afghan, 223
  Afghanistan, 219-221, 228
  Withdrawal, 224
Power Sharing Agreements, 107
Precision Bombs, 14
Pre-Nuclear Weapons, 19
Promote India China Cooperation, 182
Proxies, 151
  Haqqani Network and Quetta Shura, 151
  Hekmetyar of Hizb-e-Islami, 151
Putin, Vladmir, 85

Q

Qalal Town, 234
Qari Yousef Ahmadi, Taliban Spokesman, 14
Quetta, 221
Shura, 24, 99, 151, 222

R

Radical
  Islamic Forces, 41, 45
  Taliban Regime in Kabul, 228
Raheel Sharif, General, 189, 160
Rebellion in Balochisan, 28
Rebuilding Military/Security Forces, 182
RECCA, 239
Reconstruction
  Aid Program, 179
  And Development Project, 77
  Of Afghanistan, 129
Red Mosque Incident, 75
Regional
  Cooperation, 14, 78, 130
  Peace and Stability, 16, 125-133
  Policies, 176
  Power Dynamics, 220
  Security Complexes (RSC), 71
  tates, Interests, 72
Relapse of Afghan to Terrorism, 203-217
Religious
  Fundamentalism, 31
  Leaders, 43
  Minorities in Pakistan, 94
Rise in Insurgency, 178
Rise of
  Fundamentalism and Talibanism, 173
  Taliban, 220
  Talibanization, 130
  Pakistan, 129
Roshnagar, Mohammad Atta, 17
Rumfield, Donald, 43
Russia, 14, 49, 74, 153, 154, 155, 198
  And Central Asia, 26
  And China, 88
  China, 98

China Interests in Afghanistan, 85
Iran, China and EU, 45
Out from Afghanistan, 166
Reclaiming Central Area, 30
Returns to Afghanistan, 85-92
Withdrawal, 206
Russia's
Geopolitical and Geo-Economic Interest, 14
Proposal—Rehabilitation in Afghanistan, 86
Russian
And Afghan Cooperation, 85
Bases in-, 90
Kyrgyz Republic, 90
Tajikstan, 90
Cultural Centre in Kabul, 88
Embassy in Kabul, 85
Federation, 86
Forces in Afghanistan, 44
Funded Counter Narcotics Program, 89
Great Game, 88
Invasion, 51
Language, 88
Leaders, 87
Technology, 87
Troops, 52

S

SAARC, 57, 189
Saddam Hussain of Iraq, 44
Attack on Kuwait, 45
Government, 23
SAFTA, 182, 238
SAIL, 191
Salma Khurshid, 94
Sarkozy and Merkel, 59
Sartaz Aziz, National Security Advisor, 189
Sassanids, 187
Saudi Arabia, 24, 114, 153
And Qatar, 209
Secessionists Movement, 149
Secularism, 47
Security
And Justice, 128
Competition, 13
Environment, 151
Afghanistan, 151
India, 151
Pakistan, 151
Forces, 40, 130, 212
Of Afghanistan, 114
Serbs, 15
Shah Mohammad Qureshi, Minister, 225
Shah Shuja or Najibullah, 205
Shanghai Cooperation Organization (SCO), 79, 89, 90, 98, 236, 239
Sharia, 208
Sharma, Kavita, 19
Shia, 155
Fighters, 28
Muslims, 153, 155
Shiia Ethnic and Religious Minorities, 76
Shimla Agreement, 1971, 190
Shuja Shah Durani, 203
Silk Road, 187
SIMI, 33
Sinkiang, 203, 215
Small, Medium Enterprises, 247
Smaller Powers in South Asia (SPSA), 62

Afghanistan, 62
Bangladesh, 62
Maldives, 62
Nepal, 62
Sri Lanka, 62
Smuggling of Drugs, 34
Social and Economic Changes, 137
Soft Power Diplomacy, 65
Somalia and Yugoslavia, 154
South Asia, 42, 45
Strategic Mosaic, 43
South
Asian Region, 39
China Sea, 216
Soviet
And Americans, 112
Army, 189
Backed Afghan Government, 179
Downfall, 66
Intervention, 70, 113, 114
Intervention, 1970, 187
Intervention, 1979, 188
Invasion, 53, 63, 173
Invasion of 1979, 179
Invasion of 1979-89 and 2001 till 2014, 41
Invasion of Afghanistan, 1979, 44
Military Intervention, 12
Polls, 181
Russia, 113
Ties, 14
Troops, 14, 146, 220, 26O
Withdrawal From Afghanistan, 14
Union, 12, 18, 19, 48, 54, 86, 140, 141, 145, 151, 161, 165
Withdrawal, 200
Sponsored Jihadi Groups, 32
Stakeholders, 45
China, Russia, US and European Union, 45
State of Afghanistan, 111-121
Strategic
Depth, 163, 226
Against India, 187
Mosaic in South Asia, 46, 42
Suicide Bombing, 175
Sunni
Extremism in Afghanistan and Pakistan, 74
Extremism, (Al Qaeda and Taliban), 73
Muslims, 153
Sunnis Jihadis, 153
Super Powers, 43
SWAT
Factions, 93
Taliban, 209
Syed Tayyab Aghan, 58
Syed Yusuf Raza Gilani, 162
Syria, 37, 47

T

Tajik Faction, 24
Tajiks, 28, 76, 104
Tajiks and Uzbeks, 208
Tajikstan, 62, 65, 78, 236
Taliban, 13, 15, 17, 20, 21, 24-26, 28, 29, 45-47, 52, 58, 73, 75, 77, 78, 81, 90, 96, 97, 98, 99, 101, 102, 106, 107, 113-116, 127, 129, 137-139, 141-143, 148, 152, 163, 166, 168, 174, 175, 178, 180, 181, 187, 195, 198, 200, 204, 206-209, 211, 212, 215, 220-234
And Al Qaeda, 189

Atrocities, 13, 116
Dominance, 178
Extremists, 156
Fall of-, 137
Forces, 65
Government, 52, 53, 174, 179, 254
Government in Kabul, 24
Group, 52
In Afghanistan, 125
Insurgency, 18, 146, 220, 226
Insurgents, 139
Leadership, 24, 99, 100, 221, 222
Militancy, 220
Militants, 93, 219
Prisoners, 204
Regime, 137, 138, 148, 194, 236
Regime of Kabul, 114
Regions of Afghanistan, 16
Resurgence, 20, 220, 222
Rule, 23, 226

Targets, 28
Warrior, 52

Taliban's
Army of Suicide Bombers, 137
Fighters in Kashmir, 26

Talibanism, 129

Talibanization of
Afghanistan, 155
Regional Security, 129

Tashkent, 78

TCT-CBM, 239

Techno
Jihad, 35

Terrorism, 35

Technology Transfer (TT), 74

Tehrik-e-Taliban Pakistan (TTP), 19, 27, 75, 94, 103, 153, 209, 210, 215, 221, 222, 228, 229, 235, 236, 239, 240, 247
Hideouts, 229
Popularly Known As Pak Taliban, 153

Tej Pratap Singh, 18

Terrorism, 14, 38, 44, 49, 79, 80-82, 89, 121, 125, 152, 180
In Afghanistan, 21

Terrorist
And Militants Sanctuaries in Pakistani Soil, 190
Attack, 41, 45, 55, 153
In Europe, Africa and India, 45
Group, 25, 75, 162, 180
Organization, 27, 31, 34
Outfits, 61
Sanctuaries, 228

Terrorists
And Jihadis, 152
In Pakistan, 19

Third
Battle of Panipat, 1761, 50
World, 111

Tony Blair, British PM, 234

Traditional Societal Structure, 211

Training
Camps, 152
Of Afghan Mujahedeen, 52
Of Mujahideen, 48
Of Uyghurs, 74

Trans-border Trafficking, 74

Transformation of East Pakistan, 149

Tribal
Communities, 25, 112, 114

Conflicts, 112
Councils, 130
Culture, 135
Identity, 116
Pashtuns, 222
Tribes of Afghanistan, 15, 112
Turkmenistan, 62, 65, 91, 176, 236
Turkmenistan, Afghanistan, Pakistan and India (TAPI), 21
Gas Pipeline, 180
Project, 91, 228
Twin Towers Attach In New York, 52
Tzarist Russia, 113

U

UAE, 114
UK, Germany and Soviet Union, 66
Ukraine, 209
And Russia, 26
Crisis, 153
UN, 14, 44, 45, 60, 66, 96, 107, 137 204, 215, 216
General Assembly, 220
Office on Drugs, 104
Provisions, 115
Resolutions, 79
Security Council, 90, 96, 105, 120
UN's Role in
Combating Taliban Insurgency, 93-107
Combating Terrorism, 14
Security and Development of Afghanistan, 93
Unconventional Warfare, 31
Urbanization and Economic Development, 17
US, 12, 18, 23, 31, 42, 43, 48, 52, 54, 65, 66, 72-74, 78, 85, 97, 125, 132, 133, 140-142, 145, 152, 154, 155, 156, 157, 165, 167, 183, 190, 195, 205, 212, 216, 220, 223, 234
Af-Pak Policy, 101
Agency for International Development, 137
Aided Projects, 88
And China, 42, 49, 57
Extra Regional Power, 42
Game Plan in Afghanistan, 49
Interest, 57
And Europe, 32
And India, 22, 61, 159
And NATO Countries, 216
And NATO Forces in Afghanistan, 140, 191
And NATO Troops, 133
And Pakistan, 166, 192
And Russia, 46
And Western Interests, 154
Army, 106
Attack in 2001, 175
Bombing, 14
Carriers, 27
Combat Troops, 234
Compromise Formula, 57
Congress, 101
Consulate at Herat, Mazar-e-sharif and Jalalabad, 177
Deal with Pakistan, 73
Demand for Oil, 44
Drawdown Strategy, 126, 128
Elections, 208
Energy, 146
Extra Regional Power, 13
Flawed Stand, 20
Forces, 177
Forces in Afghanistan, 20, 95, 173, 174
Forcing Soviet Withdrawal, 175

Foreign Policy, 44
Game Plan, 54
Goal of Peace Talk, 223
India Bond, 56
India or China, 81
Influence in the Region, 89
Israel and EU and India, 210
Institution of Peace, (USIP), 226
Intelligence, 15
Intervention, 106
Invasion of Afghanistan 2001, 93, 162
Involvement in Afghanistan, 173
Led Coalition, 234
Led Coalition Forces, 221
Led Coalition in Afghanistan, 96
Led Forces, 95, 101
Led Military Intervention, 137
Led NATO Forces, 100, 107, 111
Led Operation Enduring Freedom, 115
Major Role in Afghanistan, 57
Military, 24, 56, 104
  Alliance Partners, 163
  Forces, 28
Mission in Iraq, 146
Mission, 174
Nation Building Mission-Failure, 146
Operation Enduring Freedom, 152
Pakistan and Afghanistan, 166
Pakistan Joint Operations, 41
Planning, 176
Plans, 106
Policy, 23, 199
Presence in Afghanistan, 73, 170, 233
Recurring Interest in the Region, 49
Russia Rivalry, 153
Russian Relations, 153
Sponsored Military Alliances, 54, 61
  CENTO, 54
  NATO, 54
  SEATO, 54
Troops, 95-97, 127, 137, 157, 159, 222, 234, 237
Troops Pull Out, 107
Troops Withdrawal from Afghanistan, 15
Troops –Withdrawal, 17
Troops-Phased Withdrawal-, 15
Wanted Pakistani Terrorists, 166
War Against Taliban—, 147
War Efforts, 152
War on Terror, 57, 146, 148, 152
Withdrawal, 21, 104, 204, 215, 241
Withdrawal from Afghanistan, 14, 15, 159, 173-184
US/NATO, 97
  Forces, 15
  International Security Assistance Force, 80
  Led Mission, 96
  Pull Out, 103
US—South Korea, 72
USSR, 86
Uttarakhand, 215
Uyghurs, 30
  Militants, 156
  Separatist, 74, 120
  Of Xinjiang, 119

Uzbekistan, 78
Uzbeks and Kyrgyz, 78
Uzbeks, 76, 104

V

Vajpayee, Atal Behari, PM, 190
Vietnam, 146
  Fiasco, 146
  War, 111
  Defeat of Americans, 111

W

Wakhan Corridor, 209
War
  On Terror, 55, 156, 223
  Torn Afghanistan, 50
Warlords, 173
Warrior Class, 113
Weapons
  Of Mass Destruction (WMD), 45
  Trafficking, 81
West Asia, 112, 150
Western Powers, 174
Withdrawal of NATO, 200
World
  Peace and Stability, Challenges to-. 31-38
War I, 188
War II, 113

X

Xi Jinping, Chinese President, 121
Xinjiang Province, 30, 120, 198

Y

Yousuf Raza, 62
Yusuf Raza Gilani, former Pak PM, 192

Z

Zalmay Khalilzad, 119
  US Ambassador in Afghanistan, 16
Zarang-Delaram High Way, 227
Zaranj and Delaram, 213
Zardar-Gilani
Democratic Regime, 168
  Team, 165
Zealots of Pakistan, 32
Zero Sum Game, 71
Zia-ul-Haq, Army Chief General, 163, 165